FREE YOUR MIND!

ALSO BY SIMON MATTHEWS

PSYCHEDELIC CELLULOID
LOOKING FOR A NEW ENGLAND
HOUSE IN THE COUNTRY

SIMON MATTHEWS

FREE YOUR MIND!

GIOVANNI 'TINTO' BRASS
'SWINGING LONDON' AND THE
60s POP CULTURE SCENE

OLDCASTLEBOOKS.CO.UK

First published in 2023 by
Oldcastle Books Ltd,
Harpenden,
Herts, UK

oldcastlebooks.co.uk
@OldcastleBooks
Editor: Nick Rennison
© Simon Matthews, 2023

A CIP catalogue record for this book is available from the British Library.

ISBN
978-0-85730-535-0 (Paperback)
978-0-85730-536-7 (eBook)

2 4 6 8 10 9 7 5 3 1

Typeset in 11.5 on 15.1pt Goudy Old Style
by Avocet Typeset, Bideford, Devon, EX39 2BP
Printed and bound in Great Britain by Severn, Gloucester

CONTENTS

FOREWORD

Tinto is one of the most clever and eclectic directors I have ever worked with. He is like a dog which has broken loose of his chain (or isn't too tied up) and runs free in the meadows of cinema - 'his' cinema unbound to the producer's profit. Testament to this is his almost comic book-like delirious film *Yankee*, the most atypical Italian western of its time.

After all, Tinto comes from a lineage of artists. His grandfather was a painter who married a rich Russian woman and as a young man he frequented the Parisian Cinémathèque and the Nouvelle Vague circles. A truly free, eclectic, eccentric, and neatly untidy spirit.

A madman with a great sense of humour - a very important quality, as having a relaxed atmosphere on set is a necessity for me. I am not fond of directors who rant and shout, who go on set as if they are going to war. Tinto would step in with just the right amount of grit and verve, without ever falling into conflictual anxiety.

He was like a big kid who let his dreamlike fantasies take over. Thanks to his brilliance and technical abilities, he could translate the incredible things in his head onto the silver screen.

We shot *Dropout* and *The Vacation* together in 1970 and 1971 respectively. At the time we worked with my wife Vanessa Redgrave because Tinto was dying to work with both of us.

It was one of the most bohemian experiences I ever had in cinema. Something that could only happen in the 1970s, when youth counterculture and hippie principles were still echoing in the climate.

In *Dropout* I played a lunatic who escapes an asylum and kidnaps a woman. The two fall into a dangerous attraction and, in the end, I die at the frontier while she is murdered by her husband. Tinto played the dropout: an art dealer and pornographer. In THE VACATION, the roles were reversed where Vanessa played an allegedly insane woman and I played a poacher who falls for her.

They were regenerating and liberating filming experiences. Something outside the typical Hollywood blockbuster box, where creativity is often trapped and hindered under enormous budgets.

Tinto's approach was very much inspired by the New Wave and the English Free Cinema. We would often change location on the spot and improvise. We drove around like nomads, travelling with our skeleton crew in a cramped minivan alongside the equipment. We were able to seize opportunities according to circumstances without planning.

Additionally, as good Italians, even when we were travelling around England, if there were important football matches where Italy was playing, we would run around looking for a pub or any place that had a TV to watch the game.

Many years later I asked him to appear in a film, Louis Nero's *La Rabbia*. He accepted to do a cameo as long as he had a 'beautiful lady with voluptuous breasts' sitting on his lap while he delivered his lines.

The fact is that while the critics considered him a promising genius of anti-system cinema, his films didn't initially gross much. After he threw himself into hardcore passionate romantic films with *The Key*, he found true commercial success and never looked back. Although indeed he was always intrigued by relations with sex and the link between power and sex (as seen in *Salon Kitty* with Helmut Berger).

It wasn't that he had become more serious than when we made films together. If anything, he was always serious but with that not-so-subtle hint of irony of someone who plays with being a 'master' rather than really considering himself one (although he undoubtedly is in his own way).

Some critics theorised that he was obsessed with using a big cigar as a phallic metaphor, but this is far from the truth: he just enjoys smoking cigars, simple as that. When someone becomes important there are always scholars who try to identify complex meanings where there are none. Tinto mocked them without them realising, pretending to be the stereotype that film critics had created about him.

In truth Brass is a sly cat, with a flame of sharp, critical, ironic and self-ironic intelligence which burns behind his eyes. I am the first person to say he shouldn't be taken too seriously - and he is the second. After all, as someone said, we don't laugh about what we don't love. Thank you, Tinto, thank you for letting me, part traveller on my mother's side, breathe bohemian cinema. To me, you were and are a nomad of cinema.

Franco Nero

Preface

If you lived in London in the 1960s, you might have seen him. A small, portly man in his mid-thirties with his hair brushed back, hedgehog-style. Carrying a 16 mm Arriflex camera, he might have been searching for locations for one of his films, or just shooting whatever he happened to notice. It could have been early in the morning, filming the sunrise or recording dockers at work; possibly slightly later in the day, in amongst the commuters tramping across London Bridge or recording the soon-to-be-scrapped steam locomotives coasting noisily through Clapham Junction Station. Most of the time he might be on his own, but occasionally a small Italian-UK crew would be accompanying him. But never many people, enough to fit in a couple of cars at most.

His stars were often well-known, and easily identified by regular cinemagoers. But rather than deploy them inside a studio, and film them with stage-like conventionality, he would instead show them walking through unknowing crowds, the narrative constantly teetering on the point of breaking the fourth wall between the camera's gaze and the audience's eye. They would pass through shops, arcades, galleries and nightclubs; they would get on and off buses and tube trains; everything recorded quickly and spontaneously for posterity. What we see now is a city changing as he films it. Piecing together masses of footage at the editing machine, and deploying the skills he picked up from Roberto Rossellini, his dexterous fingers assemble a narrative that moves, like the shifting lens of a kaleidoscope, from the soot-blackened, ruined terraces and dowdy street corners of north Kensington to smart boutiques, noisy demonstrations and then out into the night. We see glimpses – and more – of the cultural revolution that rocked London and the world in the 1960s: Indica Gallery, the Roundhouse, Granny Takes a Trip and even a 'happening' at the Alexandra Palace amidst the peacocks and peahens of the day, before the dream faded.

I first became aware of Tinto Brass's early films when researching my earlier book, *Psychedelic Celluloid*. Because it contains a score by The Freedom, a UK group that emerged out of Procol Harum in July 1967, this mentions *Nerosubianco*, a film considered by some to be his masterpiece. But trying to assess how much work Brass had done in London in the 1960s, or how much of the city he had caught on film at that time, took longer than expected, and became an ongoing project in its own right. As and when I could, I began piecing together an account of his endeavours. In February 2019, *Shindig!* magazine published a lengthy, and much more detailed, article on *Nerosubianco* and gradually a book began to take shape. With memories fading it seemed important to assess where Brass slotted into the hierarchy of directors and auteurs in the 1960s, and indeed how significant a figure in world cinema he might have become if the cards had fallen slightly differently for him.

None of this would have been possible without the cooperation and interest of Ranjit Sandhu, whose painstakingly assembled website on the career of Brass contains much information not accessible elsewhere. I am also grateful to the following for their time, responses and insights: Alan Sekers,

Barry Miles, Mal Ryder, David Mairowitz, Bobby Harrison, Mike Lease, Anthony Cobbold, the late Carla Cassola, Pete Brown, Stephen Frears, Ken Andrew, Don Fraser, Franco Nero and Alexander Tuschinski.

This is the story of the only European director who made four feature films in London in the 1960s.

1

VENICE

Before considering the career of Tinto Brass, we should remember that he is Venetian: from a city with its own cultural traditions that, in historical terms, only recently became part of Italy. His family trace their ancestry back to the lands on the eastern side of the Adriatic, which, for centuries, were part of the Hapsburg domains. It is uncertain whether they were ethnically Slav or German. They may even have originally been Italian, only to be subsequently 'Slavicised' or 'Germanised' during the numerous shifts of political control in that area. What is clear is that by the mid-nineteenth century his great-grandfather, Michele Brass, was resident in Gorizia (in German, Görz) where he was active in dissident political circles. He identified as Italian and was an 'irredentist', one of the many Italian-speaking citizens of Austria-Hungary who wanted the area they lived in to secede and become part of Italy.

Considering oneself Italian then, as now, did not imply being part of a homogenous culture that radiated outwards from Rome. In fact, identifying specifically with Venice was perfectly compatible with having roots in the north and east of the Adriatic, as these were areas that had once been part of the aristocratic city republic. Being Venetian, for instance, meant having a different, and in some ways more cosmopolitan, history compared to those who considered themselves Neapolitan, Sardinian or Sicilian. The prominence of the city dated back to 1082 when it was granted tax-free trading privileges throughout the Byzantine Empire. With the benefit of this concession, a string of Venetian settlements, ports and fortresses were established through Slovenia, Croatia, Montenegro, Albania, Greece, Turkey and Cyprus which combined with the city's easy access to the Alpine passes into northern Europe gave it a significant share, for centuries, of trade with China, India and Japan. Because of this network of territories, trading bases and trading arrangements, Venice enjoyed world power status for approximately four hundred years. It accrued much wealth and contained a diverse population, including a significant Jewish community, famed for their residence in 'the ghetto'. After 1453, the advance of Islam through Europe gradually eroded this position, and with the fall of Rhodes in 1522, Venice ceased to control trade with the east. But even after this the city remained a useful mid-range power, and an important player in coalitions against the Ottoman Empire. The Venetian navy took part in the Battle of Lepanto in 1571, and it fought alongside Austria and Poland in 1684.

Venice's existence as a separate state ended in 1797 when the city and its surviving possessions were traded by Napoleon with Austria, in an arrangement that saw Austrian Flanders

(Belgium) become part of France. Confirmed at the Congress of Vienna in 1815, Austrian control of Venice was noted for its suppression of Italian political aspirations, a policy that united a great many of those of Italian descent in a hatred of the Hapsburg regime. Risings that attempted to restore Venetian rule, either locally, or across its former Adriatic territories, or that even aimed at a broader 'Italian' unity, were suppressed in 1821, 1830 and 1848. The city failed too to profit from the 1859 conflict between France, Sardinia and Austria and, with its immediate surroundings, only became part of Italy (created as a state in 1861) after 1866 when, despite experiencing defeats on land and sea, Italy successfully allied itself with Prussia against Austria. Under the terms of the Treaty of Vienna, which confirmed Venice would henceforth be part of Italy, Italy was obliged to abandon any future claims to parts of Istria and Dalmatia that contained a large Italian population. These remained within Austria, and because of this, 'irredentism' there was strengthened. Most Italian citizens of what was now called Austria-Hungary identified strongly with Venetian culture: its distinct dialect, much used in Italian theatre comedies as the coarse language of common people, its annual carnival with elaborate disguises, costumes and masks (an event banned in Venice under Austrian rule) and its immense artistic tradition, personified by Titian, Tintoretto, Veronese, Canaletto and many lesser-known figures.

This was the world that Michele Brass lived in, shaping both his political views, and those of his son, Italico.[1] Born in 1870, Italico proved to be very talented at painting. He trained as an artist in Munich under Karl Raupp from 1887 and then in Paris under Jean-Paul Laurens from 1891, where he won bronze medals at the Exposition Universelle and at the Salon. Shortly after this he married Lina Vigdoff, a Russian medical student from Odessa, and settled with her in Venice. It was propitious timing. The first Biennale was staged that year, and quickly became a national and international event, superseding the gatherings of artists, architects and writers that had previously taken place at the Caffè Florian. In the second half of the nineteenth century, Venetian art was undergoing a revival. This was led by Ippolito Caffi (who died at the Battle of Lissa in 1866 whilst serving as a war artist) and galleries across Europe began exhibiting the work of painters like Eugene de Blaas (like Brass, an Austrian) and Guglielmo Ciardi. Like Ciardi, Italico Brass painted in a post-impressionist style and, once he had the funds to do so, assembled his own art collection.

His reputation spread and in 1899 one of his works was purchased by King Umberto I of Italy. In 1907 another, *The Procession Returning from the Island of San Michele*, inspired the Ezra Pound poem 'Per Italico Brass'. Resident, like Italico Brass, in the Dorsoduro area of Venice, Pound spent 4 months in the city in 1908, during which he self-published *A Lume Spento*, his first collection of verse. What appears to have attracted him to Brass's picture was the way it fell stylistically between different schools, representative neither of impressionism nor of photographic realism. To be noticed by Pound, who was only 23 then, may not have seemed of much significance at the time, but in the years that followed, with Pound championing a revolution in literature via his enthusiasm and support for TS Eliot and James Joyce this would have been no bad thing. Nor, after 1924 when he returned to Italy from Paris, would Pound's later gravitation to support for Mussolini.[2]

Granted a solo exhibition at the Venice Biennale in 1910, Italico Brass's reputation continued to grow. Supported by the journalist and critic Ugo Ojetti (another irredentist, and subsequently a signatory of the 1925 Manifesto of Fascist Intellectuals) his work was exhibited at the 1911 International Art Exhibition in Rome and later toured as part of a travelling show that visited Budapest, Berlin and Paris. In 1914, a solo exhibition in Paris followed, organised by the legendary art dealer and gallery owner Georges Petit, who some years earlier had been one of the first promoters of the Impressionists. After this his work was shown in Buenos Aires and San Francisco, where both he and Ciardi won gold medals, Brass for the picture *Il Ponte Sulla Laguna.*

His ascent into the orbit of Georges Petit took place against a background of monumental international events. War broke out between Russia, France, Britain, Belgium and Serbia on one side, and Germany and Austria-Hungary on the other in August 1914, with the Ottoman Empire added to the conflict later that year. As an Austro-Hungarian citizen, Italico Brass now found himself, theoretically, an enemy of Petit. Fortunately, Italy, his adopted country, although it was part of the Triple Alliance with Germany and Austria-Hungary, declared itself neutral. By March 1915 it had cancelled its treaty obligations, switched sides, and sensing the opportunity to make territorial gains, had declared war on Austria-Hungary (May 1915) and the Ottoman Empire (August 1915). It refrained from tangling with Germany until August 1916. Willingly granted Italian citizenship, Brass followed the footsteps of Ippolito Caffi half a century earlier, and was appointed an official war artist by the Italian high command. Posted to the Duke of Aosta's Third Army he was given the task of documenting military events on the Isonzo front. For the next three years he took part in the various advances and retreats in that area, keeping a *diario pittorico*, and emerged unscathed to be awarded an exhibition of his works, dedicated to Venice, in the Galleria Pesaro in Milan in 1918.[3]

With peace, and a considerable income from the sales of his work, Italico Brass bought the Scuola Vecchia dell 'Abbazia di Santa Maria della Misericordia (the Old School of the Convent of Saint Mary of Grace) in the Cannaregio district of Venice. More than six hundred years old, by the early twentieth century it was in an advanced state of disrepair. He began an extensive restoration, using it to store and display his large art collection, whilst commissioning additions, such as a round tower, an oriental-style balcony and some galleries inside the main hall as well as a complete redesign of the walled garden and its Gothic colonnade. For the remainder of his life, Italico Brass divided his time between painting, and being a connoisseur of sixteenth-, seventeenth- and eighteenth-century Italian and Venetian art. He also participated fully in the municipal affairs of Venice as a member of the Commission on Public Buildings, the Board of Directors for Venice's Municipal Museums and the Scientific Committee that prepared the exhibitions for Titian (1935), Tintoretto (1937) and Veronese (1939). He would be joined in much of this activity by his son, Alessandro Brass.

Born in 1898, and Italian by birth, Alessandro had volunteered for war service in 1916. He was wounded, and after the war became a lawyer in the office of Francesco Carnelutti, a significant figure in Italian commercial law. Thereafter, he pursued a legal career, leavened with politics. Like many Italian ex-servicemen, Alessandro Brass regarded the gains made by Italy at the Treaty of Versailles (Trieste, and a few enclaves in the Adriatic and Aegean) as inadequate. His irredentism translated smoothly into fascism and he participated in the October 1922 'March on Rome', an event which led to the appointment of Mussoloni as Prime Minister by King Victor Emmanuel III. In the years that followed, Alessandro, like his father, became a noted art collector whilst rising to prominence in fascist circles in Venice. By March 1939 he was considered sufficiently reliable to be appointed a delegate to the fascist 'corporate' parliament, which sat until August 1943, though it had very little actual power. He married in 1929 and had 4 sons, the second of whom, Giovanni Brass, born in 1933, would spend much of his childhood being brought up by his grandparents. Noting his prodigious appetite for drawing, they nicknamed him 'Tinto' after Tintoretto, the great Venetian artist of the 1550s.

Whatever his preferences in domestic politics, Alessandro seems to have had a reasonable grasp of the reality of Italy's position. In 1940, with the country at war with France, Poland, the Netherlands, Norway and the British Empire, he moved his family out of Venice to Asolo. Here, 32 miles north-west of the city, he had access to a property formerly owned by the Earl of Iveagh, and, prior to that, by Eleanora Duse. Regarded in the 1890s as the greatest actress of her time, Duse was noted for her relationship with Gabriele D'Annunzio, poet, playwright, novelist and leading Italian irredentist. A controversial figure, D'Annunzio was regarded by many on the Italian political right as having played John the Baptist to Mussolini's Jesus.[4] In Asolo, securely out of harm's way with his grandparents, mother and siblings, Tinto grew up in relative peace and had his first exposure to film in the local cinema, watching Charlie Chaplin silents and Walt Disney cartoons. He may have been aware too, though only a child at the time, that his grandfather, in a late creative flowering, designed the sets for the Andrea di Robilant film *Canal Grande*.[5]

Not that Italico Brass lived to see it. He passed away two months before it was released during a hectic period that saw Mussolini deposed, much of Italy become a battlefield, the government surrender to the Allies, Germany invade and occupy most of northern and central Italy, and the King and his government flee, switching sides and joining the Allies. Alessandro Brass, no longer required in a parliament that had ceased to function, seems to have been politically wise enough to see how matters would end and, although resident in a part of the country that remained under fascist rule, rejected an offer of a position in Mussolini's pro-German Salò Republic.

The Brass family survived the final stages of the war, which concluded for them when Venice was liberated by the UK 8th Army on 30 April 1945. With Alessandro's prior commitment to the Mussolini regime well-known, and employment initially denied to him, they seem to have survived for a while by distributing some of Italico Brass's art collection to various museums and even auctioning off a few pieces. (References can be found to works obtained from them by the New York Metropolitan Museum of Art, and the Cleveland Museum of Art prior to 1940. They seem to have continued this in the immediate post-war period, at a time when acquisitions from Italy were classed, in the absence of a peace treaty, as trading with the enemy, and subject to stringent taxes.)[6] With fascism vanquished, the Christian Democrats began their long period of political control, a referendum abolished the Italian monarchy and the 1947 Paris Peace Treaty stripped Italy of its Venetian outposts along the Adriatic, abruptly extinguishing the *raison d'être* of the irredentists.

By this point Giovanni 'Tinto' Brass was 13 years old, a keen amateur photographer and also a nascent film director, shooting his own amateur productions on an 8mm cine-camera he had been given as a present. In addition to this, not untypically for any boy of that age, with the onset of puberty and adolescence he had begun rebelling against his father's wielding of 'absolute authority', and a family he regarded as 'bourgeois, rich, fascist'. He also seems to have been sexually precocious, taking himself off to brothels, then state-regulated in Italy. Modelled on the French system, and introduced in Italy after the 1861 unification of the country, in Brass's account these were not significantly different from, and certainly no worse than, extremely louche nightclubs. The sense of transgression that he obtained from such adventures also transferred to his rising political consciousness, living as he was at a time when many Italians supported Palmiro Togliatti and the Communist Party of Italy (PCI). Polling 14% and winning 6 seats in the June 1946 elections, the PCI were one of the larger parties, and opposed to both the Christian Democrats and the Social Democrats. In Brass's eye, they were, therefore, politically transgressive, at a time when he was exploring sexual transgression. They were also markedly more popular in Venice (where they polled 21%) than in many other parts of the country. Their support grew subsequently, and they might have entered government later in the decade had the US not issued instructions – in May 1947, as part of the terms set for Italy receiving Marshall Aid – that Togliatti and his supporters were to be excluded from any access to control of the state, an arrangement that remained in force for many years, even when the PCI polled as high as 34% in 1976. Keeping this exclusion in place over such a lengthy period required constant political adjustments, and the result was that Italy had 47 different cabinets down to 1991, at which point, with the disintegration of the threat from the Soviet Union and the eastern bloc, matters eased off a bit.

Tinto's wayward behaviour outraged his father, who went so far as to commit his son to the San Clemente lunatic asylum in the Venetian lagoon. Built in 1844, this was a mental hospital on a tiny island that treated people suffering from various types of madness, including sexual hysteria. It also had a darker side, from what was then the immediate past: Mussolini had imprisoned his first wife Ida Dalser there until her death in 1937. Chastened by this experience, Tinto returned home and continued his studies. By 1950 he had started a law degree at the University of Padua, where he did well at his exams and, as a reward, was given a 16mm cine-camera. Around 1951 he met, through her brother Arrigo, Carla Cipriani, with whom he formed a relationship based on a mutual love of cinema. She was part of the Cipriani family who were celebrated for owning *Harry's Bar*, one of the most fashionable attractions in Venice, and a venue noted for its stellar customers: Ernest Hemingway drank there in 1948 and it was frequented by many of the stars, directors, producers and writers during the annual Venice Film Festival.

Brass's military service took him away for much of the time between 1951 and 1953, after which he returned to continue his studies at Padua. When not working at his law degree he continued to see Carla and expanded his social circle further by mixing with many local artists, including Albino Lucatello. A communist and Marxist, Lucatello was inspired by the *Fronte Nuovo delle Arti*, several of whom had fought as partisans in the armed struggle against fascism. Their manifesto was published in Venice in 1946, and they exhibited as a movement at the Venice Biennale two years later. It was a sensational show. As well as their work an opportunity arose when, due to complications caused by the Greek Civil War, the official Greek entry failed to arrive. This resulted in a vacant pavilion, which was taken by Peggy Guggenheim who filled it with modern avant-garde work from her own collection. It was the first time most people in Europe had seen Jackson Pollock or Mark Rothko outside of niche New York galleries, and proved to be something of a turning point in public awareness of modern art. The fiercely political neo-realism that had prevailed during the immediate post-1945 period now gave way to modernism and experimentalism based on abstraction, use of materials associated with modern life and mass production. Art was becoming less involved in day-to-day politics, and more observational, detached. The era of abstract expressionism had begun. Tinto Brass's politics changed around this time too, settling into a kind of anarchic non-conformism. At some point between his brief sojourn on San Clemente and his ongoing legal studies he became familiar with the work of Wilhelm Reich, a prominent Austrian psychoanalyst in the 1930s who proposed that neurosis was rooted in sexual and socio-economic repression. Reich believed, for instance, that sexual freedom could trigger political change leading to lasting happiness through society. His books *Die Massenpsychologie des Faschismus/The Mass Psychology of Fascism* (1933) and *Die Sexualität im Kulturkampf/The Sexual Revolution* (1936) were widely read studies on the nature of authoritarianism and how it oppressed the natural urges of the people.[7]

No longer the avant-garde they had seemed only a few years earlier, the members of the *Fronte Nuovo delle Arti* dispersed, and the movement lost momentum, though Lucatello, who was from Venice, remained active in the city's cultural life, and eventually won the Tursi Prize at the 1956 Biennale. In 1953, he married Giselda Paulon, the daughter of Flavia Paulon. A hugely influential figure at the Venice Biennale, Venice Film Festival and Trieste Science Fiction Festival, Flavia Paulon helped Peggy Guggenheim set up her gallery in Venice in 1949 and also owned the very highbrow film magazine *Sequenze*.[8] Through his friendship with Lucatello and Giselda Paulon, Brass got work from Flavia as a photographer at Cameraphoto, the Venetian news agency, and was engaged, during the summer of 1954, to cover the Venice Film Festival. (As it happens, this was a year with a terrific set of entries including *The Caine Mutiny, La Strada, On the Waterfront, Rear Window, Senso* and *Seven Samurai*.) He repeated this work in 1955 and 1956, and it was whilst working in this capacity that he met Lotte Eisner, the co-founder of the Cinémathèque Française. He was able to obtain Lotte Eisner invitations for prestige events – premieres, launches, press conferences and so on – and in return she suggested that if he should visit Paris, he might want to drop in and visit her at the Cinémathèque Française, where the prospect of a position was not out of the question.

Through 1956 and into 1957 Brass completed (and obtained) his law degree at Ferrara, where he was taught by Giuseppe Bettiol, a significant figure in the Christian Democrats and a leading Italian jurist in the post-war period. He made it clear to his family that he did not wish to practise law, or work in the legal profession: he wanted instead to work in film, or at the very least photography. His Plan A was to try and obtain work in Rome, where most of the producers and studios were based. He spent a couple of weeks there in July 1957 but he was rebuffed and failed to gain even the most modest employment in the industry. That done, his Plan B was to visit Paris. He did so, met Lotte Eisner and was offered an unpaid position (today we would say internship) at the Cinémathèque Française with accommodation included in a tiny, nearby flat. His job was to act as projectionist at their regular screenings and manage the screenplay library and still photograph library. He accepted. In October 1957 Carla Cipriani joined him from Venice and they married. He was 24 years old, and had worked as a news agency photographer at 3 successive Venice Film Festivals. He came from an artistic family with abundant artistic, cultural and literary connections and was now working in one of the most important creative centres of the French film industry.

Notes

(1) For a summary of Italico Brass's career in English, and examples of his works see: https://rjbuffalo.com/italico. html

(2) On Pound and Italico Brass see: https://www. nonsolocinema.com/venezia-1908-ezra-pound-e-italico. html

(3) A collection of Italico Brass's war paintings, *La Grande Guerra. I racconti pittorici di Italico Brass* by Enzo Savoia and Francesco Luigi Maspes appeared in Italy in 2018.

(4) On Duse and Asolo see: http://www.asolo.it/en/cosa-vedere-asolo/casa-duse-asolo/ The Earl of Iveagh, formerly Rupert Guinness MP, acquired a shoe making factory in Asolo in 1938. See: https://www.scarpa.co.uk/history/ Italian Wikipedia records that he *'also owned land in Italy, in the Veneto region of Asolo . Here he stayed in the house that once belonged to Eleonora Duse . During his stay in Italy in*

1938, he decided to bring together the best craftsmen in working leather and hide, founding the Società Calzaturieri Asolani Riuniti Pedemontana Anonima: SCARPA.' This is missing from his UK/US entry. Investing in manufacturing in Mussolini's Italy would have required a close and friendly relationship with local, and government level, officials.

(5)   Throughout the war Italico and Alessandro Brass loaned pictures from their collection to the Italian state for selected exhibitions and private viewings, the latter attended by leading figures across fascist Italy and Nazi Germany. Mention of this, and the appropriation of Jewish-owned items (in which there is no suggestion of any involvement by the Brass family), can be found at: https://www.lootedart.com/web_images/pdf2019/XXII_2019_BARTOLI.pdf The trailer for *Canal Grande* can be viewed at https://www.youtube.com/watch?v=L3kAqmqFIBw

(6)   For examples of post-war sales see: https://www.clevelandart.org/art/1947.210 and https://www.metmuseum.org/art/collection/search/437242

(7)   On Reich see *Adventures in the Orgasmatron: Wilhem Reich and the Invention of Sex* by Christopher Turner, Fourth Estate 2011.

(8)   Guggenheim's contribution to Venice, culture and art is outlined at https://www.guggenheim-venice.it/en/art/in-depth/peggy-guggenheim/memories/ which contains comments and recollections by Arrigo Cipriani (brother of Carla) and Giancarlo Paulon (brother of Giselda).

2

FROM THE CINÉMATHÈQUE FRANÇAISE TO YANKEE

The Cinémathèque Française was, and still is, an immensely prestigious organisation. It was founded, with an initial collection of 10 feature films, in 1936 by Henri Langlois (then only 22 years old), Georges Franju and Jean Mitry. Initially it concentrated on acquiring silent films, which, following the appearance of sound cinema earlier in that decade, were often being unceremoniously thrown away. Deemed to have no further commercial use, reels of silent film were usually melted down to extract the valuable nitrate from the stock on which they were printed. Langlois's very first acquisition was the German silent horror *The Cabinet of Dr Caligari*, and his privately run and funded organisation acted as part-cinema and part-museum, saving many films which were at risk of vanishing and preserving other related items such as cameras, projection machines, costumes, and vintage theatre programmes. Much of this was less-than-glamorous work, and involved rescuing reels of film from recycling facilities, financially strapped distribution houses, and even flea markets. It was also an entirely private undertaking. Its nearest equivalent, the British Film Institute, had been established by Royal Charter in 1933 and received a small amount of funding. By comparison Langlois and his colleagues worked with whatever resources they could conjure up themselves.[1]

During the occupation, the Vichy regime allocated them office space in the same building that accommodated the General Commissariat for Jewish Affairs. For a period, Langlois organised secret showings, in a hall named the *Musée de l'Homme*, of Soviet and American films the Germans had outlawed. Jean Rouch, at that point an engineering student, and later a prominent post-war documentary maker and anthropologist, wrote '...*In this empty Paris of the German occupation, in 1940-41, the Musée de l'Homme was the only open door to the rest of the world...*'[2] By 1942, the Germans had an outright ban on British and American films, as well as a list of French films they considered subversive. Langlois and his colleagues came up with various methods to conceal films the Germans wanted destroyed. Some hid film canisters in their homes and gardens, others, like his Jewish-German emigré and film historian colleague Lotte Eisner, secreted a cache of films in the dungeons of a chateau in the Unoccupied Zone of southern France. (From the late 1950s Eisner would mentor a new generation of German filmmakers, including Herzog, Schlöndorff and Wenders.)[3] In a country that prided itself on its cultural integrity, all of these activities contributed to the mythological status of the Cinémathèque.

After the war, the French government provided a small screening room, staff and subsidy for the collection, which initially was based in the Avenue de Messine. Here, Langlois held marathon film screenings, many of which were attended week after week, and film after film, by the cinéastes and students who would go on to create French New Wave cinema: Jacques Doniol-Valcroze, Pierre Kast, Alain Resnais, Jacques Rivette, Roger Vadim, Jean-Luc Godard, François Truffaut and Claude Chabrol. Often seated in the front row of Langlois's viewing theatre, they became known collectively as 'les enfants de la cinémathèque'.

By the time Brass arrived in 1957, Langlois was responsible for an archive of over 40,000 films, an enormous, personally assembled collection of features, shorts, cartoons, travelogues, newsreels, documentaries, experimental works and even 'home movies'. It was regularly added to as well, with production companies voluntarily depositing copies of their latest works and Langlois constantly sourcing unwanted or redundant material from distribution libraries. It was a fascinating place to work... with, importantly for Brass, unprecedented opportunities to view material rarely if ever seen in public. There was also the chance to work alongside Langlois on various projects, and by so doing, learn the art of editing and directing from scratch. One such project, and Brass's first 'credit', was a possible documentary on Marc Chagall, the legendary Russian-Jewish modernist artist, who had come up with the idea that his life might best be portrayed by making a film about his paintings. With Frédéric Rossif (with whom Langlois had made an acclaimed documentary study of Henri Matisse a few years earlier) filming began - expensively, on 35 mm and in colour - in 1952. Langlois eventually asked

Joris Ivens to supervise and edit the material. Ivens was an internationally renowned Dutch documentary maker and David Perlov, a Brazilian-Jewish student at the École des Beaux Arts (and via that a regular attendee at the Cinémathèque Française) was brought in to assist him, with Brass working alongside. At some point in the late 1950s/early 1960s the footage vanished before a final cut had been agreed and the full work is now presumed lost. Whether this was accidental or not is a moot point, as a rival effort, *Chagall* (1963), narrated by Vincent Price and directed by Lauro Venturi appeared shortly afterwards and went on to win an Oscar as Best Documentary Short at the 1964 Academy Awards.[4]

Brass also had the time and opportunity to shoot and edit his own material. An early effort from him was *Spatiodynamisme* (1958) a short colour documentary that he edited and co-directed with Nicolas Schöffer, about one of Schöffer's interactive robotic sculptures.[5] A Hungarian-French artist, Schöffer had become known after presenting the *Spectacle Spatiodynamique Expérimental*, which was exhibited at both the Théâtre d'Évreux in Évreux, Normandy and Grand Central Station in New York. Part light-show and part kinetic art, the short film featured very rapid editing by Brass. Schöffer remained fashionable for many years, and one of his self-propelled artworks is used in the promotional film for the February 1968 Brigitte Bardot song *Contact* (the B-side of *Harley Davidson* and, like that, a Serge Gainsbourg song) where she wears a Rabanne dress of the same kind featured in the films *Casino Royale* and *Barbarella*, and chants out her lyrics in the style of a robot in Fritz Lang's *Metropolis*.[6] For Brass to be involved with this type of work in 1958 was very cutting edge, and it is intriguing that his entrée into editing and directing came via documentaries about noted artists (Chagall and Schöffer) rather than any conventional dramatic themes.

Through Ivens Brass came into contact with Alberto Cavalcanti.[7] Cavalcanti hired Brass as assistant director on *La Prima Notte/Venetian Honeymoon*, a big budget Italian/French production shot in August-September 1958 in Venice with Martine Carol, Vittorio De Sica and Claudia Cardinale. After this commercial concoction he went, again as assistant director, to *India: Matri Bhumi*, screened as *India 58* in France. This was an extremely prestigious, feature-length documentary directed by Roberto Rossellini and made by him, at the invitation of Jawaharlal Nehru, in India between 1956 and 1958. Famous for *Rome: Open City* (1945), *Germany, Year Zero* (1949) and *Europa '51* (1953), Rossellini was a renowned figure in world cinema and his films did well up until his scandalous affair with Ingrid Bergman on the set of his 1951 film *Stromboli*. In 1957, whilst filming in India, Rossellini had another affair, this time with Bengali screenwriter Sonali Das Gupta, and soon after, Bergman and Rossellini separated. Rossellini returned with Gupta to Paris, where, in somewhat fraught circumstances, and once more attended by scandal, he and Brass edited the footage.[8] It premiered at the 1959 Cannes Film Festival and featured at the Moscow Film Festival that same year. Commercially it did little, but critics liked it, notably Jean-Luc Godard who proclaimed '...*Today, Roberto Rossellini has re-emerged with* India 58, *a film as great as* Que Viva Mexico! *or* Birth of a Nation *and which shows that this season in hell led to paradise, for* India 58 *is as beautiful as the creation of the world...*' [9] Rossellini kept Brass on for what was hailed in some quarters as his comeback film: *Il Generale Della Rovere*, a hard-hitting war drama set in Genoa, during the German occupation of northern Italy. Starring Vittorio De Sica, Hannes Messemer and Giovanna Ralli it was much admired and won the Golden Lion at the 1959 Venice Film Festival, subsequently getting a US and UK release in 1960-1961.

From this Brass moved on to *L'Italia Non è un Paese Povero* (1960), a government-funded, feature-length documentary about mining and mineral wealth, and the initiatives being taken to extract and distribute recently discovered oil and gas deposits. This reunited him with Joris Ivens, who directed from a commentary written by Alberto Moravia. Much liked by filmmakers, Moravia's books included *La Romana* (1947), filmed in 1954 with Gina Lollobrigida, and *La Ciociara* (1957). The latter was made into a film, *Two Women*, in 1960, directed by Vittorio De Sica and starring Sophia Loren who won an Academy Award for her performance. Later adaptations of Moravia's work would include *Le Mépris/Contempt*, directed by Jean-Luc Godard in 1963 with Brigitte Bardot, and *Il Conformista/The Conformist*, directed by Bernardo Bertolucci in 1970, with Jean-Louis Trintignant. In *L'Italia Non è un Paese Povero*, however, Ivens chose to concentrate on the poverty of the traditional Italian peasantry, and how little they received from the profits produced by the energy companies after they had vacated their land, rather than the 'progressive' message about a country being modernised. Inevitably, a clash occurred between the director and RAI TV (the production company) and the film was blocked for political reasons. Ivens took the only full-length, uncut print and gave it to Brass who took it to France for safekeeping.[10] A much shorter version eventually emerged; later accounts credit Vittorio and Paolo Taviani as co-directors with Ivens, though both brothers, then working as journalists, were originally hired, like Brass, as assistant directors.

Brass's time at the Cinémathèque Française came to end in 1960, with the organisation itself in some disarray. It lost a portion of its collection, thought to include over a hundred features, to a nitrate fire on 10 July 1959, including the only copy of the 1931 Erich von Stroheim film *The Honeymoon*. Langlois had been loaned this by the Museum of Modern Art in New York and his less than rigorous attitude to acquisition and collection and his generally unconventional methods came in for considerable criticism following this debacle. The International Federation of Film Archives (of which Langlois had been a founding member in 1938) were particularly strident in voicing their concerns, and eventually the French government stepped in. André Malraux – de Gaulle's Minister of Culture –was appointed to the Cinémathèque board and funding was provided to put the body on a more stable footing. One consequence of this was an improvement of the conditions and pay for the staff. Brass does not seem to have been under any requirement to leave but took the opportunity to do so anyway.

Having worked with Joris Ivens, Alberto Cavalcanti and Roberto Rossellini, Brass now felt ready to make his own, full-length films for cinematic release. Working at the Cinémathèque Française he had enjoyed access to the vast amount of documentary footage in their collection, much of which had never been publicly screened. With Langlois's permission, from 1959 he began editing together previously unseen newsreel material of political events and wars in the twentieth century and using it to illustrate a commentary written by himself and Gian Carlo Fusco. The end result was *Ça Ira, Il Fiume Della Rivolta*. A statement against state repression, and in favour of personal freedom, the film took its name from the song *Ça Ira*

(*It'll be fine*), one of many sung during the French Revolution. Zebra Films, the same company that had done Rossellini's *Il Generale Della Rovere*, agreed to produce. Run by Moris Ergas, their other productions around this time included *Adua e Le Compagne/Hungry for Love* (1960, with Marcello Mastroianni and Simone Signoret), *Kapo* (1960, with Susan Strasberg and directed by Gillo Pontecorvo), *Senilita/Careless* (1962, from an Italo Svevo novel with Claudia Cardinale and Anthony Franciosa) and *La Steppa/The Steppe* (1962, an adaptation of Chekhov). A Greek Jew fromThessaloniki , Ergas had survived a concentration camp and was a highly regarded producer, with a flair for literary and political subjects. *Ca Ira, Il Fiume Della Rivolta* finally premiered at the Venice Film Festival in 1964 and was released in Italy later that year. It brought Brass some acclaim, *Variety* noting '...*Well made, often fascinating, frequently a brutal montage... Film is brilliantly edited, material is vividly chosen, comment... is to the point, and the pic is technically ok...*'[11] Confirming early on the centrality of music in Brass's vision of how films should be assembled, it also came with a specially commissioned soundtrack by Italian composer Romolo Grano. A fellow Venetian, Grano had performed alongside Karlheinz Stockhausen at the Darmstadt Ferienkurse in the GDR in the 1950s and, like Stockhausen, would later become a keen practitioner of electronic music. For Brass's film he composed 18 pieces which were subsequently released on a soundtrack album on RCA. Alas, despite these promising beginnings, Italian censors denied the film an export certificate. It eventually appeared in the US in 1971 as *Thermidor*, with a narration by Ben Gazzara and Irene Worth.[12]

Whilst *Ca Ira, Il Fiume Della Rivolta* was being prepared, his next film appeared, also produced by Moris Ergas, who appears at this point to have been Brass's patron. Completed in August 1963, *Chi Lavora è Perduto/Whoever Works is Lost* was shot partly in black-and- white and partly in colour, an approach found in many of his early productions. Brass wrote, edited and directed, once more with help from Gian Carlo Fusco on the script. The dialogue was by Franco Arcalli, a friend from Venice, who had also worked on *Ca Ira, Il Fiume Della Rivolta* as assistant director. In later years, Arcalli's own credits were both eclectic and impressive, including *Death Laid an Egg*, as writer and editor, *Zabriskie Point*, editor only, and *Last Tango in Paris*, again as both writer and editor. In a plot clearly influenced by James Joyce's *Ulysses*, the camera follows a young man roaming around Venice having various thoughts, fantasies and adventures. The cast was led by Sady Rebbot, who had just starred in Godard's *Vivre Sa Vie* (1962), as the young man and Pascale Audret as his girlfriend. Tino Buazzelli (one of the narrators of *Ca Ira, Il Fiume Della Rivolta*, and a stage actor who had done Brecht's *Galileo* in Milan) and Arcalli, acting here as well as contributing to the screenplay, co-star. The film premiered at the 1963 Venice Film Festival alongside *Billy Liar, The Servant, Tom Jones* and many others. (None of these was in luck, and the Grand Prize went to a study of political corruption in Naples, *Le Mani Sulla Città/ Hands Over the City* with Rod Steiger, directed by Francesco Rosi.) Brass's film was much liked, though, and, given its subject matter, actually made for an interesting comparison with *Billy Liar*. But it was banned in Italy, for its clear mockery of social institutions, the armed forces, religion and work. When it was eventually released, with 14 minutes cut in April 1964, it did well at the box-office and Brass found himself hailed as an emerging auteur.[13] He also developed the central idea a bit further, writing another script about a day-in-the-life of a central character with a lot of Joycean inner dialogue. This time the plot was completely explicated by music, and the main role was played by a white woman who is pursued by (and fantasises about) a black man. This eventually became *Nerosubianco*, shot in London in 1967-1968.

Between the emergence of *Chi Lavora e Perduto* and *Ça Ira, Il Fiume Della Rivolta*, Umberto Eco commissioned Brass to make two documentaries, *Tempo Lavorativo/Work Time* and *Tempo Libero/Leisure Time*. Both were collages assembled from a huge variety of footage that was rapidly cut and spliced together, and matched to music from Igor Stravinsky. Not known for being a film producer – at this point he was an academic and philosopher at the University of Turin – Eco was also a member of Gruppo 63, which challenged the values of contemporary bourgeois and capitalist society, particularly the spreading of consumerism via the mass media. They sharply criticised the soporific impact of this, proposing instead 'the power of imagination'. (Eco had published *The Aesthetics of St Thomas Aquinas*, and would write a study of James Joyce a few years later.)[14] Brass's two films, both of which ran for less than ten minutes, pack in more images than most feature films do in a couple of hours. They were projected simultaneously inside a specially assembled viewing area, with visitors sitting inside, surrounded by mirrors, and overwhelmed by the experience. This was experimental cinema at its most extreme, and it is arguable that no other director, before or since, has produced material with so many images that last for a fraction of a second. In fact, these are not really 'films', they are more like kinetic art. Bewilderingly rapid montages, where images are juxtaposed in an absurd, violent, comic, satirical or sinister fashion. In terms of the rapidity with which your eyes are assaulted, there are similarities to John Latham's *Speak* (1962) (a copy of which was screened behind Pink Floyd at the Roundhouse in 1966-1967) though Latham used Pop Art designs and imagery rather than newsreel footage.[15] This was very advanced stuff – and confirmed how much Brass was influenced by Pop Art itself.

Following Ergas and Eco, Brass's next patron was Dino De Laurentiis, who brought him in to direct two of the five episodes in the portmanteau comedy *La Mia Signora/My Wife* (1964). Each of these starred Alberto Sordi and Silvana Mangano who was married to De Laurentiis. The two which were directed by Brass were written by Rodolfo Sonego who would later script *The Girl with a Gun/La Ragazza con la Pistola* (1967) and *Satyricon* (1969, with Tina Aumont). The film had music by Armando Trovajoli, and, with both stars being popular, did good business in Italy. A few months later, Brass's second film for De Laurentiis, the sci-fi comedy *Il Disco Volante/ The Flying Saucer* (1964) appeared, with Sordi, Mangano and Monica Vitti. A silly farce, it is redeemed by Brass shooting it documentary-style, on location with a large number of locals in uncredited roles. Sordi, possibly emulating Peter Sellers in *Dr Strangelove*, agreed to play four separate parts, and the end result has a distinctive, even anti-establishment slant. As with *La Mia Signora*, it was popular in Italy, and got some screenings on US TV in 1967.

His ascent continued with an invitation to be one of the co-authors of *MANIFESTO*. Written mainly by Roberto Rossellini with contributions from, among others, Bernardo Bertolucci, Gian Vittorio Baldi, and Vittorio Cottafavi, this reprised the case for art-for art's-sake, whilst noting that technological progress allowed directors to move away from social realism and that a huge opportunity existed to use film to educate audiences about their place in the world and in history. Published in Rome in July 1965, it was reprinted in *Cahiers du Cinéma No. 171* (August 1965), the edition that trailed the entries for the forthcoming Venice Film Festival.

Next came *Yankee*, a spaghetti western. Sergio Leone's *A Fistful of Dollars* (September 1964) had revived interest in the western as a genre a few years earlier by providing its producers with a return approximately a hundred times what it cost to make. Many imitations quickly followed, including such stylish works as *A Pistol for Ringo* (May 1965) and *Django* (April 1966). *Yankee* was, in fact, co-produced by the same Spanish company, Balcazar Productions, which had done *A Pistol for Ringo* (and its sequel *The Return of Ringo*) as well as the ludicrous Bond parody *Kiss Kiss Bang Bang*. They had an extensive schedule, though few of their films were seen outside Spain, Italy and France. Brass decided to shoot it in the style of a comic book, from a script by Gian Carlo Fusco and Alberto Silvestri. Filmed in Spain, it has a conventional enough plot: an unnamed gunfighter ('Yankee') falls foul of the local mobster and his gang whilst passing through a fly-blown, one-street town somewhere near the Mexico-US border. After various misadventures, the unnamed gunfighter triumphs. The main roles were played by Philippe Leroy, noted for *Le Trou* (1960) and *Senilita* (1962) and Adolfo Celi, widely seen around that time as the villain in *Thunderball* (1965). The end result is certainly good to look at (the cinematographer was Alfio Contini, who would later do *Zabriskie Point* and *The Night Porter*) and, closely following the example set by Morricone in Leone's films, there is an attractive and sparse title theme by trumpeter Nini Rosso, which was subsequently released as a single.

It was mentioned as a forthcoming release in *Variety* in May 1966. But the producers objected to Brass's cut. They wanted something conventional and easy to market, and weren't interested in flashy Pop-Art imagery that set new visual boundaries. They re-edited the film to make it more accessible (in their view) only for Brass to sue and win. Some, but not all, of his cut was reinstated. By the time this was reported in *Variety* (September 1966), *Yankee* had already been released in Italy, and would appear over the next couple of years across Europe. It is considered an interesting variant on the genre, which yielded 57 films in 1966 alone. Some cinéastes have noted that specific shots in Brass's film appear to have inspired scenes in Sergio Leone's *Once Upon a Time in the West* (1968), and Sam Peckinpah's *The Wild Bunch* (1969), both of which appeared to much greater acclaim than *Yankee*.

Brass's rise had been rapid: in nine years he had worked with Henri Langlois, Joris Ivens, Alberto Cavalcanti, Roberto Rossellini, Alberto Moravia, Paolo and Vittorio Taviani, Moris Ergas, Umberto Eco, Dino De Laurentiis, Silvana Mangano and Monica Vitti. He was 33 years old, had been the sole director of four feature films, of which two had run into trouble with the Italian censors and a third had led to a dispute with the producers over the final cut. He was considered by many the next major auteur who would emerge from Italian cinema. By comparison, at the same age Antonioni and Pasolini didn't have a single credit between them, Sergio Leone had one and Federico Fellini two.[16] French directors fared better, though, with Jean-Luc Godard and Roger Vadim having six films each by the same age, and Claude Chabrol seven. Which rather makes one wonder if Brass's spell at the Cinémathèque Française places him – in approach, style and output – much more within French than Italian cinema.

The legal case with Balcazar Productions kept Brass's name in the press and brought him to the attention of Panda Films. By the autumn of 1966 he had signed up with them to make *Col Cuore in Gola*.

Notes

(1) On the foundation of the Cinémathèque Française see: http://www.kitchensisters.org/present/archivefever/ and https://www.npr.org/2018/09/20/649236063/savior-of-film-henri-langlois-began-extensive-cinema-archive-in-his-bathtub?t=1621802444129 Also, on the formation of the International Federation of Film Archives (FIAF) see: https://www.fiafnet.org/pages/History/Origins-of-FIAF.html

(2) Quoted in *The Cinematic Griot: The Ethnography of Jean Rouch* by Paul Stoller, 1992. On Rouch see also https://www.cinematheque.fr/media/jean-rouch.pdf

(3) Herzog's recollections of this can be viewed at https://www.youtube.com/watch?v=mhc8u850eNk

(4) Some silent footage, basically rushes, can be viewed at: https://www.cinematheque.fr/henri/film/122207-chagall-dans-son-jardin-a-saint-paul-de-vence-frederic-rossif-henri-langlois-1952-1970/

(5) The film can be viewed at https://www.youtube.com/watch?v=dO0pffhB9SU

(6) *Contact* can be viewed at https://www.youtube.com/watch?v=1SE_K7SSDKg Its similarity to Brass's *Spatiodynamisme*, which appeared a decade earlier, is striking.

(7)   Ivens produced and Cavalcanti directed *Die Windrose*, a 1957 East German documentary about the struggles of women workers in Italy, France, Brazil, China and the Soviet Union.

(8)   On Brass's involvement with this film see *Under Her Spell: Roberto Rossellini in India* by Dileep Padgaonkar, 2008, p246.

(9)   Quoted at https://www.sabzian.be/film/india-matri-bhumi The film can be viewed at https://www.youtube.com/watch?v=FLrfyIBLOdA

(10) Both versions can be viewed on You Tube at https://www.youtube.com/watch?v=mWGvKLv2nLA (short version) and https://www.youtube.com/watch?v=kaQ8Uy34rsE (long version)

(11) For a full account see: https://rjbuffalo.com/1962a-ca.html

(12) It did so after Altura Films agreed a distribution deal, having previously handled *Mourir a Madrid/To Die in Madrid* by French documentarist and Cinémathèque Française collaborator Frédéric Rossif.

(13) For Brass's own view on the film see the interview at https://www.torinofilmfest.org/en/1-festival-internazionale-cinema-giovani/film/chi-lavora-%C3%A8-perduto-(in-capo-al-mondo)/5895/

(14) Gruppo 63 was primarily a literary movement, and one that wanted to continue to push forward in the same avant-garde direction that Eliot, Pound, Joyce, Proust and Kafka had taken many years earlier.

(15) A copy of *Speak* can be viewed at https://vimeo.com/159652068

(16) Among the authors of MANIFESTO Rossellini and

Cottafavi had started directing in the 1940s. Of the others Bertolucci and Baldi had just two films each to their name: Brass had four, two of which had been banned by the Italian censors.

3

'...THE CHANCE TO WORK IN LONDON...'

Run by Luigi Carpentieri and Ermanno Donati, Panda Films had been active since 1950, gradually breaking into the US and UK markets with productions like *Marco Polo* (1961) and latterly a couple of faux Bond parodies, *Goldsinger* (1965) and *The Wacky World of James Tont* (1966). They also co-produced, working on *Navajo Joe* (a 1966 spaghetti western with Burt Reynolds) and *Matchless* (1967) with Dino De Laurentiis.

By mid-1966 they wanted to make a decently budgeted film in 'Swinging London', and alighted as source material on Sergio Donati's thriller *The Paper Tomb*, which had the merit of actually having been published in the UK, in a 1958 translation by Isabel Quigly, film critic of *The Spectator*. Another of Donati's books, *Web of Violence*, had just been filmed and his other credits around this time included *Requiem for a Secret Agent* with Stewart Granger and a couple of spaghetti westerns. With what was effectively a readymade script they made an arrangement to co-produce with Les Films Corona, a Paris-based company run by Robert Dorfmann. Corona had many successes in France (and Europe) through the 50s and 60s, but despite backing directors like René Clément, Marcel Carné and Roger Vadim, like Panda, they had yet to achieve a significant hit with a UK-based film.

Brass was hired on the basis of his record as an innovative young Italian auteur, who could complete a film quickly and economically in the then fashionable 'pop' style, as evidenced in *Yankee*. Quite who approached whom, though, and when, remains unclear. According to Sergio Donati, Brass did an adaptation of the book *before* the producers had formally agreed to option it, and the option itself was only signed after Brass had shot the film. This seems unlikely: in all probability Brass was approached, worked quickly on an adaptation and even shot some of the film itself before the negotiations for the option (which may have been carried out in tandem, involving both sets of producers) were finalised, though the terms themselves may have been agreed in principle between all parties some while earlier. Once these were confirmed, at the tail end of 1966, Brass asked Armando Trovajoli to do the score and commissioned Guido Crepax to provide a set of Pop-Art cartoons that would explicate the plot.

Trovajoli was prolific (he did 15 soundtracks alone in 1967-1968) and had been active in film and music, as a jazz pianist, for many years. His music for *Bitter Rice* (1949) and *Two Women* (1960) was particularly admired. Along the way he had also worked on *My Wife* (1964), the Dino De Laurentiis portmanteau comedy of which Brass directed two episodes. His services would not have been cheap, and the fact that he was engaged to do an entire soundtrack confirms that *Col Cuore in Gola* was a film with a reasonable budget. As was common then, Trovajoli composed a main theme and used variations of it throughout the film. The vocal rendition of it, *Love Girl*, used over the opening and final title sequences, was sung by Mal Ryder, who had moved to Italy from the UK with his group The Primitives, after releasing five unsuccessful singles at home. By the time he was engaged to work on *Col Cuore in Gola* he and his band had recorded with Chris Blackwell, which may indicate that they were considered as a possible signing by Island. They had an album, *Blow-Up*, rushed out to cash in with Antonioni's film.[1] With an unusually good voice and impressive matinee idol looks, of the Engelbert Humperdinck, Tom Jones and Scott Walker type, Ryder had been spotted as having great potential in Italy. He was launched as a solo artist in late 1967 and *Col Cuore in Gola* could be seen as a preliminary step in that direction. When contacted about how he came to be hired, he recollected '...*My record company RCA got me to sing many themes when they needed to be sung in English, I also sang the theme song to* The Girl with a Gun/La ragazza con la Pistola, *a Mario Monicelli film made in 1968 with Monica Vitti...*'[2] The words for *Love Girl* were written by Audrey Nohra Stainton, wife of Greek-Italian film producer Anis Nohra. Her role was to write English language lyrics on an as-required basis for any domestically produced film that was likely to get either a US or UK release. (She also did *The Ballad of Hank McCain*, sung by Jackie Lynton, to music by Ennio Morricone, as the main theme to *Gli Intoccabili/Machine Gun McCain*, 1969.) As with the hiring of Trovajoli, the use of Mal Ryder and Audrey Stainton suggests this was seen as a film of some substance, and one that would gain a wide release.[3]

Guido Crepax was an Italian graphic artist who did comic-book-style Pop Art heavily influenced by Roy Lichtenstein. Pop Art had been formally exhibited at the Venice Biennale in 1964, and a year later Crepax became a household name across Europe with *Valentina*, his Louise Brooks-inspired creation. Drawn for the newly-launched magazine *Linus*, *Valentina* offered improbable erotic adventures and exemplified European chic for many: a mix of glamour and sensuality always staged in the most fashionable of settings. *Linus* was soon being read mainly by adults, and feature films that exploited the immense popularity of comic-strip stories quickly became very popular. By the end of 1966 both *Modesty Blaise* (with Monica Vitti) and *Kriminal* had been released and two others, *Barbarella* (a De Laurentiis project) and *Satanik* were in the early stages of production.[4]

Modesty Blaise was nominated for the Palme d'Or at Cannes in 1966, but would lose to *A Man and A Woman*, the film which made Jean-Louis Trintignant an international star. It might even be regarded, in some ways, as an influence on what Brass would try to achieve in *Col Cuore in Gola*. Both films had a comic-book feel, with shots set up to emulate the frame-by-frame plot development of the strip cartoon. Both are suspense/crime capers. Both have a lot of contemporary art, fashion and other extraneous detail crammed into them. Monica Vitti, too, provides an interesting link. As well as appearing in Brass's *Il Disco Volante* (1964) she was well-known internationally for starring roles in *L'Avventura* (1960), *La Notte* (1961), *L'Eclisse* (1962) and *The Red Desert* (1964) all of which garnered prizes on the festival circuit. Her husband, Michelangelo Antonioni, directed her in these and arrived in London in May 1966 to shoot *Blow-Up*, the first major auteur to work in the city and confirmation, if any were needed, that London was now the place to be.

With Antonioni in town, and Brigitte Bardot too (starring, with Mike Sarne, in *Two Weeks in September*) it was hardly surprising that Carpentieri, Donati, Panda Films and Les Films Corona felt that a significant London-based feature was the next logical step for their business. They had initially dipped into this market with *Matchless*, their De Laurentiis collaboration. Directed by Alberto Lattuada, this starred Patrick O'Neal, Henry Silva, Ira von Fürstenberg and Donald Pleasence and featured a couple of scenes set at the Royal Albert Hall. For their next production – *Col Cuore in Gola* – they kept Alan Sekers, Lattuada's UK production assistant, in place to assist Brass and his crew. It was a job he would occupy for the next two and a half years, through three films and a couple of aborted projects. There was no formal interview, as such, with Sekers remembering today, '...*It was all done on the shake of a hand. Most of Tinto's crew were recruited that way: it was very much like a family. Once you were "in" you knew you'd be looked after...*' [5] For mundane organisational reasons, Sekers's appointment was important – anyone foreign trying to shoot a film in the UK needed someone familiar with the country to run the daily schedule. As Sekers says, '...*I could speak enough Italian – tourist Italian really – to get by and carry out the instructions I was given on the set. If you were shooting an Italian film in the UK, rather than just some backing shots, you needed a few English crew and people who could translate Italian...*'

This was useful, but much more important was that they managed to sign Jean-Louis Trintignant for the leading role. It cannot be understated how significant a choice this was then. By 1966 Trintignant had appeared alongside most of the European greats, in *And God Created Woman* (1956) and 15 other major French or Italian productions prior to his huge breakthrough hit with *A Man and a Woman* (1966). At the point he opted to work with Brass, this was the most successful French film ever made, with massive overseas box-office takings, and a soundtrack LP that spent 93 weeks in the US album charts, peaking at No 10. What attracted him to *Col Cuore in Gola?* It appears that Trintignant had heard about the unusual approach Brass had taken to shooting *Yankee* as well as the furore about the post-production editing and cutting of the film, and on the basis of this, expressed an interest in working with him. If so, this paralleled how he got the part in *A Man and A Woman*. Trintignant did not consider himself a great actor, and hearing that *A Man and A Woman* would be mainly improvised, he approached its hitherto unsuccessful director (Claude Lelouch) and told him how much he had admired one of his films.[6] For his part, Brass's pitch to Trintignant was to stress that *Col Cuore* was about a disillusioned man (Bernard) meeting a girl with no illusions (Jane) during a day and a night in London. He hugely simplified the plot of Donati's novel to pare it down to this simple element... a murder mystery involving two characters set in a city with sordid, seedy locations. Alan Sekers remembers, *'...Trintignant was a very nice guy. Very easy to work with. I think the reason he did it was he wanted the chance to work in London and his agent had heard about this film* (Col Cuore in Gola*) being made there, so he went for it...'*

His role also fitted the persona that Trintignant projected at this time. In the 3 years that followed his huge hit with *A Man and A Woman*, he starred in 17 films. In most of these (with the exception of a solitary spaghetti western) he played bourgeois men of dubious morality or strange sexuality in elegant and ultra-contemporary settings. The part he had in *Col Cuore in Gola* chimed with this and he was happy taking the role.

For the part of the young girl Carpentieri and Donati landed Ewa Aulin. Crowned Miss Teen Sweden in 1965 at 15, she appeared the same year in *Djävulen's Instrumen* a short by Gunnar Fischer, noted for being cameraman on Bergman's *Wild Strawberries* and *The Seventh Seal*. In this she played a young girl that a jazz bassist tries to seduce after a concert. From there, she represented Sweden in a beauty pageant in Hollywood. She won, and was crowned Miss Teen International 1966, after which film work beckoned. Her debut came in the comedy *Don Giovanni in Sicilia* (*Don Juan in Sicily*), based on an acclaimed novel by Vitaliano Brancati and released in April 1967. It was directed by Alberto Lattuada, and from it she went to *Col Cuore in Gola*. Barely 17 years old when filming with Brass (Trintignant was 36), according to Sekers, '...*Aulin was very naïve, very young. Always heavily made up with lots of make-up...*'

In supporting roles were Roberto Bisacco, co-starring as David, a photographer friend of Bernard's and Vira Silenti, who was married to Ermanno Donati, as Jane's mother. Charles Kohler plays Jane's brother, Jerome, with Monique Scoazec as his girlfriend. Bisacco had just appeared with Monica Vitti in the jet-set heist thriller *Kill me Quick, I'm Cold* and Silenti had numerous credits in Italian productions, but efforts to trace either Kohler or Scoazec have failed. Given that Charlie Kohler was the name of the character played by Charles Aznavour in Truffaut's *Shoot the Piano Player* some years earlier, one wonders if this isn't a pseudonym used by Brass and/or the actor playing Jerome, as an in-joke.

Brass's script had Trintignant and Aulin being chased around London by an assorted gang of heavies played by Luigi Bellini, Skip Martin, David Prowse and Joe Zaranoff. Bellini, as Fantanicchio, had been one of Italy's few homegrown rock and roll singers in the early 60s.[7] Skip Martin, a dwarf, appeared in several highly rated UK horror productions, and whilst working on *Col Cuore in Gola* was also filming an episode of the TV drama *Adam Adamant Lives!* Prowse, universally famous now for playing Darth Vader in *Star Wars* and two of its sequels, was a weightlifter and bodybuilder who had moved into acting and would subsequently appear in a BBC TV *Wednesday Play* adaptation of Peter Terson's *Mooney and his Caravans* with John Alderton. Zaranoff was a popular wrestler: wrestling drew huge TV audiences on UK TV in the 60s, with one performer, Ricki Starr, enjoying such popularity that he secured a starring role in the Donald Cammell-scripted film *The Touchables*.[8]

With funding in place, the casting complete and a crew assembled, the film was ready to proceed by the beginning of March 1967. A batch of press releases confirms this, and also confirms, even at that late stage, that a title had not been settled on. *The Los Angeles Times* reported (on 14 March 1967) that the film *With Bated Breath* was starting in London on 27 March and would star 'the current Miss Teen International'.[9]

The film starts in a mortuary, where a family are gathered to identify the body of a middle-aged man – Mr Burroughs – who has died following a cerebral haemorrhage. We cut to Trintignant (Bernard, an actor) arriving in London. The titles, brilliantly done as a Pop-Art collage, roll to the accompaniment of Trovajoli's *Love Girl*, sung by Mal Ryder. A big rock ballad, its chord sequences, unusual instrumentation and mournful words alert us to the fact that this is going to be a human drama, and most likely one that will end in a way that at least one of the characters will regret. The melody, minus the words, and interpreted on various instruments, will occur at key moments throughout the rest of the film.

We cut to a nightclub where Trintignant is drinking. The family are there too, post-mortuary. Trintignant sees Aulin dancing and is fascinated by her. He tries to buy another drink, but the barman refuses, saying the manager is no longer extending him any credit. Trintignant says he will visit the manager upstairs and ask why: one of the manager's heavies (Luigi Bellini as Jelly Roll) notes this. Once upstairs, though, Trintignant finds the club owner, Prescott, dead. Aulin is there too, and says she didn't do it. He comforts her, opens the manager's safe and takes out an address book, gun and money. They escape as footsteps approach and drive off in Trintignant's sports car. He asks her name. She says Jane, to which he answers laconically that his must be Tarzan.

They go to Trintignant's flat. Resembling a student bedsit (which makes us wonder just how successful an actor he really is), it is decorated with massively enlarged portraits of Clark Gable, Humphrey Bogart and enormous Batman cartoons. They discuss the murder. Trintignant leaves and goes to Prescott's house. He finds an empty room with a Nazi uniform. There is a safe there that has already been opened. Jelly Roll and another heavy from the club arrive. Trintignant hides behind a curtain, but they find him. There is a *Mad* magazine poster of Alfred E Neuman on the wall behind and he replicates the gormless catchphrase of this character, saying *'What, me worry?'* After a scuffle (in which, blow by blow, the scenes are explicated by Crepax cartoons in the style of a fight in the *Batman* TV series) he shoots and kills the heavy (David Prowse) and then beats Jelly Roll senseless.

He goes back to the flat. There is a large poster advertising the *Revolver* LP on the wall. Jane comes out of the shower. They undress. There is much soft focus and they make love. The film is 20 minutes old and there have already been 3 deaths.

In the morning he wakes up, alone, when she calls him by telephone. They meet at Piccadilly Circus, where we see a busker at work entertaining the passing crowds.[10] Trintignant buys a paper. They go into a newsreel theatre, where they see footage of the Six Day War and the latest images from Vietnam. After this they walk through a CND rally in Trafalgar Square with a woman singing, very sedately, *There Will Always Be an England*. The camera pans across the demo with its crowds of students and other middle-class types, with Brass making the point as he does so that the UK is a very safe place compared with the rest of the world. Aulin and Trintignant drive away in his sports car and go shopping. They loiter outside the London Steak House, 94 Kings Road, and then arrive at a boutique, Granny Takes a Trip, 488 Kings Road.

Here Trintignant looks into a vintage Mutoscope at a set of flickering 'what the butler saw' images, and gazes at a display of classic 1966-1967 San Francisco gig posters. The sales assistant is reading *Melody Maker*. Aulin tries on a dress and Trintignant buys a huge Victorian erotica poster. They leave, and after a brief stop at an amusement arcade, head to Richmond Park. Here, we become aware that another of Prescott's gang, the dwarf, is following them. They visit an aviary. Aulin looks amazing. Trintignant is suspicious and goes to make a call from a red phone box. Whilst he does so Aulin is kidnapped. Trintignant tries to intervene, but is tripped over and beaten by the dwarf.

He recovers and takes a taxi to Earl's Court to visit Jane's brother, Jerome. Jerome's flat is full of Pop Art too, including large archery target images of the type appropriated by 'mod' culture, which seem to have come to prominence simultaneously via the artists Kenneth Noland and Peter Blake. Interestingly, the version seen in Jerome's flat can also be seen in the publicity material for *Just Like a Woman*, released in the UK on 26 February 1967. Also on display is a Mary Quant picture and a big poster for a forthcoming event at the Alexandra Palace. Whilst in the flat they get a call from the kidnappers. Jerome and Bernard leave and drive via Park Lane to the docks where they ambush and beat another heavy – an unidentified black actor – forcing him to say where Jane is being held.

Brass cuts to Bernard and Jerome arriving at Kensal Green Cemetery, and from there to the north end of Ladbroke Grove. He also cuts in footage at this point of steam trains at Clapham Junction. Next, we see Bernard and Jerome roaming around scenes of immense dereliction in Southam Street. The camera work here is tremendous and Brass uses splitscreen editing again, as he did in the opening titles. They find Jane bound and gagged in the wreckage of a house and, in a complex set of manoeuvres, shoot dead the dwarf and another of the heavies holding her, bringing the death toll to five. After Jane is released, she and Bernard run across a railway bridge and arrive in Tavistock Crescent, W11 where they catch a London RT bus. From what follows it looks as if Brass simply got on a passing bus with Trintignant and Aulin and completely improvised the next scene – he shoots Bernard and Jane upstairs, cutting to and from them (whilst they speak their dialogue) and bemused passengers. First Jane and then Bernard alight. They get separated and meet again on the Albert Bridge, where a body is being fished out of the Thames.

Finally, they arrive at a photographer's studio. There is an advert on the wall for *International Times*, but what follows echoes a similar scene in *Blow-Up*. Jane poses for the camera and takes her clothes off whilst Bernard plays the drums and does a Tarzan impersonation. They embrace and, off camera, Bernard quotes Antonioni. After they have made love for a second time, Bernard and Jane go to Indica Gallery, where the exhibition is showing some kinetic art works.

Upstairs, they find a dead man in the bath – corpse number six – and hurriedly drive away. At an amusement arcade, they encounter Jelly Roll again, and get chased by him to Holborn Station where they get on a train to Aldwych. In the ensuing melee, Jane gets away, but Bernard is pursued, in footage shot on the enormous enclosed passenger footbridge at Clapham Junction, to Clapton Greyhound Stadium where he is caught and badly beaten by Jelly Roll, assisted by wrestler Joe Zaranoff.

Manhandled into their car, Bernard escapes when the heavies crash into a police car. Both Zaranoff and Jelly Roll are killed. He goes back to the studio where Jane is doing a photo shoot. She is shocked at his cuts and bruises and looks after him. From his dark room, David (the photographer) watches Bernard and Jane via a hidden camera. We notice the poster on the wall, advertising 'The 14 Hour Technicolour Dream'. Bernard, Jane, David, Jerome and his girlfriend all go to the Alexandra Palace, to take part in this event.

They enter the huge hall amid cacophonous noise, and drift apart. The camera follows Bernard and Jane through the huge crowds and past the Exploding Galaxy Dance Troupe. Trintignant meets Mrs Burroughs and the two of them go to a small room and talk. The audience outside the room – which has large windows looking out into the hall – mill around, looking directly at the camera whilst Brass films the scene. We cut back to the main event, which Trintignant is now walking through alone, past assorted dancers, hippies, girls and mods.

In the background we see huge billowing transparent plastic sculptures and an immense dust cloud (caused by one of the bands flour-bombing their audience). Brass cuts in a flashback where we see that it was Jane who killed her father. Trintignant goes upstairs and outside to the balcony. Dawn is breaking across London. Jane is there. He confronts her about his suspicions. Coldly and deliberately, she shoots him and walks away. It turns out that Jane was the killer after all and Bernard was out of his depth. His death is the ninth and final killing in the film. Trovajoli's main theme plays, and the titles roll up the screen in a solid block of print.

After a shoot lasting no more than nine weeks, Brass and his crew wrapped *Col Cuore in Gola* in May 1967. They began the job of editing and dubbing the footage, with Brass also trying to ensure that *Col Cuore in Gola* would appear ultra-contemporary at its premiere. In the scene where Trintignant buys a paper before meeting Jane at Piccadilly Circus, the paper (*The Evening Standard*) carries on its front page the story of the SS *Torrey Canyon* – a wrecked oil tanker – being deliberately bombed by the RAF and set on fire off the Scilly Isles. This incident took place on 28 March 1967. However, when Bernard and Jane enter the newsreel theatre, they watch footage of the Six Days War, which occurred 5-10 June, after the film had wrapped. Brass clearly edited this into his director's cut sometime in June-July, so that his film would have an immediacy when released.

It premiered out of competition, at the Venice Film Festival. Opening on 28 August 1967 this had a number of high-profile formal entries, including *Lo Straniero/The Stranger* (Visconti's adaptation of Camus, with Marcello Mastroianni), *Belle de Jour* (Buñuel's study of sexuality, with Catherine Deneuve), *La Chinoise* (Godard's updating of Dostoyevsky), *Edipe Re/Oedipus Rex* (Pasolini doing Sophocles, with Alida Valli and Silvana Mangano), and, from the UK, *Our Mother's House* (a Jack Clayton suspense/horror drama with Dirk Bogarde). The jury, chaired by Alberto Moravia, awarded the Golden Lion to *Belle de Jour*; no mention was made in their deliberations, one way or the other, of Brass's film. There was, of course, quite a roster of material being screened *out* of competition, and four of these won awards too, but nothing came the way of *Col Cuore in Gola*, which, given that Venice was Brass's home town, must have felt like something of a letdown to him. Possibly, it was thought the film was just one of many London-based freewheeling crime capers. When compared to the serious intellectual fare shown at the festival, this may have seemed a reasonable line to take. Certainly, the US magazine *Films in Review*, who were present at the event, described it in their October 1967 issue as '*fatuous twiddling about, being "with-it"*' and critics elsewhere tended to dismiss it in similar terms. But this, of course, was to miss what Brass was trying to do: make a piece of Pop Art that was also a full-length feature film. Thus, he had, as would be the case in a strip cartoon, quotes from poets and philosophers embedded in the dialogue, and visual allusions to a variety of icons, ranging from comic book heroes to Hollywood stars of the 1930s and 1940s. There is also the switch, throughout the film, from colour to black-and-white and back again. Not only did this replicate the style of comic books (and Crepax's art work) it also had the benefit of reducing costs, black-and-white film stock being cheaper and available in some abundance in 1967 as productions switched 100% to colour.

As would be the case with many of his films, they weren't serious enough for highbrow critics, and were too complex and fast moving for popular audiences. For the moment, though, Robert Dorfmann in particular seems to have liked what he saw. Trintignant gave a solid performance in one of his typical roles and Aulin's image as the little girl lost who doesn't want to grow up made her an oddly childlike femme fatale. She also looks fantastic throughout the film. A chemistry was detected on screen between them and both were promptly signed by Dorfmann to star (with Claudia Cardinale) in *La Morte ha Fatto L'uovo/Death Laid an Egg*, shooting on which started almost immediately *Col Cuore in Gola* wrapped. In a more general sense too, cooperating on Brass's film seems to have been an enjoyable experience for both Panda and Les Films Corona, as in its aftermath, they co-produced *Manon '70*, with Catherine Deneuve in the main role and music from Serge Gainsbourg.

Thus, despite a muted reception, the original running time of 107 minutes remained reasonably intact and neither producer sought to make any cuts. *Col Cuore in Gola* opened in Italy in November 1967 and West Germany (as *Ich Bin Wie Ich Bin/I Am What I Am*) in January 1968. Perhaps put out by the guarded attitude of the critics, there was, oddly for a film that relied so heavily on London visuals, no UK cinema release: though a greatly reduced version (only 52 minutes long) was available there from late 1968 on 8mm, for anyone with their own home movie set up. A French release, as *En Cinquième Vitesse/In Fifth Gear*, finally happened in April 1969. US cinemas got a dubbed, full length, version distributed by Paramount (as *Deadly Sweet*) the same month, with movie theatre owners being advised by the trade journals '...*The technique of the film and the weaknesses of its screenplay make it confusing and difficult to follow...*' and '...*This will be a hard film to sell, even to today's young audiences...*' Promoted, by this point, as starring the girl from *Candy* (another Dorfmann production, and Aulin's signature role, released in December 1968), it played the US circuit through to 1970. It was screened in other countries too throughout this period and one must conclude, whatever the critics and distributors felt, that it turned a profit before disappearing from sight at the start of the new decade.

Nor was its music forgotten. Although most of Trovajoli's score remained unavailable for public purchase, the main title theme, *Love Girl*, managed to appear twice. It was included on an album released in April 1968 on CAM records, the majority of which was drawn from the films *The Seven Cervi Brothers/I Sette Fratelli Cervi* and *The Day of the Owl/Il Giorno Della Civetta*. The last of these, which starred Franco Nero and Claudia Cardinale, was another Panda-Corona production, which explains the inclusion of the track from *Col Cuore in Gola*. Around the same time, it also appeared on a double A-side single with *Amare per Vivere*, the main theme from the French thriller *Sin with a Stranger/L'Étrangère*, sung by Romuald, a popular French actor/singer. Curiously this version of *Love Girl* is by Gianni Davoli, who sings rather awkwardly in phonetic English. Quite why he was preferred to Mal Ryder is hard to ascertain, though Davoli did have some prior experience of film work. He had sung a couple of tracks on the score of *Kill Me Quick, I'm Cold*, the September 1967 crime caper comedy with Monica Vitti (and Roberto Bisacco) which also featured two songs by The Hollies.

In fact, compared to some Italian-French giallos (and, *Col Cuore in Gola* is, whatever else might be thought of it, now regarded as an early work in this genre) Brass's film got more than reasonable exposure in every respect. It premiered at a major festival, was screened publicly across Europe, got a US release and its main title theme appeared on vinyl, twice. There were many other productions made during this period that would have welcomed half as much publicity, however disappointed Brass may have been with the reception accorded his film at the time.

Notes

(1)   The Blackwell recordings (four tracks) were done with in early 1966, after which The Primitives relocated to Italy. The material was released, in France, on the Vogue label. Mal later became a hugely successful figure in Italian pop music, appearing in five films between 1968 and 1970 as well as performing on the soundtrack of three others: *Col Cuore in Gola*, *La Ragazza Con La Pistola* and *I Ragazzi del Massacro*.

(2)   Email from Mal Ryder, 9 April 2016.

(3)   Stainton was also Orson Welles's secretary at one point. See: https://www.wellesnet.com/don-quixote-orson-welles-secret

(4)   Crepax, like Warhol, did commercial art and had begun by designing record sleeves. For examples of the latter (over 200) see: https://www.discogs.com/artist/1827235-Guido-Crepax His work, with his combination of eroticism and intellectual allusions, is clearly similar to Brass. For more on his career see: https://www.lambiek.net/artists/c/crepax.htm

(5)	Interview with Alan Sekers 15 January 2019, and subsequent correspondence.

(6)	See *The Great Movie Stars Volume 2 – The International Years* David Shipman, entry on Trintignant p576-580.

(7)	Fantanicchio released eight singles, all in Europe 1960-1963. He then turned to acting, appearing in *Col Cuore in Gola* and at least one other film: *Le Bal des Voyous* (1968). But how did Brass get to cast him? One link came via Gian Carlo Fusco. In 1962 Fusco had scripted the documentary *Benito Mussolini: Anatomia di un Dittatore* for producer/director Mino Loy. Loy, in turn, featured Fantanicchio/Bellini in *Mondo Sexy di Notte/Mondo Sexuality* which filmed the same year. A clip of this can be viewed at: https://www.youtube.com/watch?v=X-IiRKN-XyA

(8)	For Zaranoff see https://www.wrestlingheritage.co.uk/wrestlerszhtm His other screen roles included appearing in episodes of *Adam Adamant Lives!* which broadcast in January and March 1967. On Rikki Starr see: https://www.wrestlingheritage.co.uk/ricky-starr Prowse's other films during this period include *Hammerhead* (1968), *Crossplot* (1969), *The Horror of Frankenstein* (1970 – as the monster), *A Clockwork Orange* (1971) and Russ Meyer's *Black Snake* (1973).

(9)	Aulin was crowned Miss Teen International on 4 April 1966 in Hollywood, at an event hosted by Adam West (then TV's *Batman*) with a guest appearance by Mia Farrow and music provided by Sonny and Cher. She relinquished the title on 20 March 1967, again at Hollywood where the hosts were Sally Field and actor-singer Noel Harrison, after which she flew to London to star in *Col Cuore in Gola*.

(10) Identified recently as Ronnie Ross, and the subject of the 1964 documentary short *Busk'n* which can be seen at https://youtu.be/-kDuomfPFkg Email from Rod Warner, 16 July 2021.

4

'...I JUST REMEMBER THE NOISE AND BEING OUT ON THE BALCONY AS THE SUN CAME OUT...'

What few realised then, but most of the film's admirers acknowledge now, is how deftly Brass took his cast and crew through London and its burgeoning 'scene' in 1967. The criticisms of *Col Cuore in Gola* on release – that it was flashy, superficial and had an incomprehensible plot – completely miss the point. Yes, the plot, which seems to start with something about blackmail, a diary and some incriminating photographs, isn't absolutely clear (as it would be, say, in an episode of a TV police series, or in any of the conventional murder mysteries of the 1940s and 1950s). But, so what? The plot in *Blow-Up* isn't particularly clear either and plenty of examples abound in classic detective fiction (notably Raymond Chandler) of near incomprehensible storylines. Dismissing it as flashy and superficial indicates that those who thought that then didn't really understand what they were seeing, and how unique it was. So, viewed today, why has the film had a kinder reception, and what makes it unique?

To begin with, and contrary to the view that his film is merely a superficial skim across 'Swinging London', Brass was fascinated by the cinematic possibilities the capital presented as a partially derelict city... the boarded-up streets awaiting demolition, the mainline steam trains that still ran out of Waterloo and the pervading atmosphere of physical decay that contrasted so markedly with the smart boutiques, galleries and discotheques elsewhere. Brass scouted many of these locations himself and shot wherever and whenever he could with great skill.

Often the owners of premises and casual spectators were unaware of what was going on, as in the scene filmed on the top floor of the RT bus. Sometimes, though, it was deliberate. The sequence where Bernard goes to Prescott's home and encounters Jelly Roll and his side-kick (David Prowse) was shot, by arrangement, at Bob Monkhouse's home in Finchley. According to Alan Sekers this was not a happy occasion, '...it was a HORRIBLE day filming there. He was awful. His wife was drunk and I'm not sure if Tom Hawkins (the location manager) didn't have his way with her. Tinto – in his nosey way – opened a cupboard downstairs and out tumbled really nasty, tacky pornography...' As to why Monkhouse was allowing his house to be used as a film set, well... at that point in the 1960s he was trying to establish himself (as many comedians do, periodically) as a serious actor. In 1962, he co-starred in a film with Anna Karina, newly married then to Jean-Luc Godard, and later did a string of TV plays including the title role in Bernard Kops's feature-length Enter Solly Gold (1965). In March-April 1967, when Brass and his crew turned up, he was filming an ITV drama, Bug, about a radio ham who suspects his wife of an affair. He was also about to be cast, as a crazy Scottish psychiatrist clearly modelled on RD Laing, in *The Bliss of Mrs Blossom*. A big budget film, this too, like *Col Cuore in Gola*, has a lengthy sequence shot at the Alexandra Palace. He really was trying very hard to go 'legit'. But relations with his wife were poor. We know today that he had a lengthy affair with Diana Dors, and probably participated in the 'parties' (which were actually orgies) at her house, commenting in later years '...*the awkward part about an orgy is that afterwards you're not too sure who to thank...*' He and his wife separated later in 1967, which, together with the affair with Dors, might explain her being drunk on the day. As for the stash of pornography: an interview Monkhouse did with *The Guardian* newspaper in 2000, looking back at his life in the 1950s and 1960s noted, '...*his autobiography is full of fantastical sexual adventures – orgies with "showgirls" and two-way mirrors and handcuffs, often with a slightly masochistic slant. In his younger years, he was famous for his collection of pornography...*' Alan Sekers's recollections certainly confirm this.[1]

Agreeing to use someone's house for a scene also saved money of course, avoiding the use of sets, and was very different to the careful, painstaking approach used by Antonioni in *Blow-Up*. Where, for instance, Antonioni spent weeks deciding which pop group to feature in one scene, Brass simply turned up at 'The 14 Hour Technicolour Dream' and got on with it. As a result, because he shot most of *Col Cuore in Gola* on the move across London, he delivered a completed film in six months at a reasonable cost.

One area that offered a terrific backdrop at nil cost was Southam Street, W10, most of which, by 1967, was empty and awaiting demolition. Alan Sekers confirms that, '...*during* my time with him we filmed quite a lot around Paddington, Bayswater, and the very rundown parts of north Westminster and north Kensington...' The same area, in slightly better condition, can be seen in a host of UK black-and-white 'kitchen sink' dramas, including Sapphire and The L-Shaped Room as well as later productions, where it appears increasingly ruinous, like Bedazzled, Connecting Rooms, Performance and Leo the Last. Southam Street had been a favourite location for street photographer Roger Mayne, who produced a huge portfolio of work there between 1956 and 1961. (Mayne was married to Ann Jellicoe, author of The Knack, the 1965 film version of which makes a strong claim to be one of the first 'Swinging London' productions.)[2]

Similarly, Brass showed a real appreciation of the grime, smoke and antique (by 1967 standards) appearance of the area around Clapham Junction. When Col Cuore in Gola was shot, many of the trains passing through Clapham, Vauxhall and Battersea were still steam-hauled. It was known that conversion to diesel and electric traction would take place in July 1967, so the last weeks of steam operation were captured by an army of photographers, amateur and professional.[3] Memorable footage was also being shot then by British Transport Films, the documentary arm of British Rail, and would be released as Rail later that year. It could well be that Col Cuore in Gola is the last feature made in the UK to show steam-hauled trains as a daily form of transport. Battersea itself is shown in the scene where Jane is abducted. It was a popular area to film in the 1960s and much of both Poor Cow and Up the Junction were shot there.

A sinister note is struck by the use of Playland amusement arcade, in Coventry Street, W1, as the base from which Jelly

Roll and his team of enforcers operate. In the 1970s, allegations would emerge placing it at the centre of a paedophile ring that preyed on young homeless boys in London. There is no suggestion that Brass, or anyone in his crew, knew this in 1967, but the membership of Jelly Roll's gang (a dwarf, a bodybuilder, a wrestler) replicates closely the type of individuals used by the Kray brothers, who were reputed to have an interest in Playland.[4]

Most murder mysteries, whether Georges Simenon in small French market towns or Dashiell Hammett in San Francisco take their reader, somewhere along the way, down sordid back streets. Brass's film is no different in that respect, but, unlike Simenon, Hammett (or Agatha Christie), he deliberately explored the emerging counter-culture of the time. Thus, the opening club scene, where Bernard sees Jane dancing, was shot at Samantha's, 3 New Burlington Street, W1. In early 1967 this had only just opened, so Brass must have been the first person to film there. It would become known as 'London's only Psychedelic Discotheque' with an E-type Jag to the side of the dance floor in which the DJ sat with his turntables. (A cramped arrangement, so much so that Jeff Dexter, then DJ at Tiles Club in Oxford Street, refused to work at the new venue. The E-type Jag doesn't, alas, feature in Col Cuore in Gola, and must have been a later addition.)[5]

The shop where Jane and Bernard buy a large poster is Granny Takes a Trip, at 488 Kings Road, SW10. Owned by Nigel Waymouth, his girlfriend Sheila Cohen and John Pearse, it had opened in 1965, and by early 1967 had a 'Jean Harlow' mural painted across its front, which we can just see in the film.[6] Sales assistant Johnny Moke (later, with Pearse, a noted figure on the London clothing and fashion scene) can be glimpsed too. It seems that Waymouth, Cohen and Pearse were keen to promote their boutique. Through 1967-1968 they repainted its frontage with a different design every few months, and the venue was also name-checked by The Purple Gang in their debut single *Granny Takes a Trip*, released on Transatlantic Records in April 1967. Banned by the BBC, but declared record of the year by DJ John Peel, it was produced by Joe Boyd the same week that he did the first Pink Floyd hit *Arnold Layne*. Allowing for the time needed for mixing, pressing and printing, The Purple Gang clearly recorded their song *prior* to Aulin, Brass and Trintignant arriving at the shop. But, fashionably clad in 1920s and 1930s gangster suits, they were photographed outside, with the 'Jean Harlow' mural well to the fore, to promote their record shortly before its release, which must have been only a few days before (or after) Brass filmed there. This makes one wonder if both events were part of a concerted PR push by Waymouth and his colleagues.[7]

Finally, the gallery Bernard and Jane visit is Indica, then at Mason's Yard, SW1. The curious piece of kinetic art that Bernard observes may be something by David Medalla, who is quoted as saying, *'...I had a double show there with Liliane Lijn after Signals closed. And many of the artists we were going to show at Signals went to Indica. It was a real arrangement, and many of the artists like Morellet went to Indica. Indica was far more informal, we were much more formal and Indica was more "hip" – a lot of people taking drugs. It was that time when people experimented with mind expanding drugs. Indica was a groovy kind of scene...'* [8] At this distance it is hard to be specific, and another contender for what Bernard is looking at might be something by Panayiotis Vassilakis (Takis) who showed there a little earlier than Medalla and Lijn. His particular piece, an 'electro-musical relief', was favourably reviewed in *New Scientist*. Indica was owned by John Dunbar and Barry Miles, and would also exhibit both Yoko Ono and Mark Boyle during Brass's spell in London.

The inclusion of Samantha's, Granny Takes a Trip and Indica in the film leads us, inexorably, to the location selected by Brass for the denouement, the Alexandra Palace and the 14 Hour Technicolour Dream. Staged on 29 April 1967, this was a large, sprawling benefit concert held to raise funds for *International Times* after its offices had been raided by the police earlier that year. Facing legal action – for allegedly publishing obscene material – the paper called in favours from its many associates, allies and friends. Among those rallying to its aid were Nigel Waymouth and John Dunbar, the former designing posters for the proposed event and the latter providing, via his gallery, several of the non-musical acts. Word of it also reached Alan Sekers, who remembers, *'...Well... I'd done some work as well for Mark Boyle (who did the light shows at the UFO Club) and through him knew that the people who wanted to stage "The 14 Hour Technicolour Dream" didn't have enough money to make it happen. I told them about this film being made and they had a meeting with Tinto who agreed to pay them £3,000 from the production monies in exchange for his being allowed to film the final sequences of his film at the event. So, I don't think it would have happened without his involvement...'*

Trying to pin down the finances of the event now, 50 plus years later, is a difficult task. The idea that Tinto Brass enabled the 14 Hour Technicolour Dream to happen is not, as far as most people are concerned, in the public domain, nor is it part of the official narrative of how the event took place. So, is it likely or is it a case of memory playing tricks?

Unfortunately, there are few people around now whom one can ask about such matters. David Mairowitz, one of the founding editors of *International Times*, could only state when approached, '...*Thanks for your request... I may have danced at the 14-Hour dream and been on any number of substances, but I'm sorry to say I know absolutely nothing about Tinto Brass or the film shot at Ally Pally... Sorry I can't be of help there...*' [9] Barry Miles, co-owner of Indica gallery, like Mairowitz involved in founding *International Times* and, as Wikipedia asserts, one of those who organised 'The 14 Hour Technicolour Dream' responded in slightly more detail, '...*I'm afraid that I have no memory of Tinto Brass, or of the producers paying money for the right to film. I wasn't involved in that side of the event and I'm afraid that the people who were – John Hopkins, Jack Henry Moore, etc – are all dead. I must say that three thousand pounds sounds like much too much money. The UFO Club used to charge one hundred, I believe. If that much was paid then it was all stolen, unless the Pink Floyd received it. I'm sorry I can't help you...*' [10] John 'Hoppy' Hopkins died in 2015, having said some years earlier about the use of the Alexandra Palace that evening, '...*The 14 Hour Technicolour Dream was a big event and a financial disaster. Most people were on drugs of one sort or another. It was a crest of a wave. It wasn't fully understood, but it was a landmark event...*' [11] Subsequent commentators have accepted this version of events, notably Julian Palacios in his book, *Lost in the Woods*, who states, '...*Two film crews were on hand to film the proceedings. Peter Whitehead, director of* Tonite Let's Make Love in London, *fought for vantage points with a film crew from the BBC, who presented a live airing of the event on BBC2...*' [12]

Given the comments of Mairowitz, Miles and Hopkins, it might seem that Alan Sekers is mistaken. But evidence from elsewhere suggests not. As indicated, Brass was not the only person wandering around with a camera that evening. As well as Whitehead and the BBC, Tutte Lemkow, a friend of

David Medalla, was there recording the Exploding Galaxy's performance.[13] To confuse things even more, *International Times* stated, in the next edition *'Receipts from the IT film of the occasion already in demand from US television companies and worldwide film distributors, are expected to gross another £5,000 within 3 months and may well amount to £20,000 in the long run'*.[14] Which film was this? Whitehead's? Lemkow's? Possibly Brass's? (One can imagine Brass stating that in exchange for his access to the event, the footage he shot would be 'their film' and released worldwide.) Or was it a completely different, and now long-lost, record of the event? It isn't clear, but BBC TV *Man Alive* broadcast *What is a Happening?*, their coverage of the event, on 17 May 1967. In this, the commentator clearly states that admission was £1 a head, and that 7,000 attended.[15] Logically, then, the gate receipts were £7,000. US journalist and *Observer* columnist John Crosby reported the weekend after the event that *'...between £7000 and £10000 was raised...'* (In relation to which, note too that Mick Farren, guitarist in The Social Deviants, who performed that evening, recollected, *'...there were about 10,000 in the audience...'*) Finally, *International Times* themselves announced a *'...net profit...'* of between £3000 and £4000. In other words, the event cost between £3000 and £7000 to stage and took, in receipts, between £7,000 and £10,000. In summary, then, if the profit was £3,000 and £7,000 was raised, the event cost £4,000 to stage. Where did they find this money?

As a benefit aimed at raising money for *International Times* it appears to have been a success, whatever happened to the money subsequently. The promoters – Hopkins, Miles and their colleagues – had thought big, and it had worked. According to record producer Joe Boyd, Hopkins chose the Alexandra Palace as the venue because it had been used before for music festivals. There was sufficient space inside to erect two stages to accommodate all the bands who wished to play, with the stages so far apart that sound quality was not unduly compromised. But, big venue equals big costs. The Alexandra Palace was huge, and in 1967 the BBC were still broadcasting from it. In fact, in 1964, the studios there (in another part of the building) had been used to launch BBC2. As can be seen in *What is a Happening?* the premises were still policed by uniformed BBC doormen, who were in charge of security arrangements for the evening. This would have cost a significant amount. There were also fairground-type rides scattered throughout the hall (a large helter-skelter is prominent) and this would have had to have been hired, and paid for, upfront, in cash. The owners of such equipment don't give it away for nothing. The organisers may not have carried insurance to cover personal injuries suffered by the audience, but they must have had to satisfy the BBC about their ability to repair any damage caused to the premises. It isn't clear, of course, what Hopkins or Jack Henry Moore told the BBC about what they actually intended staging: presumably the various mixed-media events were not mentioned, and certainly not the screening of uncertificated Kenneth Anger films in rooms off the main hall and the projection of slightly risqué films, in which nudity was prominent, onto the side wall of the main hall. They would have stressed it was a music all-nighter, rather like the trad jazz event held there (in sub-zero temperatures) in January 1963 with George Melly, Acker Bilk, Kenny Ball and Ken Colyer or the Rolling Stones Fan Club concert of June 1964 featuring The Rolling Stones, John Lee Hooker, John Mayall's Bluesbreakers, Alexis Korner's Blues Incorporated and Millie.[16]

Given the costs, and the need to raise as much money as possible, all the bands waived their fee for playing. But that still left *International Times* with the task of raising enough money in the first place to hire the premises and equipment. How did they do this? Simply, by asking for help from people they either knew or were put in touch with. Craig Sams, founder of Whole Earth Foods, recollects, '*...I ran a macrobiotic restaurant in Notting Hill in the early part of 1967... When* International Times *was busted our restaurant was the only place that dared to sell it. John Hopkins and Dave Howson approached me about the 14 Hour Technicolour Dream idea and wondered if I could help them with the money to secure Alexandra Palace. Once they had the venue booked, they said, the record companies would all want to have their bands at the event and I would get my money back in a few weeks. True to their word, I got my £400 back within a month...*'[17] There were probably others who made similar donations. But if the organisers asked Craig Sams (only 22 years old at the time) for £400 (£23k in 2022 money) how much would they have wanted from a feature-film director asking to film Jean Louis-Trintignant at their event? Given that Brass trails the concert in his film, showing posters for it, and *International Times*, in several scenes, it is hard not to conclude that an arrangement with him was reached, and that he did, indeed, provide them with £3000, as suggested by Alan Sekers. Based, then, on what was reported at the time, the event may not have happened without this money. (Or if it had, would have been smaller and staged elsewhere.) And, as for the other people filming that evening... clearly, given they were using BBC premises, they could not have asked for a donation *from* the BBC for allowing the *Man Alive* team to cover the event. (Maybe that was part of the deal? The BBC got a free documentary out of it?) Whilst they may have cut Tutte Lemkow some slack (was he 'with the band' as part of the Exploding Galaxy?) one wonders if Peter

Whitehead, shooting *Tonite Let's All Make Love in London*, was ever asked for a contribution.

Brass ended up using about 12 minutes of the footage that he shot at 'The 14 Hour Technicolour Dream'. It is interesting to compare this with the other two versions that survive. The BBC *Man Alive* team, over 30 minutes, show the Exploding Galaxy Dance Troupe in action at exactly the point in Brass's film that Aulin and Trintignant are walking past. An experimental dance drama group, the Exploding Galaxy lived as a community in Balls Pond Road, North London from early 1967 until they disbanded at the end of 1968, and were, in fact, a project instigated by David Medalla, whose show at Indica we may have seen earlier in *Col Cuore in Gola*. In Brass's film we can see a solitary cameraman filming the Exploding Galaxy, probably not the BBC (who would have used a large, multi-person crew) and therefore most likely Peter Whitehead or Tutte Lemkow. The BBC also give us some footage of Tomorrow and John's Children playing their set and an extended scene of The Flies in action, culminating in the latter case with the band throwing bags of flour at their audience, the aftermath of which Brass shows too. Peter Whitehead includes no more than 7 minutes of 'The 14 Hour Technicolour Dream' in *Tonite Lets All Make Love in London*, much of it blurred and impressionistic (deliberately so) but effective nonetheless. Amongst his footage, we see another cameraman shooting some of the crowd dancing and one would conclude, on the same basis, that this must either be Brass's cinematographer, Silvano Ippoliti or Tutte Lemkow. Based on what we hear in all three versions, the acoustics seem to have been terrible. As Alan Sekers states, in a view that is consistent with other accounts, '...*On the night it was complete fucking chaos. I don't really remember any of the bands, I just remember the noise, and being out on the balcony watching the sun come up as we filmed the final scenes...'*

The *Man Alive* commentator carries out a very revealing interview with a gang of disparaging working-class mods, whose views are comically at odds with the stoned euphoria of others at the event: clearly the 'Summer of Love' was destined to be a short-lived event even before it happened, with a backlash against its libertarian excesses (as perceived) always imminent. Whitehead shows none of this, but Brass does capture the mods, some with proto-skinhead haircuts, rolling around in the remains of one of the extended translucent plastic sculptures that Graham Stevens provided for the event. Finally, both Brass and the BBC show the Yoko Ono-devised performance *Cut Piece,* in which a young woman slowly has her clothes cut off, one small piece at a time, by members of the audience. In summary, Whitehead provides the least amount of footage of the event (despite managing to accrue the higher reputation from his coverage of it) and Brass condenses into 12 minutes more or less what the BBC show over 30. As would be expected from a TV production, *Man Alive: What is a Happening?* appeared first. But Brass's film premiered at Venice on 8 September, before Whitehead's, which was screened at the New York Film Festival, as *London Scene,* on 26 September.[18] *Col Cuore in Gola* was, therefore, the first film to show 'The 14 Hour Technicolour Dream', and, it remains the only non-documentary feature film, ever, to have been shot at a major UK music event. It is also a film in which some intriguing things 'almost' appeared, as well as one that, with slightly more luck, might have resulted in its being better appreciated at the time rather than subsequently regarded as an overlooked cult classic.

Firstly, Brass missed the arrival of John Lennon and John Dunbar. Hearing in mid-evening that the event was taking place, they drove to the Alexandra Palace from Weybridge (where Lennon lived) and were briefly captured by both Whitehead and the BBC, strolling around and standing in the main hall as the music boomed away. Had they been included in the footage edited into *Col Cuore in Gola*, it is entirely possible that Brass's film would have had an enhanced reputation on release, given the vogue for all things Beatle in 1967.

Another near miss, in this case by all the filmmakers, was Andy Warhol. Although it is not clear if he actually went inside the hall, there are accounts from audience members exiting the event in the early hours of the morning that indicate he was sitting outside in the back of a Rolls-Royce. According to Roland Frith, '...*on attempting to talk to him the front window wound down and the driver informed us that "Mr Warhol does not speak to mortals"...*'[19] This is fascinating, and the comment made to Frith (and his friends) hardly one they would forget. But, in the absence of confirmation from other sources, is it true? We know that in April 1967 Warhol and Paul Morrissey were at the Cannes Film Festival. They had arrived there to show *Chelsea Girls*. Morrissey recollects, '...*We'd taken it to Cannes to show at the film festival... They had announced it, it was part of the programme, but they hadn't given it a date. They didn't know how to screen the film. They needed two projectors and two screens, and I had to try and show them how to do it. Then they were afraid there'd be some scandal because of ten seconds of male nudity, which they'd heard about but never seen. They never screened it. They refused to show it. The first time ever that an invited film was never screened... And then we left and took it to Paris and showed it at the Cinémathèque, and then took it to London, all in our suitcases...*'[20]

The Cannes Film Festival opened on 27 April 1967. If Morrissey's recollections are broadly accurate, Warhol and his entourage probably arrived in Cannes a couple of days prior to the 27th (there are deadlines for the submission of entries), found their screening had been cancelled and then went first to London via Paris.[21] On this reckoning it is just possible that Warhol did head to the Alexandra Palace on arrival in London, and was seen by some of the audience members as they made their way home.

But, without doubt, given what many recollect about the event today, the most significant omission from Brass's footage must be Pink Floyd. Robert Wyatt, then drummer in The Soft Machine (who also played that evening) remembers, '... *The Floyd played at 4 in the morning. It must have been one of the greatest gigs they ever did, and Syd played with a slide and it completely blew my mind, because I was hearing echoes of all the music I'd ever heard, with bits of Bartok and God-knows-what. I don't understand why nobody else has ever attempted to do it since...*'[22] By all accounts, they gave an extraordinary performance as dawn was breaking. Could Brass have filmed them? To begin with, they arrived very late, at 3am, and played very late because they had started the day in the Netherlands filming a slot for the TV pop series *Fan Club*. After this they drove to the Hook of Holland, caught the ferry to the UK and then drove from Harwich to London. (The previous day they had played in a club in Stockport prior to driving to Harwich for the trip to the Netherlands; since leaving Stockport on the night of 28 April they had covered 700 miles in 28 hours.) As all the accounts state, they finished their set as the sun rose, which would imply they concluded at or shortly after 5.30am. In the final scene, shot by Brass, his crew, Aulin and Trintignant on the external balcony of the hall, the sun has (just) risen, so a timing of about 5.45am for the concluding scene seems likely. Sunrise in London that day took place at 5.36am, so, theoretically, Brass *could* have caught some of the Floyd's set and then finished his film upstairs. But it was not to be. By that point everyone was at the end of an immensely long working day and there would have been equipment and cabling still to arrange for the final shots. Probably it was too complicated to set up, perhaps Aulin and Trintignant and a few of the crew watched the band beforehand; we don't know. But, if Brass *had* caught the Floyd in action with Syd Barrett, *Col Cuore in Gola* would surely today be regarded as massively important and the definitive document of its time rather than just a superior cult film.

Which is why most commentators and connoisseurs of 1960s cinema continue to prefer *Blow-Up*. Even in 1967 this was something Brass's colleague Alan Sekers was aware of '... *Incidentally, early on in the preparation of* Col Cuore in Gola *I remember we all went to see* Blow-Up *in what must have been its first cinema run. Tinto was rather upset afterwards as Antonioni had tackled the same themes that he was planning to portray, albeit in a more pretentious way...*' In fact, some scenes in Brass's film were shot *before* either he or anyone in his crew had seen *Blow-Up*, notably the sequence where Aulin/Jane is posing as a model in David's studio. Because of their similarity to Antonioni's film, though, everyone watching *Col Cuore in Gola* subsequently thought Brass was copying his fellow countryman. It is clear he wasn't. But, in the spring of 1967, such considerations remained in the future. Ever anxious to move on quickly to his next project, Brass secured funding from Dino De Laurentiis for two more London-based films, one of which, *Nerosubianco*, would be his masterpiece.

Notes

(1) *The Guardian* interview (20 August 2000) can be read at
     https://www.theguardian.com/theobserver/2000/aug/
     20/features.magazine27 Monkhouse was actually quite
     good in *The Bliss of Mrs Blossom*, but further significant
     roles eluded him and it represented the peak of his
     straight acting ventures.

(2) Mayne worked extensively as a stills photographer in
     film and TV with his work being used in the BBC series
     Landmarks 1964-1965. In 2017 The Photographers Gallery
     produced an excellent appreciation of his work in their
     magazine *Loose Associations*, which notes, p38 '*By 1967,
     Southam Street had become a vast Victorian shell, every pane
     of every house – at least the ones that were standing – smashed;
     it made a bleak urban canvas for Jean-Louis Trintignant's pan-
     European crime drama With Heart in Mouth.*'

(3) Including Alan Grange, one of the audience members
     at 'The 14 Hour Technicolour Dream' who notes at
     http://www.ukrockfestivals.com/14-hour-tech-dream-
     menu.html '*...I was there after hitch hiking from Hartlepool
     and spending the morning train spotting at Waterloo – still
     steam locos until July...*' *Rail* was made by Geoffrey Jones,
     who, like Brass, was much praised for his ability to edit
     rapidly and cut images to music. It can be viewed via
     the BFI website: http://www.screenonline.org.uk/film/
     id/1319220/index.html

(4) The Kray brothers reputedly used a dwarf, Roy 'Little
     Legs' Smith, a London street-busker, as an enforcer. Smith,
     who also managed to appear in The Beatles' *Magical
     Mystery Tour*, was the subject of the biography, *Little Legs,*

Muscleman of Soho, written in 1989 by George Tremlett. On his website https://thejohnfleming.wordpress.com John Fleming, former Film Section Editor of *International Times*, states '...*The other character I remember was a dwarf called Roy "Little Legs" Smith who was a busker himself, but he also used to collect money for street performers. A busker would play the queues in Leicester Square and Little Legs would go along collecting money in, as I remember it, a hat...*' In an odd instance of art imitating life, Brass has a scene in *Col Cuore in Gola* where a busker is 'playing the queues' but cuts away before we can see if anyone is collecting money in a hat.

(5) On Samantha's see http://lesenfantsterribles.adrianstern.com/samanthas.pl# It opened in November 1966, with *London Life* magazine reporting on 22 October that it would be opening shortly with '*a James Bond décor*'.

(6) On Granny Takes a Trip see https://agnautacouture.com/2012/12/16/granny-takes-a-trip-a-boutique-everybody-wanted-to-be-seen-in/ which has the mural and a couple of film clips. Also http://dandyinaspic.blogspot.com/2011/07/granny-takes-trip.html which has similar and a floor plan of the layout in 1967 showing the Mutoscope that Trintignant inspects.

(7) Pink Floyd recorded *Arnold Layne* (their debut single) on 29-30 January 1967. It was released on 10 March and, though banned, reached no 20 in the UK charts. Despite much airplay *Granny Takes a Trip* failed to replicate this success. Nigel Waymouth, part-owner of the boutique, was a graphic designer who had recording ambitions of his own: 1967 would see him, as part of Hapshash and the Coloured Coat, release an album, *Featuring The*

Human Host And The Heavy Metal Kids. For examples of his graphic design, some of which can be seen in the background of Brass's film see: http://visualarts. britishcouncil.org/collection/artists/hapshash-the-coloured-coat

(8) See https://www.sothebys.com/en/articles/artist-david-medalla-talks-beatles-rolling-stones-and-londons-1960s-experimental-art-scene On Takis: see *New Scientist* (22 December 1966) and the article *The Sounds of Tomorrow*, stating that along with John Cage and Iannis Xenakis he was one of the most promising musicians of the century. Mason's Yard – a small courtyard/cul-de-sac in London SW1 – also hosted The Scotch of St James, one of London's ultra-fashionable music venues in the 1960s, but not, alas, seen in Brass's film.

(9) Email, 23 May 2019.

(10) Email, 31 May 2019. However... the UFO Club used the basement of the Gala Berkeley Cinema at 31 Tottenham Court Road, W1. This was owned at the time by Kenneth Rive, who via Gala Film Distributors was the main UK source for European and world cinema films for many years. As a sympathetic host, with other interests in the arts, he may have charged the UFO Club a less than commercial rent for use of his premises.

(11) Quoted at: https://www.bbc.co.uk/music/sevenages/events/art-rock/pink-floyds-14-hour-technicolour-dream/

(12) See *Lost in the Woods: Syd Barrett and The Pink Floyd* by Julian Palacios (1998) p140.

(13) Lemkow, also a dancer, choreographed the dance sequences in *Casino Royale* (1967). His filming at 'The 14 Hour Technicolour Dream' (which has yet to appear in the

public domain) is confirmed in *London's Arts Labs and the 60s Avant-Garde* David Curtis 2020 p75.

(14) See *International Times*, 19 May 1967.

(15) This can be viewed at https://www.youtube.com/watch?v=kOC13xE9gwE

(16) Information on The Rolling Stones concert, including photographs, can be found at: https://flashbak.com/the-rolling-stones-all-night-rave-alexandra-palace-6th-june-1964-364431/

(17) Quoted at http://www.ukrockfestivals.com/14-hour-tech-dream-menu.html For more on Craig Sams see: https://www.craigsams.com/blog/2016/12/21/larry-smart

(18) *Tonite Lets All Make Love in London* had a soundtrack album, which appeared on Andrew Loog Oldham's Instant label in July 1968. Containing pieces of dialogue/monologue from the film most of the music features artists signed to Oldham's sister label Immediate (Chris Farlowe, the Marquis of Kensington, Vashti, The Small Faces) none of whom appeared at the Alexandra Palace. It does contain, though, the Pink Floyd track *Interstellar Overdrive* which the band played at 'The 14 Hour Technicolour Dream'. However, the version on the record is not the same one that appeared on their debut album *The Piper at the Gates of Dawn*. It was an earlier recording, made in January 1967 specifically for Whitehead and his film. See *Random Precision: Recording the Music of Syd Barrett 1965-1974* by David Parker, 2001. See also article in *Shindig!* 69, July 2017 which notes that Whitehead's role at the time was to film interesting images of London and its scene for Italian TV.

(19) See http://www.ukrockfestivals.com/14-hour-tech-dream-menu.html

(20) Quoted at https://warholstars.org/chelsea-girls-2.html

(21) Where *Chelsea Girls* was shown privately at Robert Fraser's flat. See *Groovy Bob: The Life and Times of Robert Fraser* by Harriet Vyner, 1999. It seems the screening was facilitated by Prince Stanislas Klossowski De Rola, one of the Rolling Stones entourage who dated Tina Aumont – briefly – in late 1966. For more on his career, see: https://www.formidablemag.com/stash-de-rola/

(22) Quoted in *Lost in the Woods: Syd Barrett and The Pink Floyd* by Julian Palacios, 1998; also in *Wrong Movements: A Robert Wyatt History* by Michael King and Robert Wyatt, 1994.

5

'...HE ALWAYS HAD ENOUGH MONEY IN HIS ACCOUNT TO START HIS NEXT FILM...'

With *Col Cuore in Gola* wrapped and in the editing suite, Brass considered his next project. Impressed by the experience of living and filming in London, and well aware of how many auteurs, stars and producers were flocking to the city, he set up his own independent production company, Lion Films, to make London-based films, and, specifically, to turn some of his own ideas into quality features. With the script already written, resurrecting his 1963 project *Nerosubianco* and relocating it to London was an obvious possibility. Brass discussed it with writer Goffredo Parise who had worked with him on *La Mia Signora/My Wife*. Parise, a novelist, and like Brass from the Veneto, had adapted the 1898 Italo Svevo novel *Senilita* for the screen in 1962 as *Careless*. Svevo's book had been much liked at the time by James Joyce and the film adaptation, shot on location in Trieste with Claudia Cardinale and Anthony

Franciosa, won Mauro Bolognini the Best Director prize at the San Sebastian Film Festival. It also managed to get a UK release, as well as the usual range of bookings in Italy, France, Spain and Germany. Parise liked Brass's idea of a film based on a woman being pursued around a city by a man (the plot of *Senilita* is fairly similar) and with this endorsement Brass approached Dino De Laurentiis for production funds.

Which is not to say that the approach was either complex or lengthy. Brass's style, according to Alan Sekers, was short and to the point: '...*Tinto's way of raising funds was that he would go to a producer and say "I've got a script..." and would reach for his pocket, at which point the producer would say "No problem. I'll fund the film" (!) Tinto shot very quickly once he had the money and usually only spent about 50% of whatever was allocated. So: he always had enough money in his account to start his next film. You were always paid in cash as well, usually by his wife, who ran the financial side of things...'* It helped that De Laurentiis already knew how economically Brass could work. By 1967 De Laurentiis was one of the most active producers in Italian cinema, with as many as eleven films being shot and prepared for release at any one time. But, though well-known to US and UK audiences as the man behind quality art-house releases like *Riso Amaro/ Bitter Rice* (1949) and *La Strada* (1954), he had yet to make anything that could be described as a 'Swinging London' film, despite latterly funding popular fare like *The Battle of the Bulge* (1965), the Bond spoof *Kiss the Girls and Make Them Die* (1966) and *The Bible... In the Beginning* (1966). His comedy thriller *Matchless* (1967) had been partly shot in London, but it struggled to get a UK release. In the meantime, of course, rival producer Carlo Ponti had won tremendous acclaim with *Blow-Up*, which, by May 1967, had won the Grand Prix at Cannes, been nominated for a couple of Academy Awards and was on its way to earning twelve times its production costs. Thus, the potential that might accrue from a shrewd investment in a London based film with UK and US releases was obvious. In the end, with *Col Cuore in Gola* a promising start to Brass's UK career (and pencilled in for a screening at the Venice Film Festival later that year) the idea sold itself with De Laurentiis's only enquiry, on being told the scope of the project, being *'why London?'* (Presumably this was on grounds of cost: it would always have been cheaper to keep the crew in Italy, and shoot there.) To which Brass responded *'Because it suits me...'* De Laurentiis agreed to advance sufficient funds to make two films and Brass was left, virtually to his own devices, to shoot whatever he wanted.

With help from Francesco Longo, Brass quickly drafted a detailed, 120-page treatment based on the earlier *Nerosubianco* outline, but with the location switched to London and the plot itself being further explicated and propelled by contemporary pop music rather than traditional Italian folk tunes. Part-script (though there was little actual dialogue) and part-shooting schedule, there were, in what was a very radical approach to storytelling in cinema, four distinct strands to the work. Firstly, all the action would take place in the course of a single day as the central character moves around a large city. Secondly, the narrative would switch seamlessly between the external dialogue and songs experienced by the main character and their own interior monologue. Thirdly, the viewer would be uncertain as to how much was actually happening and how much was imagined, and fourthly, the central character would be an unfulfilled, and white, bourgeois woman fantasising sexually about a possible relationship with a black man.

The similarities of the first three elements here to the plot of James Joyce's *Ulysses* are marked, as is the connection between Joyce and, noting Brass's initial discussion with Parise, Italo Svevo. Both Joyce and Svevo had lived in Trieste and been frequent visitors to Venice. Brass was familiar with their work. Like Joyce much of his film would be about sex with a stress on sexual freedom, but unlike Joyce (and Svevo) it would be told from a woman's point of view. The film would also, with its rejection of bourgeois social norms, owe a significant debt to the political theories of Wilhelm Reich. Reich had died in jail in the US in 1957, but by the 1960s was undergoing something of a revival. He was getting mentioned in publications like *International Times* and was attracting a number of new adherents to his views, particularly among those who subscribed to the anti-psychiatry theories of RD Laing. He had even leached into the pop counter-culture via Dino De Laurentiis's film *Barbarella*, where one of the characters, Durand Durand, is clearly modelled on Reich and operates an orgone accumulator, a device invented and used by Reich in the 1940s that supposedly increased sexual pleasure and improved mental and physical wellbeing. Thus, by giving his film a Reichian slant, Brass was being both radical and reflecting contemporary views.[1]

What emerged from Longo's and Brass's reworking of the script to accommodate this was a film with four key characters: the woman, the black man about whom she would fantasise, her husband, bourgeois too, but willing to let her discover herself, and the pop group, whose songs would replace dialogue as a way of advancing and explicating the plot. There were few supporting parts and, as with *Col Cuore in Gola*, most of it would be shot 'on the move' around London. But could it be done? A film with a Reichian plot, shot in the style of *Ulysses*?

The task of selecting the group – who would need to carry the entire film – began early. Of necessity this had to be an act that could compose and perform, at short notice, over a dozen original songs. It was a big ask – given that relatively few groups at that time wrote a significant amount of their own material – so it had to be someone of status, or if not status, an act that had just emerged on the scene and who appeared to have immense potential. In some ways, then, finding the right band was harder than casting the acting roles. In this respect the link with De Laurentiis was helpful. As a major film producer, he was constantly being sent press releases and copies of debut recordings by the managers and promoters of pop acts. This was de rigueur then across the industry. In April 1967, for instance, Carlo Ponti and Selig Seligman – producing *Smashing Time* – agreed a non-speaking role in the film for the new EMI group Tomorrow, as a tie-up for the release of their single *My White Bicycle*. Later, when the film was in the editing stage, they were lobbied by manager Don Arden, and duly inserted a few snippets of music from his latest act Skip Bifferty, just signed to RCA, into the soundtrack. Both groups were mentioned on the film credits.

The first suggestion for the band came, therefore, from De Laurentiis. He had been sent a cassette tape of The Bee Gees whose single *New York Mining Disaster 1941* was at that point doing quite well. (It eventually reached No 12 in the UK and No 14 in the US.) The tape was passed to Brass who demurred. In the words of Alan Sekers, '*...Robert Stigwood, their manager sent a cassette tape (very modern in 1967) to Dino De Laurentiis asking him, I think, if they could appear in any of his films. Dino* sent it to Tinto who played it and didn't think the music (or the type of group they were) would be suitable. Which I think was entirely right...'. It's worth mentioning that when De Laurentiis was sent the cassette, Robert Stigwood had just become Brian Epstein's partner in NEMS, the company that handled The Beatles and Cilla Black. With Epstein then the most successful pop promoter in the world, a tie-up with him via Stigwood would have been hugely beneficial for De Laurentiis and indicates that Nerosubianco was regarded as a project of some significance.[2]

With the Bee Gees proposed and rejected, the next group that seems to have been considered were Procol Harum. Piecing together the sequence of events that led to this, though, after the passage of more than 50 years, and with the recollections of the surviving participants in Brass's film patchy (to say the least) is not a straightforward task. For his part, Alan Sekers recollects, '...when we first started planning Nerosubianco, A Whiter Shade of Pale hadn't even been released...' This is quite clear: planning the film started prior to 12 May 1967, the day that Procol Harum released their first record. Produced by Denny Cordell, this entered the UK charts two weeks later after massive airplay on the network of 'pirate' radio stations that surrounded the UK. A neat promo-film was made to accompany it by Peter Clifton and Richard Mordaunt with images of the band's original line-up in a ruined stately home, intercut with footage of the hostilities in Vietnam.[3] Their manager at that point was Jonathan Weston, and if he were acting as other managers did then, he would have approached a range of film producers, with copies of the promo-film, his group's record and a press release, asking if his charges might be considered for appearances in their forthcoming production. Indeed, the group were signed up for a film very early on in their career. The UK music press announced on 24 June 1967 that Procol Harum, and their keyboardist Matthew Fisher, would be contributing some music to the film *Separation*, a low-to-medium-budget feature made by Jack Bond and Jane Arden. A study of a woman, her relationships and eventual breakdown, it was shot in and around London in a mixture of colour and black-and-white and had a particularly effective scene where Mark Boyle's light show was projected to the music of Procol Harum's *Salad Days*.[4] The possibility that either Weston approached De Laurentiis or De Laurentiis (or Brass) approached Weston about appearing in *Nerosubianco* appears entirely possible. For Weston and the group, though, the problem that emerged very quickly was the sheer level of success that *A Whiter Shade of Pale* was enjoying. Quite simply it was the biggest debut single of all time, bigger than The Beatles, bigger even than Elvis back in 1956. By the end of June 1967, it was on its way to being No 1 in the UK (for five weeks), France (for nine weeks), the Netherlands, Germany, Italy, Spain and Australia and had just started selling heavily in the US where it would peak at No 5 that summer. This was unprecedented and demanded more than just the type of routine, route-one, pop management that would be accorded any hopeful act.

According to Bobby Harrison, then drummer in Procol Harum, '...*Things went pretty well until A Whiter Shade of Pale became such an enormous hit. At that point Tony Secunda and Denny Cordell basically took the group over and decided who should stay and who they wanted out... we ended up taking them to court. Cordell in particular had very fixed ideas about what we should do, what we should look like and the type of music we should play...*'[5] Part of the logic behind the Cordell-Secunda putsch stemmed from the naivety, or just plain lack of experience, of Weston who was booking the group into gigs at a fee of £60 (when they were roaring up the charts towards the No 1 slot) whilst hiring a limousine (at £250-£300 a time) to transport them to the venue. Most other acts in such circumstances went out for £500 a night. Cordell had already produced hits for The Moody Blues, Georgie Fame and The Move (who were managed at that point by Secunda) but the level of success presented by the debut Procol Harum release was of another dimension completely, and presented immense opportunities. Both Cordell and Secunda were ruthless. By mid-July Weston had been ousted, as had Harrison and guitarist Ray Royer. A subsequent court settlement (announced on 12 August 1967) guaranteed Harrison and Royer royalties in perpetuity on everything they had recorded with Procol Harum up until the time they left the band.

The new version of Procol Harum would be touring the world and 'breaking' the US market, a strategy that required endless months of recording, rehearsing and select prestige concerts. There was no space in this schedule for the numerous film projects that had only recently been attached to the group. John Heyman, producer of *Privilege*, *Boom* and *Secret Ceremony*, wanted them for the Wolf Mankowitz-scripted *Seventeen Plus* which had a budget of £750k (roughly £22.5m today) and the group themselves planned, rather speculatively, their own 'Beatles style' film. Neither was made.[6]

This being the case, if Weston had any knowledge in June-July 67 about *Nerosubianco* it appears to have stayed with him when he was sacked. The remainder of Procol Harum, Secunda and Cordell were neither aware of it nor even concerned about it, supposing they were aware of it at all. Harrison and Royer decided to stick with Weston and after auditions another group was quickly assembled with bass guitarist Steve Shirley joining from the defunct West Midlands act The Boss Men and keyboardist Tony Marsh from Neil Christian and The Crusaders. (In another of the coincidences which litter this narrative, Marsh had previously played with Screaming Lord Sutch in whose ensemble he had been replaced by Matthew Fisher, later to join Procol Harum.)[7] By late August 1967 they had adopted the name The Freedom and were rehearsing in Weston's house in Hertfordshire where they attempted, without much success, to write new material.

At this point - if not earlier - Mike Lease enters the narrative. Though only 22, he had a significant reputation as a keyboardist and multi-instrumentalist. After a couple of years paying his dues on the road with The Zephyrs, a typical band of the time who released five singles on EMI/Columbia and managed a couple of brief film appearances, he released a solo single on Pye and then became a producer and arranger, initially at the newly launched, and very fashionable, Decca subsidiary label Deram. His credits there included the label's debut release, *Happy New Year* by Beverley (previously folk singer Beverley Kutner of The Levee Breakers and later married to John Martyn); *Summer of Last Year* by The Pyramid, an outfit that included a pre-Fairport Convention Iain Matthews; and arranging the strings on The Move's *Here We Go Round the Lemon Tree* the August 1967 flipside to their huge hit *Flowers in the Rain*. Somewhere along the way he had also teamed up with drummer Peter Trout, later of Denny Laine's Electric String Band (another Deram act), in Studio G's Beat Group. This was an outfit put together by Denny Cordell to record instrumental tracks that could be sold to film and TV companies and used

in their forthcoming productions.[8] According to Bobby
Harrison, '...both Jonathan and me wanted Mike Lease. I knew him
from his work as an arranger at Deram and thought he was very
good. So, Jonathan asked Mike to join the group. My recollection is
that the film had something to do with it too: I think the producer
was telling Jonathan that if we didn't get our act together, he'd get
another band to do the music...' Today, Lease recollects that the
core members of The Freedom (at that point Harrison, Royer
and Weston) were definitely aware of the film 'at least as early
as August, probably before' which logically can only mean that it
first appeared (to them) as a project in June-July 1967 whilst
Harrison and Royer were still in Procol Harum. As Lease says,
'...I was actually approached months previously, long before Tony
was invited to join the band...' [9]

It was certainly true that by September 1967 De Laurentiis
was losing patience and was indeed threatening to get another
group. Both Lease and Ray Royer confirm as much, albeit
with differing recollections of the context. Royer is quoted,
'...we had never even played a gig when, in the autumn of 1967, our
manager Jonathan Weston was approached by Italian film director
Dino De Laurentiis. He was looking for a group to write and perform
the soundtrack for a projected film of his which at that point was titled
"Attraction". The choice was between either us or Steppenwolf. We got
the job but we had to change our keyboard player in the process. Our
management then came back with Mike Lease, who was an absolute
genius...' [10] As can be deduced from Lease's comments, and
the recollections of Alan Sekers, Royer is mistaken about when
Weston first knew of the film. But this merely confirms that
Royer and Harrison were not necessarily aware of everything
their manager was doing: Weston, like so many band managers
of the period, only told his charges what they needed to know,

and usually only just before they needed to do it. Mike Lease, interviewed in 2019, concurs that Steppenwolf were mentioned as the alternative.[11]

As with the Bee Gees, this shows how significant a production De Laurentiis was anticipating. Steppenwolf would clearly have had the capacity to do the *Nerosubianco* score – between 1968 and 1974 they sold millions of records, became world famous for *Born to be Wild*, and had their music featured in both *Easy Rider* and *Candy*. Signed by Dunhill records in August 1967 they would have given De Laurentiis enhanced connections with Hollywood via Lou Adler, the owner of the label, and a hugely well-connected figure in US music and film circles. Having produced many hits for Johnny Rivers, Barry McGuire and The Mamas and the Papas, by the summer of 1967 Adler was also financing *Monterey Pop*, the DA Pennebaker documentary film of the music festival. Thus, as with the earlier potential partnership between Stigwood, Epstein and De Laurentiis, an Adler-De Laurentiis link-up would have yielded significant possibilities, even if bringing the band across to the UK would have been both expensive and complicated by the need to get visas. (Similar difficulties had resulted in Carlo Ponti dropping the idea of using The Velvet Underground in *Blow-Up*.)

Sensing the importance of the situation and not wanting to be dumped a second time, Weston, Harrison and Royer finally prevailed on Mike Lease to stop his session work and join The Freedom. He did so, and for a very brief period, like Procol Harum, they were a five-piece, with two keyboardists. But after no more than a week in this incarnation it became clear Lease couldn't work with Marsh who was jettisoned. With Weston now convincing De Laurentiis that they could do the work, The Freedom were formally announced for the production on

14 October 1967. Alan Sekers remembers, '...once *The Freedom were confirmed a great deal was spent on them – their clothes for the film were done by Mr Fish: the boutique run by Michael Fish in Clifford Street...*' Being kitted out in the latest gear by *Mr Fish* was indeed expensive. Opened in 1966, and located midway between New Bond Street and Savile Row, the boutique was decidedly top-end with a clientele that included Noel Coward, James Fox and Vanessa Redgrave. Buying a shirt there cost at least £8 in 1968 (allowing for inflation, £260 in 2022) and De Laurentiis bought The Freedom a multitude of outfits, some custom-designed. For Harrison and Royer though, it was second time around; Harrison recollects, '...*I'd got stuff in Mr Fish before when I was in Procol and had met The Beatles there when A Whiter Shade of Pale was tearing up the charts. I remember everyone being introduced and shaking hands with them...*'[12] Next, the group were installed by De Laurentiis in a palatial and very expensive town house in Mayfair for the duration of the shoot.

Finally, they were booked into Olympic Studios to rehearse and record all the material that would illustrate Brass's plot with Glyn Johns and Eddie Kramer, the hottest music engineers in the UK at that point. Between them they had worked with Chris Farlowe, The Rolling Stones, Eric Burdon and the Animals and The Jimi Hendrix Experience. Immediately prior to the *Nerosubianco* sessions Kramer was mixing Hendrix's *Axis: Bold as Love* and Johns had completed The Rolling Stones' *Their Satanic Majesties Request*. Whilst working with The Freedom they would be simultaneously doing Traffic's *Mr Fantasy*, *Music in a Doll's House*, the debut album by Family and The Small Faces classic *Ogdens' Nut Gone Flake*. These arrangements confirm how central to Brass's (and De Laurentiis's) vision the group were, and how important their role would be in the film itself. They started work immediately.

During the five months it took to confirm the group, Brass started casting the acting roles. Clearly, the film would revolve around the character of Barbara, the leading woman. No fewer than 60 actresses were considered for this part. Whoever was selected had to be comfortable with nudity and a plot that set out to break a number of long-standing taboos. After due deliberation, Anita Sanders, a glamorous Swedish model who had moved into acting roles, was chosen. She was 25 and had just co-starred in the heist movie *Assalto al Tesoro di Stato/Assault on the State Treasure* after starting out with unbilled slots in *Juliet of the Spirits* and *The 10th Victim*, the latter now regarded as one of the great Pop-Art extravaganzas of the era and confirmed as the film that inspired Mike Myers to devise his Austin Powers alter-ego. According to Alan Sekers, Anita Sanders was '... *very cool, very Swedish...*' In a film with little dialogue her lack of traditional acting skills was no encumbrance, and in any case, most Italian film productions then were dubbed into whatever language was required for the country they were being exhibited in. There was no overriding need for those appearing in them to declaim memorably, or even to be word perfect with their dialogue. They simply needed to look good, not be self-conscious, start and stop speaking when required and follow whatever instructions they were given on set. Everything else would be sorted out in the editing and dubbing suite. As a model who had done numerous fashion shoots in the preceding seven years, she looked extremely striking and confident in the part. But she was also serious about the film's message and coming from a country where attitudes towards nudity were much less inhibited, she appreciated, probably more than anyone else on the cast, what Brass was trying to achieve.

The part of the black man about whom the woman fantasises (and who represents her release from bourgeois norms) went to Terry Carter. He could sing and act and had first been noticed in Broadway shows like *Mrs Patterson*, in 1954, alongside Eartha Kitt, and *Kwamina*, staged in 1961, with Sally Ann Howes. Between these he had appeared in 92 episodes of *The Phil Silvers Show* as Private Sugie Sugarman, at the time a radical casting, given that much of US society remained segregated. In an interview in the mid-1960s Carter had described his acting career as '... *waiting for the phone to ring...*' If so, after a run of TV parts he must have been anxious for a call, because, by early 1967, he had begun a stint as a newsreader. A 1970s CV of his states how he got the part in Brass's film: '...*while summering in Rome in 1967, Terry was sent by the Morris Agency to meet Italian producer Dino De Laurentiis and avant-garde art film director Tinto Brass, who asked him to star in his movie,* Nerosubianco *(aka* Black on White *or* Attraction*), set in London. Since he was still a TV newscaster, Terry had to request a 13-week leave of absence from his news anchor job, in order to work in the film. Although it was an unprecedented request for Westinghouse, he got it. Before long, he realised that his first love was acting...*'[13] *Nerosubianco* would be very different to his previous work, though the plot of *Kwamina*, an inter-race love story, told in music, does have similarities. Alan Sekers recollects, '...*I don't think he could really figure out what was going on. (But neither could some of the Italian actors, either.) Terry Carter wasn't a happy bunny for much of the shoot, it was hard enough for him just being in Europe, let alone in something as experimental as this...*'

Nino Segurini played Paolo, the woman's husband, someone dull and conventional who is sufficiently enlightened, however, to allow his wife the chance to become liberated. Segurini had already co-starred in *Una Bella Grinta/The Reckless* and *Una Questione Privata*, both notable works in their day. The former won an award at the Berlin Film Festival in 1965 and the latter – set among anti-Nazi partisans – would be remade by the Taviani brothers in 2017. Umberto di Grazia completed the cast. For him this was one of eight features that he was billed in around this time, most being spaghetti westerns, though he also managed appearances in *Barbarella* and the Vanessa Redgrave-Franco Nero drama *A Quiet Place in the Country*.

Interestingly, Brass made an addition to the shooting crew he had deployed on *Col Cuore in Gola*, recruiting Nick Saxton as production manager (London). Prior to this Saxton was credited as camera operator (one of three) on the half-hour-long, black-and-white documentary *Anatomy of Violence*, directed by Peter Davis, about the 'Dialectics of Liberation Congress' held at the Roundhouse, London between 15 and 30 July 1967.[14] Saxton's obituary states that he worked on *both Separation* and *Nerosubianco*, which, given the definite involvement of Procol Harum in the former and possible involvement in the latter, does seem to confirm a connection of some kind between the two films. As with 'The 14 Hour Technicolour Dream', the Dialectics of Liberation Congress was a major event, reviewed by *International Times*, and referred to as legendary for many years afterwards. A very 1960s thing – it brought together US, UK and European intellectuals to discuss the origins of social violence – many of the papers given at the event were collected together and published in a bestselling 1968 Pelican special. Attendance at it was certainly not cheap. Flyers allude to the possibility of concessions, but, even if some were made, assuming most of the attendees paid the full fee (15 guineas), and the estimate of around 5000 people attending was accurate, this would indicate takings of circa £70,000 (over £2m in 2022). Those fortunate enough to be able to attend – and many were presumably academics or media people, whose employers paid for them – participated in lectures and debates with R D Laing, Allen Ginsberg, Stokely Carmichael and Herbert Marcuse. (Some thought it odd, given that the participants were discussing issues to do with the traditional nuclear family, that there were no women speakers.) *Anatomy of Violence* captures the generally argumentative atmosphere and includes some intriguing shots of Carmichael, who, with UK black activist Michael de Freitas aka Michael X positioned next to him on stage, engages in a vigorous dispute with a white member of the audience. Like 'The 14 Hour Technicolour Dream', coverage of the event was not restricted to one film crew: another, led by Robert Klinkert from the Netherlands and London-based Iain Sinclair, was present, filming the event for West German TV (WDR) as *Ah! Sunflower!* the footage of which mainly featured Ginsberg in his role as a roving ambassador for the counter-culture. (Sinclair, then a poet and subsequently a noted 'psychogeographer', would confirm some years later that the fee he earnt from WDR was sufficient to buy him a house in Hackney.)[15] Given Brass's earlier involvement with *International Times*, the hiring of Saxton may well have been a conscious effort to increase the director's access to people, buildings, events and 'happenings' that could be used as the backdrop to *Nerosubianco*, to enhance its credibility as a truly contemporary film.

Notes

(1) In *Barbarella* Durand Durand is played by Milo O'Shea, whose starring role as Leopold Bloom in the screen version of James Joyce's *Ulysses* was greatly admired at the 1967 Cannes Film Festival. Faithful to the text and atmosphere of Joyce's novel, the film adaptation was shot in the Dublin of the mid-1960s, its 'updating' not causing problems to the viewer.

(2) Chronologically, The Bee Gees arrived in the UK from Australia on 6 February 1967, signed a management deal with Robert Stigwood on 24 February, did their first session in the UK (backing Brian Epstein act Billy J Kramer) on 4 March and began recording their debut LP, *Bee Gees First*, on 7 March. Their debut single, *New York Mining Disaster* 1941 appeared on 14 April. It seems likely that the cassette tape Stigwood sent De Laurentiis contained a selection of tracks designed to promote *Bee Gees First*, which eventually appeared – with a cover from Klaus Voormann, who also designed the sleeves for *As Is* (Manfred Mann) and *Revolver* (The Beatles) – on 14 July.

(3) This can be seen at https://www.youtube.com/watch?v =z0vCwGUZelI

(4) Released in March 1968, a contemporary review of *Separation* (which is described as being in the tradition of *Blow-Up*) can be read at https://procolharum.com/ separation_260368.htm The segment with Procol Harum's music and Mark Boyle's light show can be viewed at https://www.youtube.com/watch?v=qW3QcEsLbtA

(5) For this and all subsequent comments: Interview with Bobby Harrison, 1 May 2019.

(6)   *Seventeen Plus* was announced in *The New Musical Express* on 23 September 1967. See https://procolharum.com/y/yan_nme_230967.htm

(7)   On Shirley and The Boss Men see http://www.historywebsite.co.uk/articles/InBetweenTimes/Page9.htm Between leaving The Boss Men and joining The Freedom, Shirley auditioned unsuccessfully for The N Betweens, the group that later became Slade.

(8)   This was not uncommon at the time. The Pretty Things, who enjoyed some commercial success from 1964 to 1966, also recorded 'library' music under the pseudonym Electric Banana. In this guise they appeared, memorably, in *What's Good for the Goose* (1969) alongside Norman Wisdom. Their material continued to turn up on the sound track of numerous film and TV productions well into the 1980s.

(9)   For this and all subsequent comments: Email from Mike Lease, 9 December 2018.

(10) See *Procol Harum: Beyond the Pale* by Claes Johansen, 2000.

(11) On the involvement of Steppenwolf, Charlie Wolf, the current tour manager of John Kay and Steppenwolf, responded to an email enquiry about this on 12 December 2018 '...*John Kay's response: If so, I never heard about it. JK...*'

(12) On Mr Fish see https://masonandsons.com/blogs/style/a-peculiar-fish The cost of Mr Fish outfits is confirmed at http://dandyinaspic.blogspot.com/2011/07/mr-fish.html and http://sweetjanespopboutique.blogspot.com/2012/06/dandy-fashion-michael-fish-and-simon.html

(13) For Carter's comments, and much else on the preparation of the film, see https://rjbuffalo.com/1968a-ne.html

(14) The film can be viewed at https://www.youtube.com/watch?v=88M60oBU-Ms and at https://allenginsberg.org/2011/07/dialectics-of-liberation-1967-asv-9/ The Penguin special paperback of the event was edited by psychiatrist David Cooper, who co-authored *Reason and Violence: A Decade of Sartre's Philosophy*, with RD Laing, and like Laing was an advocate of anti-psychiatry. Finally: all the main participants were recorded and their contributions released in a series of spoken word albums on the short-lived Liberation label. See https://www.discogs.com/label/247848-Liberation-Records-7 Though limited in terms of how many people attended the event, the Dialectics of Liberation Conference was a critical event in the UK's counter-cultural history, particularly within revolutionary politics, black awareness and feminism.

(15) A clip of *Ah Sunflower!* is at https://allenginsberg.org/2011/07/iain-sinclair-ah-sunflower-footage-asv-10/ Sinclair was active from early on in the London Filmmakers Co-op and also published poetry. His house was used as their London residence by the folk-rock band Dr Strangely Strange, during the period they recorded for Island and Vertigo records, 1969-1970.

6

'...I SHOULD HAVE BEEN MORE THAN A LITTLE SUSPICIOUS WHEN OUR MANAGER SUDDENLY BOUGHT A FERRARI...'

Officially, filming began in late October 1967. However, careful viewing of the footage in the opening scene (in a park) shows summery conditions, with background trees in full bloom. One wonders if – whilst waiting for The Freedom to confirm their availability – Brass did some establishing shots as early as August. In this context, the recollections of both Mike Lease and Alan Sekers that the location for the opening scenes was not, as viewers would suppose, Hyde Park in London, but Woburn Abbey, is intriguing. Coincidentally this venue hosted the Woburn Abbey Pop Festival, from 26 to 28 August 1967, the first ever outdoors UK pop event, and, amongst those appearing were the Bee Gees, the only time they ever played at a major UK music festival.[1] Did Brass, on hearing this event was taking place, head to Woburn Abbey, and using some of the hippies who were hanging around, shoot some material, which he then edited into the footage at a later date? Given how he slotted shots of the Six Day War into *Col Cuore in Gola*, it seems possible.

For the duration of the shoot the crew were based at a large flat in Cadogan Place, Belgravia. Owned by an Indian businessman, this was partly used as a dormitory for the crew, and partly as a set and sound stage. The agreement with the owner was that whatever Brass and his crew did, and whatever alterations they made, it had to be returned to the owner in exactly the same condition at the end of filming. This was quite a neat arrangement, and more economical than hiring hotels for the crew and booking an existing studio. Italian journalist Nerio Minuzzo confirmed this and observed how Brass operated as a director on the film: '...*He starts at impossible hours... He often leaves, hunting for images, when it is still dark. Four cars and a van: all fifteen people, including the actors, squeeze inside, together with the Arriflexes, the tripods, the lamps... There is an abundance of film. We start from Cadogan Place, where an apartment serves as an office, an interior set, and a dormitory for half the crew. No one knows where the day will end. Sometimes the director jumps out of the car, looks around, finds that the light is right, the place is good. In two minutes, the tripod is in place, the reflectors are in position, and one of the crew kindly offers to divert passers-by... Often, there is no permission to shoot, and if a suspicious policeman arrives, the order is to lie: We're Italian journalists! We're making a TV documentary! As an excuse, it wouldn't mean anything, but the explanation is rather unusual, and it is provided in English with help from Brass, a ragged beatnik...*' [2]

The group were often present too. Brass would explain to them via an interpreter the type and tone of music required for the scene, and it fell to Mike Lease to transpose these requests into songs and arrangements, adding whatever string-quartet backings, harpsichords and other pop-Baroque flourishes were required at a later date. As he says, '...*Virtually all the composing was done concurrently with the filming/recording. It was very hectic indeed. In fact, I had never known such sustained pressure in a professional capacity, and it went on for months until completion. We often liaised through an American interpreter, a really nice woman, who would give us an English-language précis of the ideas that Tinto wanted as the lyrical basis of each song. We would then embody this with the music as quickly as possible... He would often challenge some of the lyrics, which to him conveyed the wrong impression of his meaning, sending us back to the drawing board – he spoke very little English. To get a more correct meaning was usually my task, none of the others had a political clue...*' [3] The job of writing the lyrics usually fell to Steve Shirley, who also provided lead vocals. Bobby Harrison also confirms the pressure they were under to turn-out suitable backing tracks: '...*Out of everything I did, working on* Nerosubianco *wasn't what I ended up getting the most enjoyment from, but it was certainly the hardest and most complex music I ever played, waltz times, the lot...*' [4]

The crew, cast and band were also accompanied by journalists who reported enthusiastically about what was being filmed. Italian magazine *L'Europeo* carried a piece on 9 November 1967, drawing comparisons with the work of Buñuel and Joyce, in the case of the latter specifically mentioning *Ulysses*. Brass himself described The Freedom as '...*a didactic choir, in the manner of Brecht...*' and confirmed his intention was, by framing everything in a style that was '...*a little bit Freud, and a little bit Joyce...*' to show how women's role in society was changing because of a partial shift in economic power between the sexes.

Less cerebral coverage came that same month from *Melody Maker*, who reported, in some detail (with an accompanying still photo taken in a scene shot in Porchester Baths): '...***IS THIS THE ULTIMATE*** *in publicity exposure? A pop group appearing in the nude? In fact, they're not completely unclad, despite appearances. They're wearing panties under their guitars. And, in another sense too, they've not yet bared themselves to the public. They have yet to issue a record. The photograph is a shot from a film sequence. The group is called Freedom, a breakaway faction from Procol Harum. The film, made for Dino De Laurentiis, and directed by Tinto Brass, is called* Attraction. *They're hoping it will be shown at next year's Cannes Film Festival, and Freedom have written fourteen songs for it. They are managed by Jonathan Weston, a twenty-three-year-old ex-public schoolboy from Rugby. The film, he hopes, will launch the group in a big way in America. "It wouldn't get past the censors in Italy," he told Michael Bateman. "It's very symbolic. You might say phallic. Chicks lying around with no clothes on. But mind you, from the rushes I saw, the scenes are very tastefully done. It's a fantasy about a woman, her husband, and her lover. The woman's got some kind of sexual conflict, and practically everyone she sees in the film she sees dressed and undressed." The girl's fantasy world is reflected by cutting into a gigantic happening and environmental light display which was filmed at the Roundhouse at Chalk Farm. Burps, coughs, sneezes and other noises are transmitted by way of an oscilloscope on to three closed circuit TV screens. Sound impulses are turned into light impulses, and the resulting pictures in colour are mixed together. The music is in the same style, blending electronic sounds, harpsichords and a string quartet. It's unusual for a group to make a film before a record, but Freedom is not the usual sort of outfit. They're militantly anti-commercial, and go on about how beastly the business is. Mike Lease, Welsh and twenty-one, is the arranger. He has a classical*

*background, and tried to flee the pop scene, but was hauled back
into it by manager Weston. "I hate the percentage scene, the publicity
scene, and all this rubbish. You get a whole lot of middlemen, and
many of them are just parasites. But if you're not commercial you can't
have money to hire recording studios, vans, equipment, and you can't
survive." If the nudist gimmick caught on, would they repeat the act on
stage? Lease thinks not: "It's not my scene." Steve Shirley, described in
Freedom's publicity as "a heartbreaker", says he'd be too embarrassed.
Bobby Harrison, former Procol Harum man, and a likely footballer
who was in West Ham's nursery side, says he'd do it if the money was
right. And small, fuzzy-haired Ray Royer, billed as "a mystical dreamy
elf-like man" who claims to have twice gone "round the magic circle of
meditation", feels much the same way. "I'd strip off if I wanted to, but
it would have to be spontaneous. This Saturday maybe..."'*

This was trite, and underplayed what Brass and the band
were actually trying to do, but it was good coverage, especially
as the circulation of UK music papers at the time was in six
figures. Weston's comments here allude to possible difficulties
getting the completed film past the censors. He may have been
right: other people had commented as much and word had
even reached De Laurentiis, who was upset when he saw some
of the rushes. Aware of the fate that had befallen Warhol's
Chelsea Girls at Cannes that summer, he flew to London to
remonstrate with Brass, asking that he cease shooting material
that would make obtaining a release certificate difficult. In
response to De Laurentiis asking, '...*Can you tell me, where can
we distribute such a film? In Sweden, maybe, and then where? Are we
only going to show it to friends?*' Brass simply shrugged, saying, '...
We'll cut it, we'll cut it...' With the film having a lowish budget,
De Laurentiis chose not to pursue the matter and may also
have reasoned that given Brass was a good editor, maybe he

could cut the offending scenes in such a way that the censors wouldn't object after all.

Midway through the shoot, The Freedom were invited to play at a New Year's Eve party at Dino De Laurentiis's house on the French Riviera. They drove all the way there from London, with Mike Lease remembering the event well: '...Yes, this was our first gig. Apparently, Dino's daughter had asked her father for us, and was our biggest fan. It was a beautiful mansion overlooking the Med. We stayed there for the best part of a week, in luxury. The majority of the clientele gave off, to me, a distinctly "mafioso" atmosphere – very well-heeled and shady. This was probably a totally false inference on my part, they were probably just wealthy businessmen from southern Europe, after all. We performed all of the film music plus a couple of other compositions, and things went fine until midnight, when I launched into "Auld Lang Syne", baffled by the non-existent response from the audience. I'd forgotten that it meant nothing to people from this neck of the woods!'

Early in the New Year, as filming came to an end, The Freedom made their UK live debut at Sussex University on 28 January 1968.[5] They appeared as support act to Traffic, an ideal pairing, given the similarities in sound and song structures between the two bands at that point. A little later Brass wrapped the shoot, and by February the footage was being worked on in the editing and dubbing suites. The Freedom completed their contribution to the score and the various cast members recorded their dialogue, such as it was. Brass brought in Gian Carlo Fusco, with whom he had worked on *Chi Lavoro e Perduto/Those Who Work Are Lost* and *Yankee* to compose the voice-over 'interior' thoughts of Barbara and her imagined exchanges with the other characters that occur throughout the film. Fusco was a skilled writer, compared by some to Jacques

Prévert or even Jean Genet.[6] He had written several novels set in fascist Italy and also worked extensively as a journalist and screenplay writer. He made occasional acting appearances too and can be seen briefly in *Nerosubianco*. His other film credits included the commentary for *Mondo Nudo/Naked World*, a considerable box-office success and one of the burgeoning genre of 'mondo' films, a somewhat grotesque free-wheeling documentary series spawned after *Mondo Cane/A Dog's Life* won the Palme D'Or at the 1962 Cannes Film Festival. Many sequels and blatant cash-ins to this appeared, with various low-budget US and Italian productions continuing to this day. Although the 'mondo' genre was essentially sensational, it was by virtue of its trashy ethos part of the breaking down of barriers that occurred in the 1960s, and its films attracted a fair number of well-known composers and writers. Producing a deadpan, observational script for one of its productions was no easy task.

Brass worked frantically and *Variety* reported on 8 May 1968 that he had finished assembling his cut of the film, which ran at that point for 120 minutes. The intention was to screen it at Cannes. The festival itself ran for two weeks from 10 May and among the official entrants that year was a veritable cornucopia of 1960s pop cinema: *Charlie Bubbles*, *Here We Go Round the Mulberry Bush*, *Joanna*, *Petulia*, *Girl on a Motorcycle*, *Wonderwall* and *Revolution*. But, in the first of what would be several reversals, the screenings were abandoned after a few days, with *Variety* reporting that François Truffaut, Jean-Luc Godard, Claude Berri, Claude Lelouch and Louis Malle were insisting that the festival close to show solidarity with the Sorbonne students and striking workers. A month later, Roman Polanski, an exile from Communist Poland, was quoted as saying those directors were *'...idiots... people like Truffaut, Lelouch and Godard are like little kids playing at being revolutionaries...',*[7] which was a fair point, but one which failed to put in context the general turmoil across France that year. Though Truffaut, Godard et al were sincere – for the main – in their support for political change, part of the reason events had reached such a level in the first place was down to high-handed action taken by the government against the film community.

For them, their dispute with de Gaulle and his ministers began on 9 February 1968, when the Minister for Culture, André Malraux, dismissed Henri Langlois from his position at the Cinémathèque Française, changed the locks on the building, and appointed Pierre Barbin as his replacement. Truffaut, Godard and others responded by withdrawing permission for their films to be shown at the Cinémathèque, and were quickly joined in this by Charlie Chaplin, Roberto Rossellini, Richard Lester and Orson Welles. Within a week there were demonstrations taking place in the street outside, these being dispersed by police baton charges. By 23 February *Cahiers du Cinéma* was campaigning for Langlois's reinstatement, and had collected signatures supporting this from a massive array of the cultural greats of the time: Michelangelo Antonioni, Ingmar Bergman, Luis Buñuel, Peter Brook, Alfred Hitchcock, Elia Kazan, Akira Kurosawa, Pier Paolo Pasolini, Satyajit Ray, Andy Warhol, Jean-Paul Belmondo, Brigitte Bardot, Catherine Deneuve, Marlene Dietrich, Jane Fonda, Katharine Hepburn, Peter O'Toole, Toshiro Mifune, Gloria Swanson, Samuel Beckett, Truman Capote, Max Ernst, Eugène Ionesco, Pablo Picasso and Jean-Paul Sartre. Although Malraux backed down, and Langlois was reinstated on 22 April, wider protests began elsewhere as other grievances were brought into play involving both factory workers and students.[8] By the time the Cannes Film Festival was underway, eleven million people were on strike across France, with the prospect very much in the air that the de Gaulle government might collapse and be replaced by a socialist-communist coalition. It was deeply ironic that the convulsions that shook France in 1968 started, in part at least, from a dispute at the Cinémathèque Française and that these had the result of preventing a widespread appreciation of *Nerosubianco*, a revolutionary film made by one of its former staff. (And one which would surely have been heralded, by Godard, Truffaut, Berri, Lelouch and Malle, as a work of the utmost significance, had they managed to see it.)

The impact of the Festival being abandoned was that out of the 28 scheduled films, only 11 were shown. In the festival catalogue itself Brass's film is not listed as either being entered into the formal competition, or screened 'out of competition'. Which is not to say that it wasn't screened. Brass himself confirmed that it was, some years later in *Film International* in 2011: '...*the film was rather successful at Cannes. Some producers from Paramount were quite taken with* Nerosubianco *and invited me to Paramount...*'[9] It seems that just as he shot wherever he wanted on location, Brass simply turned up at Cannes and screened *Nerosubianco* in an invitation-only fringe event that he and De Laurentiis quickly organised for various significant industry figures. One wonders today though, given what a groundbreaking work the film was, whether De Laurentiis shouldn't have arranged something a bit more significant? We know now that *Nerosubianco* would have compared favourably with any of the better-known offerings and giving it such a limited and restricted exposure, 'events' notwithstanding, seems curiously perfunctory and self-defeating. Perhaps the reason they took such a route came down to trying to ensure that whatever happened it was at least *seen*. After all, Warhol had relied on the organising committee to screen *Chelsea Girls* only to come away disappointed.

For the moment, though, expectations remained high. Partly due to their work on the film, The Freedom secured a recording contract with Mercury Records. Their debut release, *Where Will You Be Tonight*, appeared on 7 June 1968. Primarily a US label, Mercury moved energetically into the UK and European market around this time, signing up Aphrodite's Child and The Eyes of Blue, among others, and generally spraying quite a lot of money around.[(10)] In the words of Mike Lease, '...*I'm not sure what led to the Mercury deal, there was very little information given to us. I know that there was a huge advance paid, of which we (at least I) saw nothing. I should have been more than a little suspicious when our manager suddenly bought a Ferrari, driving around London streets in 1ˢᵗ and 2ⁿᵈ gear – yes, it was the real deal!*' Around this time, Alan Sekers went with Brass to see De Laurentiis at his office in Rome. The purpose of the meeting – which Sekers did not actually witness, sitting outside whilst it took place – appears to have been to tie down arrangements for the formal release of *Nerosubianco*, and to release the funding for *L'Urlo*, the second part of the Brass-De Laurentiis deal. There was also a need to tie down Brass's trip to Hollywood to meet Paramount, as well as an interesting anecdote, discussed later, connecting De Laurentiis, Stanley Kubrick, Brass, *Waterloo* and *A Clockwork Orange*, the significance of which was not appreciated at the time. For the moment, as regards *Nerosubianco*, everything seemed to be on track. Brass flew to the US, met Paramount and by the summer of 1968 was back in London arranging *L'Urlo*.

The first of a series of real blows that would ultimately lead to the film being almost completely forgotten occurred when Brass was in America. The Italian tax authorities – ironically, given Mike Lease's comments about the clientele at the New Year's Eve Party – seized control of the various De Laurentiis companies, suspecting massive and systemic tax evasion. De Laurentiis himself fled Italy to avoid arrest. Bobby Harrison remembers, '...one day Jonathan told us that Dino had been done for tax evasion and everything got shelved at that point...' The non-release of the film brought other matters to a head. Mike Lease was annoyed with both the management of the band and the conduct of his colleagues once they began playing gigs to publicise their Mercury single. '...At this time, I did nothing other than the Nerosubianco project. I was responsible for all the arrangements, co-composition, recording, production and editing. Although Jonathan Weston managed to credit himself with production, this is entirely fallacious. He basically didn't have a musical clue... I decided to leave Freedom sometime after a gig in the summer of 1968. We were headlining at a college. When I joined the band, the roadie was Harvey Bramham. I wasn't altogether happy about his involvement, having known him previously. After the first couple of months, his homicidal driving persuaded me to give the band and the management an ultimatum – either he was sacked or I would leave the band. He was dismissed. Apart from his being a thief, I had realised that he was also supplying drugs to Ray and Steve, which was becoming increasingly problematic. At the college gig, this chicken came home to roost. At one point, Bobby and I were playing the agreed song, Ray was playing a different song and Steve yet another different item, both of them apparently oblivious of the cacophonous result. The audience were mystified, although some thought it was "far out". The problem was obviously drug-related, and I found out they were still in

contact with Harvey, and were reluctant to address the problem. So,
I turned this over in my mind, becoming sickened by the whole scene
and eventually decided to quit...'

With the film not forthcoming and Lease – the main
composer and arranger in the band – departing, The Freedom
struggled on and made the best of things. Robin Lumsden,
a former colleague of Harrison's in the pre-Procol Harum,
Southend-based outfit The Powerpack, was recruited to
replace him on keyboards, and the group set about trying to
write commercial material. But worse was to follow. Firstly,
in October 1968 – echoing Jonathan Weston's comments in
Melody Maker a year earlier – the Italian censor refused to grant
the film a certificate unless substantial cuts were made, on
the grounds that the material was too explicit. Then, about a
month later, The Freedom were dropped by Mercury and their
attempt at a hit single, *Kandy Kay*, only struggled out on the
tiny Plexium label, which was distributed by EMI. Similar to
the type of stuff being done then by outfits like The Tremeloes,
it was competent but a step down from the heights they had
reached with Mike Lease, and it sank without trace.

In the meantime, attempts continued to try and salvage
the film. In Italy *ABC* magazine, for which Gian Carlo Fusco
wrote, carried no less than 30 pages about its non-appearance
in their December 1968 edition, proclaiming it a masterpiece
that was being needlessly blocked by the censors. Perhaps that
had an effect. The Italian tax authorities hadn't actually shut
down the De Laurentiis network; they let it continue running
under their supervision, and had a clear interest in maximising
the revenue that could be generated, however distasteful some
might think the films. To get a version, any decent version, of
Nerosubianco released Brass returned to Italy from the UK and

went back to work in the editing suite. Nino Segurini came with him and was shot – dressed as a priest – holding up a board on which was written *Proibito* immediately prior to the scenes that were either being deleted or obscured with a rotating psychedelic design. Some replacement footage was added too, from Brass's collage documentary *Ça Ira, Il Fiume Della Rivolta* which depicted war atrocities, murders, ranting dictators and the like. By including fragments of this, Brass made a point about the censors: they found despotism, murder and genocide less objectionable than the nudity that was being removed from the film. By February 1969, Brass had cut 44 minutes, and a version running 76 minutes and dubbed in Italian was passed by the Italian censor. He also produced a slightly different 80-minute version (which is better and truer, one suspects, to his original vision) dubbed in English for distribution in the UK and US. To tie in with the film appearing in Italy, the score found its way into the public domain too, and was released as an album on Atlantic. Containing 10 of the tracks composed by Lease and The Freedom, only 8 of which were actually in the short version of the film, this was better than nothing, and in its way quite prestigious... after all, at that point Atlantic hosted Led Zeppelin and were about to sign Yes.[11] Not that The Freedom knew this at the time or would profit from the arrangement. They disintegrated as a band in the first weeks of 1969 with Royer, Shirley and Lumsden all vanishing from the scene, Weston searching out other opportunities and Harrison being left with the name and the chance to rebuild the act along lines he felt more comfortable with.

All that was now left was to get the English language cut of *Nerosubianco* into the cinemas. The shortened version was marketed to interested distributors at the May 1969 Cannes

Festival and a bid came in from Radley Metzger. He bought the rights to screen it in the US via his company Audubon Films, and other arrangements were made via a Columbia subsidiary. Metzger and Audubon had been distributing European art-house films in the US since 1961. Many of these featured nudity and sex scenes considerably in advance of anything being shot in the US (or UK) and as a result were often classed – quite wrongly in many cases – as adult erotica and shown at cinemas that catered to a clientele that wanted to watch such material. Typical of these were *I, a Woman* (1965) and *The Libertine* (1968), the latter starring Jean-Louis Trintignant. Metzger also directed his own films, and after an initial critical success with *Dark Odyssey* (1961) had noted the profits made by most erotic films and had modified his directing efforts to accommodate that genre. One of these, *Carmen, Baby* (1967), was a colossal hit and in July 1969 he followed this up with *Camille 2000* which featured brilliantly designed modernist sets, plush photography, good camerawork and use of colour, all in emulation of the glossy pop style of contemporary Italian features. The cast were well-known to film enthusiasts: Danièle Gaubert, Nino Castelnuovo (from the 1964 mega-hit *Les Parapluies de Cherbourg/The Umbrellas of Cherbourg*), Eleonora Rossi Drago and Roberto Bisacco. Interestingly, Drago had been in Brass's *Il Disco Volante/The Flying Saucer* and Bisacco had co-starred in *Col Cuore in Gola*. Thus, when Metzger bid for and won the rights to *Nerosubianco*, he knew that it wasn't a sex film per se, and he was familiar with Brass's work and reputation. It was the closest to a sympathetic release and distribution that the film would get, albeit not necessarily in theatres that would attract a mainstream audience. Metzger ordered a large number of prints and when these were delivered

Nerosubianco opened in the US in October 1969, by which time the slightly shorter European version was being screened in West Germany, Austria and Spain.

The involvement of Columbia is intriguing. In April 1969 they acquired the distribution rights for *Model Shop*, a US feature from French director Jacques Demy (whose big breakthrough had been *Les Parapluies de Cherbourg/The Umbrellas of Cherbourg*) in which a woman meets a man in a city, in this case Los Angeles, and has a brief, casual relationship with him. Starring Anouk Aimée and Gary Lockwood (for whom this was the follow-up to his appearance in Kubrick's *2001: A Space Odyssey*) Demy's film had music by the US band Spirit, who also appear on screen. The similarities to *Nerosubianco*, which was planned and filmed first, are very striking and it may be that Columbia saw Brass's film as a companion piece to Demy's, playing the same venues and targeted at the same audiences.[12] The final curiosity in *Nerosubianco*'s long and uneven journey to a release of sorts was the absence of any official credit for Dino De Laurentiis as producer. His name does not appear on either of the versions that made it into the public domain. Why would this happen? Did De Laurentiis try and curry favour with the Italian authorities by formally disassociating himself from the film? Or was it the case that De Laurentiis, who often produced films on an uncredited basis, wanted to make tracing his liabilities rather problematic for the taxman? Alternatively did De Laurentiis agree to disown the film to reduce his tax liabilities? *Nerosubianco* was not shown formally at Cannes in 1969, which seems to indicate that De Laurentiis was no longer involved by then and that the tax authorities were merely selling the film to interested buyers to meet their costs in dealing with his case and with no interest in the film's artistic standing. Which is a great shame. For a second consecutive year *Nerosubianco* was denied the chance to compete with its many rivals, which in 1969 included *Easy Rider*, *If...*, *More*, *Head*, *The Trip*, *Gli Intoccabili/ Machine Gun McCain* and *Isadora*. All became well-known, some sensationally so, whilst Brass's film slid into obscurity.

Around the time that Metzger appeared on the scene Harrison relaunched The Freedom with Roger Saunders and Walt Monaghan, recruiting them from the defunct mod act The Washington DC's. They quickly secured a deal with BYG, a French label, and in June-July 1969 recorded an album, *Freedom at Last*, at Orange Studios in New Compton Street using the mixing console that had been built and operated (until his suicide) by Joe Meek at 304 Holloway Road. Label owners Jean Georgakarakos and Jean-Luc Young produced and the band began gigging immediately. According to Harrison, '*...I really wanted a heavier sound. I formed a new version of Freedom with Roger Saunders and Walt Monaghan from the east London outfit The Washington DC's. We got a residency at The Bridge House Tavern, Canning Town and were signed up by BYG records, a French label. We did quite well in France: Claude Nobs got us a lot of work. We recorded an album Freedom at Last and were invited over to appear at the massive pop festival at Amougies, in Belgium in October 1969. I remember us flying there and back the same day! We played as support to Pink Floyd which we found a bit scary given how huge a band they were at that time. The festival was filmed by Jérôme Laperrousaz and released in two parts: Music Power and European Music Revolution...*' (13) As *Nerosubianco* opened in cinemas across the US, and much of Europe too, Harrison and his new colleagues began carving out a new career for themselves, and The Freedom finally got on with establishing themselves as a gigging band.

Notes

(1) Details of the Woburn Abbey Festival are at https://www.
     bbc.co.uk/news/uk-england-beds-bucks-herts-40926916
     and http://www.ukrockfestivals.com/woburn-67.html It
     seems that a couple of the acts were filmed by Peter Clifton
     with the material slotted into his 1973 documentary *Rock
     City*. Given that Clifton also shot the original promotional
     film for *A Whiter Shade of Pale*, with both Bobby Harrison
     and Ray Royer, the idea that Brass was hanging around
     Woburn too doesn't seem that peculiar.

(2) For this and much else on *Nerosubianco* see https://
     rjbuffalo.com/1968a-ne.html

(3) Interview with Mike Lease.

(4) Interview with Bobby Harrison.

(5) See http://www.45worlds.com/live/listing/traffic-sussex-
     university-1968 The gig took place on 28 January 1968,
     when Traffic were promoting their *Mr Fantasy* album,
     and high in the singles charts with *Here We Go Round
     the Mulberry Bush*. (The title song for the film of the same
     name.) Admission was £1.

(6) Prévert seems a particularly apt comparison. A poet, his
     lyrics were often recited as songs by some of the great
     chanteurs and chanteuses of the 1940s, 1950s and 1960s.
     Prévert supported left-wing causes and wrote many film
     screenplays.

(7) Quoted at https://variety.com/2018/vintage/news/cannes-
     1968-student-protests-festival-closed-1202797967/

(8) For more on the Malraux-Langlois contretemps see
     https://www.newyorker.com/magazine/2003/10/20/
     after-the-revolution-4

(9)   Quoted in an extensive interview at http://filmint.nu/
      if-history-runs-cinema-can%E2%80%99t-keep-walking-
      an-interview-with-tinto-bras/ The majority of the piece
      concerns *L'Urlo*.

(10) The Eyes of Blue were immediately featured in *Connecting
      Rooms*, a film funded by David Hemmings's company
      Hemdale. Like *Nerosubianco* it had difficulties getting a
      release, as the momentum of Swinging London faded.

(11) See https://www.discogs.com/The-Freedom-Nerosubianco/
      release/4306738

(12) The trailer for *Model Shop* can be seen at https://www.
      youtube.com/watch?v=Ppg7w8XfYR4 Spirit recorded 11
      tracks for the film, produced by Lou Adler, which didn't
      get a formal release until 2005.

(13) A version of this can be viewed at https://www.youtube.
      com/watch?v=dfGr23WeE5I. The film had a troubled
      history, with its release subject to an injunction from
      Pink Floyd. Accounts of The Freedom's career written in
      the 1970s tended to refer to them as 'short-lived': see the
      entry for Procol Harum in *The Encyclopaedia of Rock Vol
      2 From Liverpool to San Francisco* 1976 p 274-275. Actually,
      The Freedom recorded and released five albums between
      1967 and 1972, two of which were on the UK's prestigious
      Vertigo label.

7

'...FOR THE SCENE AT THE ROUNDHOUSE WE HAD A COUPLE ACTUALLY HAVING SEX...'

So... what is the film actually like? *Nerosubianco* begins with Barbara and her husband Paolo driving around London. She wants a break and some time by herself. She feels repressed and he agrees to her request. He drops her off at a large park, probably Hyde Park although most of the footage that follows was clearly shot at Woburn, possibly earlier than October 1967. On the soundtrack a gormless middle-class voice intones various pseudo-political phrases whilst asking repeatedly 'Who's in charge?' This framing device plants the Reichian idea that political rhetoric is, of itself, sterile, and that revolutionary change only occurs in society when people alter their personal behaviour. To emphasise this point, Barbara notices many uninhibited young people, including a young woman draped, serpent-like, around a tree. We see a close-up of a Hieronymus Bosch painting, and symbolically one of the young people offers Barbara an apple. Whilst this occurs The Freedom play their opening number, *The Better Side*. Brilliantly filmed, the band are shot from the middle distance, playing at various levels within an enormous oak tree. This required significant logistical arrangements, with the drums and Hammond organ needing to be winched on to the lower branches and somehow kept in place. According to Mike Lease an official from the Duke of Bedford turned up querying if they had the owner's permission: they didn't, of course, but continued anyway. *'...Tinto was obviously the boss and quite unpredictable. As I mentioned before, he ignored officialdom/bureaucracy for every scene. For example, for the "tree" filming, we simply invaded Woburn Park and started setting up the instruments in the tree, this was quite difficult to set up and "hairy", particularly for the lads in the higher branches, Ray and Steve. I was on one of the lower branches because the Hammond was so heavy and difficult to manoeuvre around. It was a whole day's work and very dangerous – Tinto was particularly good at getting others to take risks. An official eventually arrived, puzzled, and demanded to see our authorisation. Tinto pretended to send off his assistant to get the (non-existent) approval certificate, then assured the man that he had personally got permission from the Duke of Bedford, in broken English, until the man was convinced and went off satisfied, forgetting that he hadn't seen the evidence. This was typical of Brass – an arch-manipulator, though very likable...'* A visual masterpiece, in which the music complements the action perfectly, the end result is similar to the 1970 Apple album cover design for *John Lennon and the Plastic Ono Band*.[1]

From here, Barbara begins her odyssey across the city. Starting among the overgrown tombstones in Kensal Green cemetery, she travels by tube, sees a black man (or thinks she does) and fantasises about being naked and chased through the woods by him. We see a poster advertising the film *To Sir, With Love* (released in the UK on 27 October 1967, and a huge commercial success) with the face of Sidney Poitier being momentarily prominent and echoing the image of the black man that she thinks she has seen. Barbara walks the streets of central London, visiting boutiques and passing advertisements for *International Times* as well as Frank Zappa and Bob Dylan posters that were common at that time. In a nod to Freud and his views on the importance of sexual dreams and fantasies, a disembodied voice on the soundtrack recites readers' letters from a sex magazine and we assume that similar frustrated thoughts are passing through Barbara's imagination. The Freedom perform their second song, *The Truth is Plain to See*. We see some enormously enlarged Guido Crepax, Pop-Art images of *Valentina*, and Barbara fantasises, like a comic-book heroine might, about encountering the black man in a narrow alleyway.

Next, and just 15 minutes into the film, she visits a hair salon. The receptionist is played by a young Janet Street-Porter and The Freedom perform *Butt of Deception*. Halfway through the song the women clients have all acquired gigantic pantomime cows' heads and we switch to a domestic residence (Barbara and Paolo's) where a full-sized (real-life) cow, symbolic of Barbara and her status in the marriage, is lying awkwardly on a bed. Her husband has called for a doctor, and Barbara is medically examined, fantasising as this occurs that the GP is now the black man she saw in the city. She leaves and takes a trip on a river boat.

As she does, we see barges, tugs and warehouses, showing that the Thames was still a working river then. Barbara imagines (or sees) people engaged in domestic disputes inside the buildings that she passes, including a woman committing suicide, the message of the sequence being that society as a whole is unhappy and in conflict. The Freedom are glimpsed in the windows of passing buildings performing *Relation*. Barbara fantasises about killing her husband. Her daydreaming continues and she imagines she is back in her flat with her husband. The images of these scenes, almost Pop-Art masterpieces in their own right, are shot by Brass and his cameraman in ultra-modern but sterile interiors, intercut, Andy Warhol-style, with Esso and Coca Cola logos that confirm the commodification of their marriage. Barbara buys an *International Times* and arrives at a traditional municipal steam baths for the scene referred to in the November 1967 *Melody Maker* article. In both extant versions of the film this has clearly been edited, and, from the Italian language version, almost deleted. The Freedom are there too, playing *Childhood Reflection* whilst surrounded by a group of naked women. Not surprisingly, they recollect this scene quite clearly. In the words of Bobby Harrison, *'...we had no clothes on... I told my Mum about it and she was very shocked, being a strong Catholic...'* Mike Lease, for his part, says *'...Tinto could be occasionally violent. He had a truly obnoxious assistant director who would lose no opportunity to finger, etc the (many) naked girl extras in the various sets, and generally be a complete pain in the arse. After one of these transgressions, Tinto called him over and floored him with a cracking right cross, leaving him quite docile for a while afterwards...'* Harrison's comments are especially ironic given that we also see Barbara and Paolo in bed together surrounded by Catholic imagery and cut to more of Crepax's *Valentina* pictures whilst a voice explicates Catholic religious teaching on the soundtrack.

The daydreaming ends and we are back at the scene on the boat. She arrives at a funfair. What follows is very heavily edited;

one assumes therefore that most of the 40 minutes removed by Brass to get the film past the censors occurred in the sequences shot in the steam baths and funfair. The Freedom play *We Say No*, lots of young people appear adorned with body art and face painting until an elderly woman machine guns a crowd of them. We switch from images of sexual antics to images of executions in footage that suggests forthcoming state repression, and an establishment backlash against liberty. It concludes with some shots of the same long, thin, translucent plastic sculptures that were displayed at 'The 14 Hour Technicolour Dream'.

Barbara emerges and arrives at Trafalgar Square where a large anti-Vietnam rally is being addressed by Tariq Ali. Simultaneously with Ali's use of violent political rhetoric the interior monologue on the soundtrack switches to comments about sexual torture, Brass once more making the Reichian point that violent politics and abusive sex are interrelated. Barbara sees the black man again. The Freedom appear, apparently in the midst of the crowd, performing *At Last*. How did they manage it? Mike Lease explains: '...*Clever editing, this. We filmed on a normal "tourist" day, not in the middle of the anti-Vietnam demo! Tinto spliced it all together convincingly. At Trafalgar Square, several policemen, very suspicious, came on heavy about Tinto not having permission to film there. Within 15 minutes they were all smiling and joking and obviously flattered to be unpaid extras on the set...*'[2] To highlight the point being made about political turmoil, Brass edits in documentary footage of Hungary 1956, the Cultural Revolution, battles between the police and anti-Mosley demonstrators in Cable Street in 1936 and the Sharpeville massacre. The sequence ends in an art gallery (actually the room in the flat in Cadogan Place that served as a set) where a young Chinese man tries to get Barbara to take one of Mao's 'Little Red Books'. The black man intervenes, and forces the Chinese youth to accept instead *The Autobiography of Malcolm X*.[3]

The Freedom pass on a bus playing *Born Again* and we arrive at the Roundhouse, where within the huge space, cordoned off by enormous white sheets, Mark Boyle's light show is taking place. A woman is wired up to various bits of medical machinery and people - including Gian Carlo Fusco - are providing spit and phlegm that can be placed on slides and projected, at enormous magnification, onto the surrounding screens. The set contains some very modern, transparent, plastic furniture. A woman, Graziella Martinez, dances. In the words of Alan Sekers, Boyle came to be involved because he '...had a project called "Son et Lumière for Bodily Fluids and Functions," and he was looking for a venue to do a new version. He had performed at the ICA and I put Tinto in touch with Mark who proposed a "happening" to be held without spectators, but just "to be" for its own sake...' Just prior to filming this, Boyle and Martinez had performed a piece - *Lullaby for Catatonics* - at the 1967 Edinburgh Festival, as part of a mixed-media event with The Soft Machine. Indeed, when Brass shot *Nerosubianco*, Martinez had just returned from Paris where she and The Soft Machine had performed together.[4] The minute or two that we see here of Boyle's light show and Martinez's dancing is thus of some archival importance, the only known record of it on film.

Nor was this the only time that the Roundhouse staged a mixture of avant-garde film and music. In October 1966, John Latham's 11-minute-long animation *Speak* - an op-art and graphic design piece assembled from thousands of split-second colour compositions - was screened there, during a performance by Pink Floyd. This particular event, a concert to celebrate the launch of *International Times*, was attended by Michelangelo Antonioni, Monica Vitti, Marianne Faithful and Paul McCartney, among others. A year later, at exactly the same point that Brass began shooting *Nerosubianco*, Pink Floyd would record half an hour of improvised instrumental music at Latham's request for use in another of his films, only for him to reject their efforts as unsuitable.[5] This sequence in *Nerosubianco*, then, is very much 'of its time' and Brass remains the only director to stage and include a Roundhouse-style event of this type within a feature film, whilst at the same time presenting it in a sympathetic and non-exploitative fashion.[6]

Barbara passes through the scene and we cut to London Bridge, which is jammed with thousands of commuters. The black man is following her again. The crowds are immense and she goes into a pedestrian underpass. She pauses at a photo-booth, has her picture taken, and then walks away without collecting the prints. The black man retrieves them, calling to her *'Hey Lady! You forgot your pictures!'*, (the only dialogue spoken by Carter in the film), then chases after her. Thinking she is being harassed by him, a group of sharp-suited city gents – all wearing bowler hats – pin him up against a wall. Barbara moves on.

She reaches the Natural History Museum and walks around the enormous Diplodocus skeleton. Large pictures showing family groups of naked prehistoric people fill the background. They contrast with the crowds we have just seen milling around in the city outside. The black man approaches her again, and she escapes to the lavatory, where we see, as she opens one cubicle after another, enormous images of Frank Zappa, Allen Ginsberg and Gregory Corso. Throughout this her interior monologue continues, with a detached, ironic voice reading out the text from a women's underwear catalogue. She arrives in Soho. There is a fight between a white man and a black man. Barbara stands on a street corner. The wall behind her is plastered, many inches deep, with posters advertising gigs and concerts. We can pick out advertisements for PP Arnold and The Dubliners, both of whom enjoyed chart success in late 1967.[7] Brass edits in a shot of the English Heritage plaque at 28 Dean Street, W1, confirming Karl Marx's residence there. Barbara stands by a poster of Marcel Marceau, and momentarily wears similar make-up.[8] By this Brass implies that her trip through London is a type of mime, and, that women generally are obliged to perform a role in a man's world. She walks through a sex shop and into a strip club. As with the steam baths and funfair, this scene is heavily cut in both the Italian and UK language versions. She fantasises that she is the stripper, that her husband is too restrained and that the black man who follows her is a voyeur. She has – or she fantasises about, we cannot tell – a gynaecological examination, and, after a dream sequence with her husband in a taxi, arrives at an art gallery.

Here we see a sculpture exhibition showing mannequins, some of which are arranged in sexual poses, and a group of young people covered in body paint collapsed in a corner. David Cobbold, then a young artist at the Royal College of Art, provided the mannequins and confirms, '...the sculptures were commissioned especially for the film and destroyed afterwards. They were made in plastic sheeting over a chicken-wire armature and spray painted... I met Tinto, quite large and fat with a brush haircut. His wife was very small. We called her Mini Mouse. Unusual couple. On the set it seemed like organised chaos...' [9] The Freedom are playing The Game is Over wearing, as they do so, some of the outré costumes purchased for them in Mr Fish. With that song still playing we arrive back at the Roundhouse. In a circular set created by hanging vast, elongated white sheeting from the roof of the building, The Freedom continue to play and we see several close-ups of them as they do so. In the background a couple appear to be having sex on an inflatable mattress. According to Alan Sekers, this was the first time unsimulated sex had ever been filmed in the UK, albeit the editing barely shows it. '...For the scene at the Roundhouse we had a couple actually having sex (which must have been a first in a commercial film) on an inflatable couch with their bodies linked up to a lot of scientific equipment monitoring their brain and body activities whilst the light show consisted not of oil being moved around by heat but bodily fluids instead. The machinery used to monitor all this made a huge amount of noise. Very avant-garde and very 60s... There was a randomly chosen boy and a randomly chosen girl wearing only electrodes and heartbeat monitors, connected to an oscilloscope, onto which was trained a video camera. The image of the oscilloscope would be projected by a black-and-white Eidophor television projector. All the equipment needed technicians, in white laboratory coats, and people looking after the brain monitors and so forth, and tuning the oscilloscope. Mark Boyle would occasionally dash in to get a smear of bodily fluid onto a slide, which was projected behind the couple. The boy was called Kumo Spyder, and he had been hired as a truck driver for the film crew... he was always up for anything. The girl who had volunteered got slightly cold feet. Tinto was perfectly happy with the result, and then had Nino Segurini and Anita Sanders walk through the event as part of the plot...'

In fact, we see Barbara being chased around the circular set by her husband after which she returns to the park where the film began. Here the black man finally meets her and, symbolically, she bites an apple. Once again, the park is full of liberated young people and The Freedom are seen as they were at the start, scattered around a huge oak tree playing *Attraction*. This changes into *With You* and the film moves to a simple, raucous finale. Paolo arrives in his car and Barbara runs to meet him, looking much happier than she did at the start of the film. They depart. The music carries on. The camera swings to show a wintry horizon in fading light. The Freedom run out from behind the camera and dance around as they disappear into the distance. Then the crew run out too and finally Tinto Brass stumbles after them, remonstrating that they should return, as the music pounds on. The light fades and a solid block of print – the credits, an idiosyncratic piece of graphic art in its own right – moves slowly up the screen.

This is the best version we have of *Nerosubianco*, as shot by Tinto Brass in London in 1967-1968. In comparison with other films made then, there is nothing else even remotely like it. It is told entirely from the woman's point of view, and Sanders is the opposite of the 'dolly bird'-type actress then common. Musically, The Freedom are central to the narrative and not incidental, as bands generally were in films like *Here We Go Round the Mulberry Bush* and *Smashing Time*. Although other productions like *Wonderwall* and *The Committee* would deploy music in a sympathetic fashion, neither of these had a band appearing throughout *and* singing songs that highlight and propel the plot. Some might argue that Godard's *One Plus One/ Sympathy for the Devil* (shot after *Nerosubianco*) covers similar territory... London... the 1960s... race issues... a rock band. Yes, it does. But is it more entertaining? And what intellectual point is Godard, ultimately, trying to make?

For anyone interested in the history of London as a place, the details that Brass shows of the metropolis at that time are fascinating, and, as with much of the footage in *Col Cuore in Gola*, provide us with a visual record of a now vanished city. The boutique where Barbara tries on clothes and The Freedom perform (nearly) naked is Early Bird, 20 Park Walk, London, SW10, now long gone and occupied by the Park Walk gallery. Throughout the film we see several images of the '*Wool Mark*' design, created by Franco Grignani in 1963 for the International Wool Secretariat. An iconic example of 1960s graphic and commercial art, it won several awards. Grignani exhibited alongside Francis Bacon, Jasper Johns and others, had a show in Brass's home town Venice in 1967, and, when *Nerosubianco* was being filmed, was in London designing a set of now much-admired book covers for Penguin paperbacks. Attempts at locating the funfair Barbara visits, Luna Park (a London version of the main attraction in Coney Island USA), have foundered. Nobody seems to know where it was. But Porchester Steam Baths, where much of the footage was cut from the Italian version, still operates, as Porchester Spa, in Queensway W2, as does the Roundhouse.

The brief London Bridge scene shows the 'old' bridge which was sold to a US millionaire in April 1968; this may be the last time it was used as a location by a feature film. As in *Col Cuore in Gola*, the Aldwych branch of the Piccadilly Line stood in for the scenes on London's tube, though neither film is formally credited as being shot there. The line closed to the public in 1994, but is still retained today for film work. David Cobbold's sculptures were displayed in Axiom Gallery, 79 Duke Street, W1; just off Grosvenor Square, very near the house where The Freedom were accommodated for the shoot. At the time Brass filmed it was an up-and-coming place where promising young artists would be shown:

John Walker, painter and printmaker, Malcolm Carder, a modern, installation-type sculptor who – like Grignani – also designed book jackets for Penguin (some of them brilliant) and kineticist Liliane Lijn, who moved in the same circles as Gregory Corso and William Burroughs, all exhibited there in 1967-1968. Axiom shut in the 1980s and the site is now occupied by a coffee shop.[10] The inflatable chair and mattress seen in the Roundhouse sequences were designed by Quasar Khanh, a French-Vietnamese furniture maker who launched these as part of his 'Aerospace' range in early 1968. As an example of the immediacy of the pop era, this couldn't have been improved on by Brass.[11]

The script Gian Carlo Fusco provided for the interior monologues also has a backstory, particularly the passages where an off-screen voice carefully and precisely reads out letters discussing the sex problems experienced by their authors. Did he create this himself, or was it based on material that was publicly available at the time? In London, in 1967, similar stuff was being published by Oz and International Times. A more likely candidate, though, is Mayfair magazine, launched in 1966. For many years this carried a feature, 'Quest', which explored 'the laboratory of human response' via fictional interviews with supposedly ordinary people in which graphic descriptions of sexual encounters were discussed. These were actually written by Graham Masterton, then deputy editor, and later an author of sex manuals and science fiction novels. Masterton and Mayfair were also publishing the work of William Burroughs in 1967-1968, so the magazine itself would have been seen – loosely – as part of the wider anti-establishment liberalisation that was occurring and not so different from some of its counter-culture cousins.[12]

A word needs to be said as well about the clothes purchased in Mr Fish for The Freedom. The costumes worn by them at the second and climactic scene in the Roundhouse are clearly lengthy, flowing 'man skirts', a style made famous by the boutique. Officially that fame began with Mick Jagger wearing a half-length version at Hyde Park in July 1969 and was consummated when David Bowie wore a complete one on the cover of his album *The Man Who Sold the World* (November 1970). We can clearly see here, though, that the first outing for this line, which, in keeping with Brass's film, played with ideas of gender identity and stereotyping, was via The Freedom, in *Nerosubianco*.

Sadly, efforts have failed to determine the location of the hair salon where we see Janet Street-Porter. According to Alan Sekers, her involvement arose '...*probably through her husband, Tim Street-Porter, a well-known photographer back then. We would have met her through Anthony Haden-Guest, our route into much of what was going on in London then. He knew Tinto from places like the Arts Lab at 182 Drury Lane (where people like JG Ballard and Yoko Ono put on readings and performances). Tinto really liked exploring all that cutting-edge stuff...*'[13] The Arts Lab opened in September 1967 with Graham Stevens, R D Laing, the Exploding Galaxy, Michael X and a screening of *Chelsea Girls* all appearing/performing there in the first couple of weeks. [14] Much of the material Brass uses in *Nerosubianco* and *L'Urlo* overlaps with this, and the Italian magazine *ABC*, which also covered Brass's films in some detail, even ran an article on the Lab on 3 March 1968.[15]

By 1967 Street-Porter had already appeared – uncredited, as a girl dancing in a club to The Yardbirds – in *Blow-Up*. Now, she managed to appear, again uncredited, in *Nerosubianco*, which directly competes with Antonioni's acclaimed work for the accolade of best 'Swinging London' film. A few months later (February 1968) she became editor of *Petticoat*, a weekly colour magazine for adolescent girls that covered fashion, sex, careers and relationships in a way that was then considered modern, frank and liberal. In that sense, her appearance chimes with her day job and the points Brass was making in *Nerosubianco*. She provides other connections too. With her husband, Tim Street-Porter, she had studied architecture alongside Pink Floyd's Roger Waters and Nick Mason, and both the Street-Porters had been to parties at 101 Cromwell Road, a huge nineteenth-century terraced house in a parade of seedy hotels, where a large number of artistic, creative and musical types from Cambridge had lodgings, including, at one point, Waters. Later, just after Waters had moved out, several of the participants in the July 1967 Dialectics of Liberation Conference, an event filmed by Nick Saxton, were accommodated there, and the address became famous for a lengthy party at the Conference's conclusion. Accounts differ slightly on the dates, but by the late summer of 1967 Syd Barrett had taken up residence in 101 Cromwell Road, after which he became increasingly estranged from the group, and Waters in particular.[16] One wonders if Barrett, and various hangers-on from the Dialectics of Liberation Conference, were still living there whilst *Nerosubianco* was being filmed? Perhaps they were, but as with many of the faded memories (and connected with them, many of the unreliable narrators) of that time, such matters are now impossible to determine. With this amount of background detail and interlocking connections, though, and the prominent use of Mark Boyle's light show, *Nerosubianco* could be legitimately regarded as part of the cinematic canon of work associated with Pink Floyd and The Soft Machine. It was certainly exploring the same territory, with some of the same people, at the same time.

One notes too, scenes pioneered in Brass's film that would be repeated, with much greater acclaim by other directors, in subsequent years. The image of an elderly pensioner machine-gunning young hippies was used by Lindsay Anderson in the finale of *If...* The scene where the black man (Carter) finds himself ambushed by a gang of men in bowler hats, looks not unlike Alex and his gang ambushing the hapless tramp in Kubrick's *A Clockwork Orange*. In another parallel with *A Clockwork Orange*, the intercutting of war atrocity footage and images of dictatorships occurs in Brass's film some three years prior to its use by Kubrick. Even the general 'feel' of the film makes one wonder if *Nerosubianco* should be regarded as the prototype of the late 1960s/early 1970s mod-pop 'pilgrim's progress' sub-genre in which the central character (or characters) wanders through a city, country or landscape encountering all the fashionable people and problems of the day. Antonioni did this with *Zabriskie Point* (filmed after Brass's work) and Lindsay Anderson certainly followed suit with *O Lucky Man!* in 1971-1972 which also deploys Alan Price and his band as a *Nerosubianco*-style Greek chorus.

After it had missed critical acclaim at Cannes in 1968 and 1969, Radley Metzger did his best to market the film when it opened in the US, initially sending it out as a double bill with the 1959 UK feature *Sapphire*, a London-set drama about a mixed-race girl who can pass as white.[17] Which wasn't a bad match at all, albeit *Sapphire* is nothing like *Nerosubianco*, and is very conventional in tone. A few months later, in February 1970, *The New York Times* ran an extensive profile of Anita

Sanders, but, however the film was presented, the reviews were poor. Critics simply didn't 'get' it and were puzzled by how Brass had chosen to edit and score the material. But Columbia persevered, releasing the film in Denmark, the Netherlands and Japan in 1970. It finally reached the UK in November 1973 as a second feature (now cut to only 59 minutes long) and Australia in 1974. The *Monthly Film Bulletin* considered, '...*as presented here with extensive cuts it is an incomprehensible shamble neither sexy enough for the exploitation market nor fashionable enough for art-houses...*' As to details of where it was exhibited in the UK, none survives, though a brief existence as a supporting feature to the soft-core sex comedies of the time seems likely.

In the US Metzger made no changes to the prints. He just kept screening them and patching them up whenever they needed repairs. By the early 1970s *Nerosubianco* was playing the late-night cinema circuit across the US, in the type of environment graphically depicted, some years later, in the film *Taxi Driver*. In fact, well aware of how he could maximise his income, he released it under a variety of titles including *Attraction*, *Black on White* and *The Artful Penetration of Barbara*. Customers at the type of venue that screened adult films (or anything late night) no doubt assumed that these were all different productions. This generated a substantial income, little of which was seen by Brass, Sanders, Carter or The Freedom. Ranjit Sandhu, then a cinema projectionist, states, '...*We can do a rough calculation: maybe thirty tickets sold each hour; multiply that by twelve hours and the total would be about 360 tickets a day, which is far greater than the business that an average cinema enjoyed. In 1970, ticket prices at porn cinemas were about $5 each, which is about $1,800 a day, or well over half a million dollars a year, gross, and operating expenses were minimal...*' And here *Nerosubianco* remained for a decade with the prints being gradually hacked about and shortened until, after the final bookings at a Maryland drive-in in early 1979, they finally wore out and the film vanished from sight completely.

By then Tinto Brass – exhausted after three years of costly and debilitating litigation in which he had tried and failed to retain control of *Caligula* – was on his way back to London to shoot *Action*, which would be his last feature solely based in the UK. The way the other participants in *Nerosubianco* dispersed was in many ways a perfect illustration of how quickly the optimism of the 1960s faded into the grey reality of the 1970s. Anita Sanders starred in another six films before retiring in 1976. Terry Carter finally returned to full-time acting when cast in *McCloud* (a US TV series spin-off from *Coogan's Bluff*) which started filming in August 1969. His later work included some of the 1970s blaxploitation thrillers, notably *Foxy Brown* (1974, with Pam Grier) and he remained busy in film, theatre and TV. Procol Harum soldiered on to 1977. The Freedom, as reinvented by Bobby Harrison, finally fell by the wayside in 1972. Harrison's later venture, SNAFU, folded in 1975 after which he didn't record for twelve years. There are reports that Mike Lease was contacted by Denny Laine after leaving The Freedom, and in the autumn of 1968 was briefly involved with Balls, a group whose membership shifted so frequently that consistent live work was never a possibility. They recorded a demo for release on Apple – which duly appeared two years later on another label – and in September 1969 were even suggested as candidates for the score of *The Magic Christian*. By then Lease was long gone, having returned to Wales where he became a music teacher.[18]

As for Jonathan Weston, after ending his involvement with The Freedom, he worked on the 1969 West German TV special

Love You till Tuesday which was intended to make a star out of David Bowie. It didn't, but it did include an arrangement of *Space Oddity*, which, rerecorded, became Bowie's breakthrough hit that year. Some of it was even shot at the Mr Fish boutique. [19] Later, he emerged as manager of folk singer Shawn Phillips who went on to have some success in the US. In the UK, though, Phillips became best known for composing the theme music to the long-running TV series *World in Action* about which he later stated, in words showing that he shared the experience of Mike Lease and Bobby Harrison when it came to Weston and money, *'...I'd like to set you straight if I may. Jonathan Weston had nothing to do with this piece of music. In fact, he walked into the session, as we were finishing up. I improvised it on the spot with Mick Weaver, and John Sheppard, the series producer, paid for the session. At the time, I was not a member of the British Musicians Union, and there was some question as to how I'd get paid, but Granada told John that night when he called them, that I might make, oh... £2-3 pounds at the most. So, Jonathan said we could put his name down as composer, and if anything came in, he would give it to me. Never did any of us dream that this music would run for more than 30 years. It was only 20 years later that I found out Weston had been collecting the royalties all those years...'* [20]

There was even a typically 1960s finale for Harvey Bramham. After being sacked by The Freedom he became roadie and driver for Fairport Convention. In May 1969, whilst he was at the wheel, their van crashed killing three people. He was found to have been asleep whilst driving and was jailed for manslaughter.[21] On his release in 1970 he fell in with Francis Morland, regarded as *'...a rising star in the London art world of the 1960s...'* and, at that point, a contemporary of Peter Blake, David Hockney and others. But Morland also dabbled in drug smuggling on the side, using the exhibiting of his work at overseas galleries as a cover for transporting various substances. In 1971 he was arrested in the US. Bramham – to whom Morland entrusted the finances of their business – escaped but was found, extradited and jailed in the US from 1976 to 1979. Via *Nerosubianco* and Harvey Bramham we have, then, a route into *Performance* territory: the crossover between transgressive sexuality, violent crime, art, music and the wider counter-culture that characterised so much of the late 1960s with its gallery of characters like Groovy Bob Fraser, the Krays, David Litvinoff and Lucian Freud.[22]

But, to row back a decade, in the summer of 1968 with the film wrapped, edited, scored and available for viewing by privately invited studio executives, distributors and producers, Tinto Brass remained very much the man of the moment. Based on his success in delivering *Col Cuore in Gola* and *Nerosubianco*, he was invited to Hollywood to meet Paramount Pictures.

Notes

(1)　Recorded much later, in September 1970, the cover photograph for this was taken by Dan Richter, a US mime artist-actor-photographer who appeared in Kubrick's *2001: A Space Odyssey*.

(2)　The brief clip showing Tariq Ali must have been filmed on 22 October 1967. The demonstration shown proceeded, despite police warnings, from Trafalgar Square to the US Embassy at Grosvenor Square. Brass appears to have shot the earliest extant footage of the event. At the time Ali was employed as a journalist by the lifestyle magazine *Town*: owner Michael Heseltine. Vanessa Redgrave was at

Trafalgar Square too that day, but isn't shown in the film. For more on this see: https://www.marxists.org/history/erol/uk.secondwave/grosvenor-square.pdf

(3)   The scene turns out to be an in-joke directed at Jean-Luc Godard: a close examination of the film, frame by frame shows that the red book being seized from the youth is not actually by Chairman Mao, but is the script for *La Chinoise*, a drama Godard released in August 1967 about left-wing political activism. A copy of *The Autobiography of Malcolm X* can also be seen in Godard's film, as can quite a bit of Pop Art, used to explicate the plot. *La Chinoise* is available via the BFI and its original trailer can be watched at https://www.youtube.com/watch?v=Ts7HBWQXWfA

(4)   http://pinkfloydarchives.com/SM/SMdates.htm has Martinez and The Soft Machine, alongside Martine Barrat's dance company, at Ste-Genevieve sur le Tobogan, Theatre des Champs-Élysées on 6 and 7 October 1967.

(5)   Latham's *Speak* can be watched at https://vimeo.com/159652068 Pink Floyd recorded, abortively as it happened, backing music for another John Latham project on 20 October 1967. See *Random Precision: Recording the Music of Syd Barrett 1965-1974* p101.

(6)   The Roundhouse was certainly getting a lot of film exposure at this time, turning up in *Escalation*, directed by Roberto Faenza showing a performance at the venue by The Crazy World of Arthur Brown (filmed 18 August 1967) and the US spy thriller *Hammerhead* which opens with a staged theatrical event with occult overtones.

(7)   Particularly The Dubliners, with *Black Velvet Band*, which sold heavily August-December 1967.

(8)   Marceau was in London on 30 October 1967, performing

at the Saville Theatre, Shaftesbury Avenue, and later being featured on the *Eamonn Andrews Show*. Like Milo O'Shea, he also appeared in *Barbarella*. His medium, mime, seemed to acquire a cachet around this point. The Arts Lab, Drury Lane hosted many such events, including an evening with 'Mark Boyle's Sensual Laboratory and Graciela Martinez (sic) introducing David Bowie' in late 1967.

(9)   Email from David Cobbold, 17 September 2019.

(10)   On Axiom see http://www.haenlein.com/projects/misc/axiom/index.htm

(11)   Examples of Khanh's furniture can be seen at http://www.voicesofeastanglia.com/2013/07/quasar-khanh-inflatable-furniture.html and https://www.youtube.com/watch?v=rYixzEE3Xf8 Khanh also designed the Quasar Unipower, a completely square 'cube car' with a glass body and inflatable plastic seating. Emblematic of the 1960s, only 15 were built, making it typical of a decade Khanh and others, would later look back on as a period when '...*the sky was the limit – at that time anything was possible...*' The car can be viewed at https://www.youtube.com/watch?v=29u543fIX5g There isn't one in *Nerosubianco*, but it does appear in Michel Audiard's 1970 comedy *Elle boit pas, elle fume pas, elle drague pas, mais... elle cause!* See https://www.facebook.com/watch/?v=2182635602055399

(12)   For more on Masterton and *Mayfair* magazine see https://www.grahammasterton.co.uk/pdf/penthousearticle.pdf An interview with Masterton (who later worked for Bob Guccione at *Penthouse*) providing further detail about his relationship with William Burroughs can be read at https://realitystudio.org/interviews/interview-with-graham-masterton-on-william-s-burroughs/   The

financial difficulties faced by *International Times* in early 1967 were caused by a police raid of their offices on 9 March. Searching, allegedly, for pornography, the police took away much of the material and equipment needed to produce the magazine.

(13) It proved impossible to contact Janet Street-Porter whilst researching this book. Her autobiography, *Fall Out: A Memoir of Friends Made and Friends Unmade* (2006), which covers this period, makes no mention of her appearance in *Nerosubianco*. However, it does state (page 78) that she and her husband met Quasar Khanh circa 1967-1968 *'when Tim was commissioned to photograph his blow-up furniture'*. Perhaps her involvement was due to this? The book also notes that Tim Street-Porter worked as an assistant film editor at this time.

(14) Haden-Guest – a veteran socialite – wrote the captions for *Birds of Britain*, the 1966 coffee table book by advertising photographer John Green. It sold 50,000 copies. See https://www.abebooks.co.uk/servlet/BookDetailsPL?bi =30582755060&searchurl=an%3DJOHN%2BD %2BGREEN%2BAND%2BANTHONY% 2BHADEN%2BGUEST%2BAND%2BDAVID %2BTREE%26sortby%3D20&cm_sp=snippet- _-srp1-_-image3 and https://www.snapgalleries.com/ portfolio-items/john-d-green/ In a contemporary echo of what Brass was showing in his films it pushed the idea that Swinging London was really based on women coming more to the fore in society than had previously been the case.

(15) See *London's Arts Labs and the 60s Avant-Garde* by David Curtis 2020, particularly p41 which notes Brass and *Nerosubianco*.

(16) Comments about this, from Nigel Lesmoir-Gordon and David Gale, can be found at https://authorsinterviews. wordpress.com/2015/08/22/here-is-my-interview-with-nigel-lesmoir-gordon/ and on the Blog *Men on the Border* (30 December 2013) at https://www.facebook. com/MenOnTheBorder/photos/laing-part-8-the-101-cromwell-road-apartment-that-syd-barrett-and-david-gale-sha/594237037315096/ Checking various published accounts, Pink Floyd had no recording or performing commitments on either 26, 27 or 30 July 1967 so the idea that Syd Barrett attended the Dialectics of Liberation after-party at 101 Cromwell Road on or around 30 July 1967 appears entirely possible.

(17) *Sapphire* concerns the murder of a mixed-race woman who can pass as white, and the attempts by the police to track down her killer. Directed by Basil Dearden, later noted for *Victim*, it starred Nigel Patrick and Yvonne Mitchell.

(18) https://garagehangover.com/denny-laines-electric-string-band/ states of Laine circa October 1968 that *'Around this time, he reunites with Mike Lease, who is working with John Martyn's wife, singer/songwriter, Beverly Kutner. Lease agrees to help Laine audition bass players and drummers for a new version of Balls but despite finding suitable musicians, including drummer Peter Phillips, the line-up never settles'.*

(19) It can be seen at https://vimeo.com/211318045 Bowie subsequently signed to Mercury (May 1969) releasing his debut single, a completely rerecorded version of *Space Oddity*, on 11 July 1969.

(20) Phillips claims to be owed at least £189,000. See: https://shawnphillips.wordpress.com/music/soundtrack/world-in-action-main-theme-1977/ His quote can be found at

https://www.thisismyjam.com/song/shawn-phillips/
world-in-action-theme and the theme itself can be heard
at https://www.youtube.com/watch?v=f35K-sGe9mo For
his part, Mick Weaver contests that Phillips was not the
sole author: it was a collaborative effort. See: https://
www.youtube.com/watch?v=95qLDc7zwYY

(21) Six months. See: https://sites.google.com/site/quiteearly
onemaymorning/

(22) On the connection between Bramham and Morland see
http://gangstersinc.ning.com/profiles/blogs/exclusive-
the-art-of-smuggling-by-britain-s-first-drug-baron Morland
reflects on his career at https://www.vice.com/en/
article/bnpezd/francis-moreland-the-gentleman-
drug-smuggler-772 A further account is provided – in
some detail, and drawing in a veritable cornucopia of
London characters – by Stewart Home at https://www.
stewarthomesociety.org/art/trip.htm This notes that
Morland exhibited at the Axiom gallery in 1969. Home
suggests that Morland may have been involved in drug
activity as early as 1966. One wonders if he was the person
supplying Bramham with the substances that were then
passed on to members of The Freedom in 1967-1968.

8

'...GET ME BREZHNEV...'

Stanley Kubrick's *A Clockwork Orange* premiered in New York in December 1971. It opened in the UK a month later. Box-office takings were excellent and reviews were exceptional. Today, it is regarded as one of the defining films of its time and still retains, when watched half a century later, the visceral impact that audiences admired so much when it appeared. Like many cinematic triumphs, though, it passed through several permutations before appearing on the screen with various different screenplays, producers, directors and stars being considered. It 'did the rounds' of film production companies in London and Hollywood for at least five years prior to Kubrick starting work and, in that time, the only other director to come close to making it was Tinto Brass. Precisely how close he came might still be a matter of conjecture for some, but, after reviewing a great deal of material in the public domain it

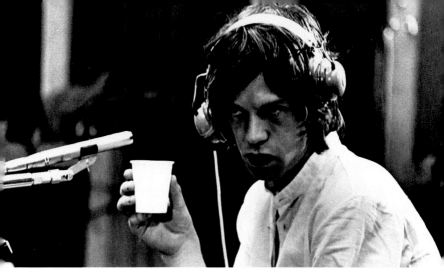

A pensive Mick Jagger during the filming of Godard's *One Plus One*, 1968. He was considered for the lead in an early version of *A Clockwork Orange*, with his suitability for this being discussed by Paramount and Tinto Brass in Hollywood.

A poster for the legendary *14 Hour Technicolor Dream*, held at the Alexandra Palace in April 1967. Publicity for this is shown on more than one occasion in *Col Cuore in Gola*, and Brass would conclude his film at the event: the only time a feature film has ever been shot at a major UK music festival.

The owner, Michael Fish, outside Mr Fish. An immensely famous, and expensive, London clothes boutique, its unisex costumes would be worn by The Freedom in *Nerosubianco*, some years prior to their being made famous by Mick Jagger and David Bowie.

That
"Candy"
girl
is at it
again...

and
again...

and again...

FILMS DISTRIBUTING CORPORATION PRESENTS

JEAN-LOUIS TRINTIGNANT
That man from "A Man and A Woman"

EWA AULIN
That "Candy" girl

in

Deadly Sweet

With ROBERTO BISACCO / CHARLES KOHLER / MONIQUE SCOAZEC / LUIGI BELLINI

And With VIRA SILENTI / Screenplay by TINTO BRASS
(Freely taken from the novel "THE PAPER TOMB" by
Sergio Donati and published by Arnoldo Mondadori)

Produced by ERMANNO DONATI and LUIGI CARPENTIERI / Directed by TINTO BRASS / COLOR / A FILMS DISTRIBUTING CORPORATION RELEASE

(X) Persons under 16 not admitted

Col Cuore in Gola eventually appeared in the US in 1969, with this poster advertising it and giving the impression it was a sequel to *Candy*, the film that made Ewa Aulin an international star.

Brass made much use of pop-art and cartoons in both *Col Cuore in Gola* and *Nerosubianco*. Here Jean-Louis Trintignant gets ready to crib a line of dialogue from *Mad magazine*.

Anita Sanders in *Nerosubianco*. A former fashion model, she spent much of the film looking like this. She starred in another 8 films, but none of them gave her a role where she explored Reichian ideas of sexuality and politics in the manner of James Joyce.

The US release poster for *Nerosubianco* from late 1969. Despite its delayed appearance, the film actually did quite well at the box office. But it remained unrecognised as a ground-breaking cinematic work.

A 1968 Arts Lab poster advertising Mark Boyle and Graciela Martinez. Both feature in Brass's masterpiece, *Nerosubianco*, in sequences shot at the Roundhouse.

Terry Southern in conversation with Dennis Hopper outside the Chelsea Hotel, 1969. Southern wrote an unused script for *A Clockwork Orange* and also intersected with Brass via his work on *Barbarella*, with Jane Fonda and *Candy*, with Eva Aulin.

David Hemmings resting between engagements in London, 1968. Due at one point to star in *A Clockwork Orange*, with Brass one of several directors connected with the project.

The famous Jean Harlow mural on the front of Granny Takes a Trip, 488 King's Road SW10 in early 1967. Part of this is visible in *Col Cuore in Gola*, with Brass also shooting scenes inside the boutique.

You say you want a revolution? Vanessa Redgrave and Tariq Ali just prior to an attempted march on the US Embassy in London, 1968. Brass caught Ali speaking in Trafalgar Square in *Nerosubianco* and Redgrave later agreed to star in two of his films: *Dropout* and *La Vacanza*.

Brass and crew on location for *La Vacanza*.

Tina Aumont's appearance in *L'Urlo* alternated between fashionably elegant and demonic, as seen here. As well as working with Brass, her career at this time also saw her involved with French avant-garde filmmakers, Bernardo Bertolucci and hanging out with rock musicians Jimi Hendrix and The Rolling Stones.

A publicity shot for the Radha-Krishna Temple London taken when they signed to Apple and recorded their August 1969 hit single *Hare Krishna Mantra*. Their brief appearance in *Dropout* would be the only footage of them in a feature film.

Scottish folk-pop band Middle of the Road worked on several film soundtracks, including Brass's *Dropout* and Carlo Ponti's *The Priest's Wife* prior to their huge international hit with *Chirpy Chirpy Cheep Cheep*.

Jane Fonda at the August 1969 Isle of Wight Festival. Around this time she rejected an approach from Dino de Laurentiis to appear in *Barbarella Goes Down*, a sequel directed by Brass.

Franco Nero, Vanessa Redgrave *en famille* in 1970. They made 4 films together, including two for Brass, *Dropout* and *La Vacanza*.

A bloated-looking Jim Morrison in 1971. His death that year brought an end to attempts by several producers and writers to build a feature film around him, one version of which would have been *40 Days in the Wilderness*, directed by Tinto Brass.

seems likely that, other than Kubrick, he was indeed the only person who came near to being given the job. That being the case, it illustrates once again how highly regarded Brass was in the late 1960s and early 1970s and how significant an auteur he seemed at that time.

We know that the screening of *Nerosubianco* at Cannes in May 1968 impressed a couple of executives from Paramount. They had backed De Laurentiis on *Danger Diabolik* and Brass's ability to combine London settings, violence, permissive sex, music and Pop-Art trappings on a low budget with a clear focus on youth, led to them considering him as director of *A Clockwork Orange*. They flew him to Hollywood, most likely in June-July 1968, where he spent about 10 days discussing the project, for which either David Hemmings or Mick Jagger, or both, had been considered as leads.

Anthony Burgess's book was published in 1962 and had many admirers. Andy Warhol shot a version of it, *Vinyl*, in June 1965. It was little more than a home movie featuring various members of his entourage (Ondine, Edie Sedgwick) and few saw the film. That same year, according to Burgess, Mick Jagger paid $500 for the film rights.[1] Burgess who was, apparently, hard up, appears to have sold 'the rights' more than once to different parties. At the point Jagger did this The Beatles had cleaned up at the US box-office with *A Hard Day's Night* and *Help!* Consequently, The Rolling Stones were looking for a similar film project, and *A Clockwork Orange* suited them, enhancing their 'bad boy' image, with Jagger and the group cast as Alex and the Droogs.

A Clockwork Orange was one of two films they considered at that time. In September 1965, Peter Whitehead shot footage of them on tour in Ireland. Edited together as *Charlie is My*

Darling, this premiered at the Mannheim Film Festival in October 1966. A perfectly watchable and interesting hour-long, black-and-white music documentary, it was screened as a UK entry alongside Peter Watkins's *The War Game* and Whitehead's *Wholly Communion* (Ginsberg and other poets at the Albert Hall). Both of these were commended by the Jury, who awarded the Grand Prize to Jiri Menzel's *Ostře Sledované Vlaky/Closely Observed Trains* at what was a very intellectual event. The lack of attention received by *Charlie is My Darling* seemed to affect the band and their management, and the result was that the film never got a theatrical release.

As for how Jagger got involved in the first place, it seems that the starting point may have been Michael Cooper. A photographer, Cooper was working with gallery owner Robert 'Groovy Bob' Fraser at his gallery in Duke Street, Mayfair in 1964. Fraser was one of the earliest people to exhibit Warhol in London, so it seems likely that Cooper heard about Burgess's book in the context of it being an explosive, groundbreaking novel that Andy Warhol was much taken with. By 1965 Cooper was closely aligned with The Rolling Stones, a semi-permanent member of their entourage and effectively their official photographer. He was also becoming widely known on the London scene, so much so that Antonioni based the character played by David Hemmings in *Blow-Up* on him. It seems entirely possible that Cooper told Jagger and the group about the book and its cinematic potential, and that Jagger, on this basis, bought his option from Burgess. Other sources confirm that Cooper was active in disseminating the work. Terry Southern (another friend of Fraser's) states, '...*Michael turned me onto* A Clockwork Orange *and so I took an option on the book and was going to write a screenplay. Then David Hemmings came out with*

Blow-Up *and the agency said "We'll package this thing with David Hemmings because he's hot..."* [2] Confusingly, Southern stated his *'bargain basement'* option with Burgess of $1,000 against a final price of $10,000 was arranged via Si Litvinoff, and that David Puttnam, then agent for photographer DavidBailey, and Sanford Lieberson *'set up a development deal'* at Paramount who *'underwrote a draft written by Southern and Cooper'*. If this was so, it implies that the Puttnam-Lieberson-Southern-Cooper version of *A Clockwork Orange* was lined up (most likely at some point in early 1967) as a project for Goodtimes Enterprises, the production company set up by Puttnam and Lieberson. Goodtimes' first credit would, in fact, be *Performance*, a study of violence, sexuality and youth culture starring Mick Jagger that began filming in September 1968.

For his part, Sandy Lieberson (a US agent who handled the affairs of Peter Sellers and The Rolling Stones) recalls that he was given a copy by Cooper, and *'...I thought, "My God!" I had to go back and read it a couple of times, but I was stunned by the power of it, so I made enquiries into the rights...'* [3] In yet another variation, it seems that Burgess's agent put Lieberson on to Si Litvinoff (Terry Southern's lawyer) who had optioned the book with his business partner Max Raab for just a few hundred dollars. *'...I knew Si,'* Lieberson continues, *'so I approached him and said, look, I'd like to put a film together with Michael Cooper as writer and director...'* [4]

Thus, as well as Jagger, both Southern and Litvinoff had options and Lieberson was making enquiries too. The proposal – throughout much of 1966 and 1967 – was to make the film with Jagger and his colleagues using a Terry Southern script with Cooper directing. (Cooper was then 23 years old and had no cinematic experience.) In terms of dates, Southern probably

wrote his screenplay after modifying *Casino Royale* and prior
to beginning work on *Barbarella* (a De Laurentiis production)
and *Candy* (which starred Ewa Aulin). Thus, a date of late 1966
through to early 1967 seems likely for his input, with Lieberson
confirming: '*...We decided where it was going to be shot, it was going
to be almost all Soho, there was a rawness to Soho at that point which
doesn't exist today. We had picked out the site for the Korova Milkbar,
which was some weird kind of Chinese restaurant-bar. It certainly felt
possible to recreate the atmosphere of the book in a much more gritty,
dirty way, more realistic than Kubrick's approach... I also think that
our instinct was that the language had an importance as great as the
visual...*'

Si Litvinoff remembers things differently. '*...I was separately
obsessed with making a film of* A Clockwork Orange, *which I had
optioned in 1966 and after much time spent with Nic Roeg, knowing
that he had written screenplays, was an extraordinary cinematographer
and wanted to direct, I believed that Nic could be an ideal director of
the film, which I conceived as low budget, that is, if financial backing
had the same faith as I did...*' Apparently, '*...Terry Southern...
suggested that I read an English novel titled* A Clockwork Orange
*by Anthony Burgess... When I read the book I was electrified with
excitement... This book read like music to me (and, as I later found
out, to some of The Beatles and to some of The Rolling Stones)... I
visualised a movie opening with a futuristic monolith of a building
darkened except for one lit-up apartment wherein a young man is
playing with a snake and listening to Brahms or Schubert or better
still, my favourite, the chorale, Ode to Joy, from Beethoven's Ninth
Symphony. I was hooked and almost immediately started my quest
to acquire the rights... Being able to tell Deborah Rogers, who was
the agent for Burgess, some of the higher-profile clients I represented...
and being able to tell her that I wanted Terry to write the screenplay*

helped enormously. The fact that no one else was interested (despite all that is in print of people who say they sought the rights or held the rights) also helped and by March of 1966 I had the option...' Thus, according to Litvinoff, there were no proper options granted on the book, prior to his. He also implies that Burgess may have made some money on the side by selling others 'options' pre-March 1966. *'...Yes, I know that it has been printed that Burgess in interviews* (Playboy *and* Rolling Stone)... *said he sold the rights for $500... Bear in mind that that... (my option of)... $1,000 was only for the first year and Burgess was to receive – and did receive – more $1,000 payments as well as the full-exercise price payment. Add those payments to his percentage of net profits, sales of the suddenly famous book as well as new interest in his other books and a new career as a screenwriter and celebrity and you will see how fraudulent his $500-sale-price statement was – and is... I also can include... the payment he received for a screenplay of* Clockwork...' [5]

Litvinoff concludes by stating that Burgess's screenplay was 89 pages long, a bit on the short side for a major feature film. Particularly one that was a literary adaptation. Presumably Burgess wrote his script after Litvinoff had optioned the book, implying it was written summer-autumn 1966, some months prior to Southern producing his version. According to Litvinoff, then, by late 1966 *A Clockwork Orange* would have been directed by Nic Roeg from an Anthony Burgess script with Mick Jagger starring – the rest of the group not figuring in this account. At this point Roeg's qualifications were certainly better than Cooper's: he'd been cameraman on *The System*, *Fahrenheit 451* and *Casino Royale*, as well as lightweight UK pop-music programmers like *Just for Fun* and *Every Day's a Holiday* and had also written the screenplay for *A Prize of Arms*, a 1962 heist film.

Except, as Litvinoff recollects, no one wanted to fund a film by an unknown director starring Mick Jagger. '...*After many failed attempts beginning in 1966 of trying to get financing for the film with Mick Jagger to star, Terry and I were... at the opening party for Antonioni's film* Blow-Up...' (December 1966) '...*and we talked to David Hemmings... who was going out to Hollywood to star in* Camelot *and he instantly agreed to star in* Clockwork. *He knew the book and loved it. A few days later I flew out to LA to see if I could get financing. I went to the set of* Point Blank... *to see if the director John Boorman would be interested. I had seen a movie he had directed for a rock group and I was impressed that in my opinion he was able to make something out of nothing. Despite the fact that in my heart I really wanted Nic Roeg to direct and Mick Jagger to star, I was not getting anywhere with the studios with that desire. Well, again I got a fast yes from Boorman who also knew and loved the book...*'

By January-February 1967, then, Jagger had been dropped by Litvinoff and replaced by David Hemmings (ironic, given his most prominent role had been inspired by Cooper) and Nic Roeg had been edged out by John Boorman. The film Boorman '...*had directed for a rock group...*' was Catch Us If You Can. Released in August 1965, it starred The Dave Clark Five, who in terms of record sales were at least as prominent in the US at that point as The Rolling Stones.[6] Alas, attempts at selling Boorman + Hemmings + Burgess to the studio executives in Hollywood came to nothing. Nor did trying to interest anyone in a combination of Jagger and Ted Kotcheff, a Canadian director who had made Life at the Top. By the summer of 1967, Litvinoff was back to making '...*many trips to London to try my efforts there with the Roeg-Jagger package...*' using either the Burgess or the Southern script. It seems, by this point, Brian Epstein was on board too, offering the involvement of the NEMS organisation (himself and Robert Stigwood) with the possibility of some Beatles songs thrown into the mix. But it was still to no avail. A further complication – to getting any version made – was the approach then exercised in the UK by the British Board of Film Censors. *A Clockwork Orange* was an extremely violent book that included two controversial rape scenes, one by Alex and his gang of an adult woman, and another, by Alex, of two pre-adolescent girls. Terry Southern states, '*...I wrote the script and sent it to Stanley Kubrick, who promptly had some kind of reaction against it and rejected it. So we started putting it together independently of Stanley, but what we didn't realise was that we'd have to get the script cleared by the Lord Chamberlain... and the British Board of Film Censors refused to clear the script on the basis of its violence and bad language...*' Leaving aside Southern's comments about Kubrick, Litvinoff gives a similar account '*... The problem was that the "censor" Lord Trevelyan would give the film an X rating which would preclude all of the huge number of Mick's teenage fans from buying theater tickets and hence investors were so wary of that economic loss that they would not finance it...*'

Thus, by mid-1967 or thereabouts, matters had ground to a halt with the realisation that even if the film got made it couldn't be widely shown anywhere in the UK. But, to return to Southern... in his account he wrote his screenplay semi-independently once he had an 'option' on the film (Litvinoff would have said that legally he didn't) and seems to have shown it to whoever he thought might be able to make the film. Kubrick therefore comes into the picture in early 1967, but initially rejects the film. At that point he had yet to complete *2001: A Space Odyssey* after which he planned to make *Napoleon*, an epic of immense proportions. Litvinoff had distractions too, having just started producing his very first film, *The Queen*, a feature-length documentary about a New York drag-queen beauty contest.[7] Whilst the Roeg-Jagger option remained a possibility, with funding now being provided by wealthy clothing manufacturer Max Raab, whose company The Villager had pioneered the preppy Ivy League look from the mid-1950s, Litvinoff also explored other options.

On 2 February 1968, he wrote to John Schlesinger, trying to interest him in the project: '...*This film should break ground in its language, cinematic style and soundtrack (the Beatles love the project and Mick Jagger and David Hemmings have both been keen to play Alex). After you've read the script and novel, I'm sure you will see the incredible potential we all see in this project...*' [8] Again, he failed. Schlesinger wasn't taken with the idea (replying, diplomatically, '...*I am not sure it's the sort of subject I particularly want to tackle...*') and in any case from April 1968 would be busy on *Midnight Cowboy*. Similar approaches were made at the same time to Roman Polanski and Ken Russell, though it is not even clear if Russell ever knew about it and if the 'approach' went any further than his agent. Inevitably, the news that Litvinoff was now considering a different star and director reached the ears of Jagger, Cooper and The Beatles. The same month that Litvinoff wrote to Schlesinger they drew up a petition which they sent to Terry Southern, presumably thinking that he wielded a decisive influence on whatever might happen, asking that Jagger be reinstated in the main role. The signatories to this included Anita Pallenberg, Donald Cammell and James Fox, all of whom were, by that point, under contract with Jagger to make *Performance*, as well as Cooper, Peter Blake, Robert Fraser, Marianne Faithfull, Christian Marquand and all four Beatles.[9]

The hubris here is extraordinary. Leaving aside the commitment to *Performance*, a few weeks after signing the petition Cooper and Fraser left the UK with a film crew to tour India in a bus à la Ken Kesey (or The Beatles in *Magical Mystery Tour*) where they would make the film *Tantra: Indian Rites of Ecstasy*, funded by Jagger and with Sandy Lieberson as co-producer.[10] Kenneth Anger was along for the ride too with Nick Douglas – a public school-educated hippy/antique dealer – credited as director. The idea was to rendezvous with The Beatles during their visit to the Maharishi Mahesh Yogi at his ashram in Rishikesh, and film a major counter-culture documentary about eastern religion and life, with The Rolling Stones doing some of the music, possibly in the same way that Brian Jones would record various Moroccan musicians in Joujouka a few months later. Very little of this materialised. Kenneth Anger (who supposedly shot the best footage) decamped early on in the trek and when the bus finally reached Rishikesh, The Beatles had already left. By May 1968 Cooper, Douglas, Fraser and their crew were back in the UK. The film itself finally emerged as a 27-minute-long travelogue in October 1969 and got only a very limited distribution.

The reality was that through 1968 and 1969, The Rolling Stones, and Jagger in particular, had other fish to fry. Would they even have had the time to make *A Clockwork Orange*? Apart from *Tantra: Indian Rites of Ecstasy* and *Performance*, the band would be filmed by Jean-Luc Godard (in June 1968) for *One Plus One*, with preparations for *The Rolling Stones Christmas Special* starting shortly afterwards. They were also due to provide some music to Kenneth Anger's *Invocation of My Demon Brother* after which Jagger and Richards would shoot sequences for *Umano Non Umano* (made by Anita Pallenberg and Mario Schifano, an Italian Pop-artist Fraser had exhibited at his gallery) with Jagger then heading to Australia to star in Tony Richardson's *Ned Kelly*. In early 1968 some of this would have been known to Litvinoff and Raab, so it was hardly surprising that they carried on looking for a way to make *A Clockwork Orange* and took no action on the petition from Jagger and co.

By the summer of 1968, Litvinoff had moved to London to start work on *All the Right Noises*, starring Olivia Hussey in her first major role following *Romeo and Juliet*. Raab co-produced, and was also beginning to put together *Lions Love (and Lies...)* in the US. Directed by Agnès Varda, this featured Warhol 'superstar' Viva alongside James Rado and Gerome Ragni, the writers of *Hair*. At this point Roeg was wrapped up in preparations for *Performance* and Kubrick, having turned down Southern's script for *A Clockwork Orange*, and with the post-production of *2001: A Space Odyssey* almost complete, was toiling through the preparation of *Napoleon* for which he hoped to have David Hemmings in the title role, with much of the film shot on location in eastern Europe.

This was the moment, when most of the principal figures in the putative filming of Burgess's book were otherwise engaged, that Brass states he was approached by Paramount. It seems clear that Litvinoff wasn't involved with this, as, when asked about the role of others in trying to get *A Clockwork Orange* made, he dismissed any notion '...*that David Puttnam set it up at Paramount, which never happened; that Paramount put it in turnaround, which never happened... Film history continues to be created by third parties who were not at the dance...*' Which all seems clear enough until one considers that *A Clockwork Orange* was doing the rounds of Hollywood as a property without an attached director, and at least two different versions of the script. Paramount may have thought that, if they could interest Brass, they could acquire one of the screenplays (note here that in Hill's biography it is specifically stated that Paramount underwrote one by Southern and Cooper) and start production. They distributed De Laurentiis's output in the US and in terms of fashionable London-based films had already released *Smashing Time*, *Sebastian*, *Up the Junction* and *Only When I Larf*. They also had *The Bliss of Mrs Blossom* and *Barbarella* waiting to premiere. With his De Laurentiis connection and a reputation, from *Col Cuore in Gola* and *Nerosubianco*, for completing creative, boundary-pushing, youth-orientated films at a modest cost, Brass ticked a number of boxes. We should note too that, whatever the strict legalities, Paramount may not have been unduly concerned about Litvinoff who in mid-1968 was a small standalone producer. In the last resort, Paramount probably reasoned that, if they could get a director on board, they could brush Litvinoff to one side, or even pay him off, and do *A Clockwork Orange* themselves.

In terms of an actual date for Brass's trip to Hollywood to discuss *A Clockwork Orange*, an examination of press reports, interviews and chronologies suggests June-July 1968 as being most likely. Alan Sekers recollects, '...*I went to a meeting circa '68-'69 with Tinto at Dino De Laurentiis's office. Dino was planning a film of Waterloo with the co-operation of the Russian government, and there were lots of models of sets and so on lying around. Tinto went inside and I waited. He came out and said "You'll never guess what happened in there". "What?" I asked. He replied: "Dino took a call from Paramount saying that Kubrick was planning a film about Napoleon that would be filmed in Hungary with the cooperation of the Hungarian government. Paramount wanted assurances that Dino's film wouldn't overlap with their production. Dino told them it wouldn't and everything would be fine. He then put the phone down, picked it up again and said to his secretary, 'Get me Brezhnev', and was put through and asked Brezhnev to put pressure on Hungary to change its mind about helping Kubrick"...'* We know that De Laurentiis began planning *Waterloo*, which Paramount distributed, in 1968 after he had reached agreement with Mosfilm, the Soviet film-funding organisation. Most of the film was shot by the summer of 1969, and its release took place in October 1970. The meeting Sekers refers to, then, must have been after the May 1968 Cannes Film Festival but prior to De Laurentiis fleeing Italy once his tax affairs were under investigation. Given that The Freedom were told circa June 1968 that De Laurentiis had been 'done' for tax evasion and that De Laurentiis was absent from Italy for quite some time after this, a date of June 1968 for this meeting in Rome seems likely, with Brass flying to the US to meet Paramount afterwards. In a 2000 magazine interview Tinto stated, *'...I should have made* A Clockwork Orange, *in '68. The Americans really liked* Nerosubianco, *which I had filmed in London. So, they invited me to the States where I was received in great pomp at Paramount. I remember that in the production's home office there was an infinite hallway... filled with doors of dressing rooms and on every door was a nameplate: an incredible parade with the names of every old and famous celebrity in American cinema, both actors and directors. Traversing this longest of hallways I came upon the nameplate with my name: Tinto Brass. I too had been inserted into this Olympian species. I stayed in the United States for ten days to assess a project to make a film with Paramount – even though I had come to America already having in mind the overriding idea to make* The Howl *with Gigi Proietti. I didn't wait for another occasion to put it to them. The project that they proposed to me was to film* A Clockwork Orange. *I read the book and really liked it; however,*

I had in mind Proietti and my project. Then I said to the producers, yes, I like your idea; I agree to film A Clockwork Orange, *but first I want to make* Howl...' [11]

What transpired during the 10 days Brass spent in Hollywood? The only account we have comes from Italian writer Piernico Solinas, a friend of Brass whose brother Franco Solinas was celebrated for the screenplays *The Battle of Algiers* and *Queimada/Burn!* It seems that discussions with Paramount reached a point where casting the leading role was considered and a senior executive (unnamed) was against Mick Jagger on the basis that he didn't *look* like a conventional leading man. Paramount wanted someone better-looking. Brass defended Jagger, urging the executive to take his wife to see *One Plus One* and get her opinion on how pleasing or displeasing Jagger was. Was the executive Robert Evans? Head of Production at Paramount in mid-1968, he had been brought in to rebuild the studio's fortunes in 1966, quickly making it the most successful in Hollywood with films like *Barefoot in the Park*, *The Odd Couple*, *Rosemary's Baby*. [12] Presumably Evans/Paramount saw the potential in *A Clockwork Orange*, but weren't convinced about Jagger. Brass could only have made his comments about Jagger *after* Godard had filmed The Rolling Stones for *One Plus One*, (which he did 4-10 June 1968) thus confirming late June-early July 1968 as the date for Brass's presence in Hollywood. Interestingly, given the discussion on how suitable he was for the role, Mick Jagger was actually in Los Angeles at more or less the same time as Brass. From 6-25 July 1968 he was at Sunset Studios, 6650 Sunset Boulevard, finishing work on the *Beggars Banquet* album, after which he was available in the UK until *Performance* started shooting in September. Sunset

Studios are less than a mile from Paramount, so if Brass had agreed to start work, and Paramount had been minded to use Jagger, *A Clockwork Orange* could have been filmed partly in LA and partly in London July-September 1968.

Brass's main concern, though, appears to have been his prior commitment to make a second film for De Laurentiis. The impression he gives now is that he tried to make *A Clockwork Orange* conditional on his existing deal with De Laurentiis. Why did he do this? Well, possibly because by the time he was in Hollywood, De Laurentiis had been busted by the Italian tax man, and the funding of *L'Urlo/The Howl* suddenly looked parlous. In any event, Paramount were having none of it and the prospect of waiting around whilst everything – money, script, a cast and locations – was carefully put into place for *A Clockwork Orange* held no appeal for either party. The logistics certainly weren't perfect. Hemmings might have been available later in 1968 and then not for another twelve months. Or, if Paramount were reconciled to using Jagger, that implied either shooting almost immediately or waiting until at least March 1969. As to which script might have been used, possibly Brass would have kept the Southern screenplay. By summer 1968 Southern was busy on *Easy Rider*, but his script for *Barbarella* had been used by De Laurentiis, so he would have been an acceptable author and was bankable. Add into the mix that Tinto wanted to return to the UK to make *L'Urlo/ The Howl* (whoever funded it) and it became apparent that *A Clockwork Orange* was likely to be a long haul, and it dropped back, accordingly, into being 'a future project'. Indeed, with neither Paramount nor Litvinoff managing to progress matters, Brass apparently still harboured some hopes as late as the summer of 1969 that he would return to the film.

Ironically, what really killed the idea was De Laurentiis becoming very heavily involved in the production of *Waterloo* starring Rod Steiger as Napoleon. The most expensive film in the world then, its progress and scale had the unforeseen effect of making it impossible for Stanley Kubrick to raise finance for his *Napoleon*. As the comments from Alan Sekers about De Laurentiis calling Brezhnev to ensure that cooperation with Kubrick was withdrawn show, Kubrick also found himself blocked in his efforts to shoot on location in eastern Europe. With trouble raising funds and no agreement on where he might film the enormous battle scenes he envisaged, Kubrick began considering alternatives to *Napoleon*. Si Litvinoff recollects, *'...Sometime in late 1969 and early 1970... I started to receive visits from some LA-based Warner Brothers executives always inquiring about* (A) Clockwork (Orange) *and when our New York lawyer Bob Montgomery said that a New Jersey accountant had made a $100,000 offer for the rights for some anonymous person, I intuited that it was Kubrick, to whom Terry Southern had given the book many years earlier... When I refused the New Jersey deal I knew that I would hear from someone other than him, at first, someone to ferret out information... I just continued to go forward preparing for production until John Calley... who was a friend of mine and who was as close to Stanley Kubrick as anyone could be and who was running Warner Brothers, telephoned me and became the intermediary for a deal to ultimately be made by us with Warner's...'* Thus, by early 1970, and mindful of their own difficulties in trying to get the project started, Litvinoff and Raab signed up to do *A Clockwork Orange* with Warner Brothers, Stanley Kubrick directing. Neither the Burgess nor the Southern screenplay was used, Kubrick writing his own adaptation. Litvinoff concludes, *'...Although it was not my original dream, it all turned well with Nic (Roeg) quickly able to...*

(do)... Walkabout, and Stanley Kubrick making Clockwork, *a big box-office hit... I have always thought that any of the directors I had asked to do the picture would do it successfully. The difference is that they thought it was dark and Kubrick did it in bright white light...'*

A Clockwork Orange finally appeared in December 1971 and went on to be nominated for 7 BAFTAs, 4 Academy Awards and 3 Golden Globes. But it was considered such a controversial film that it failed to win in any of the categories concerned. It did, however, get an award – for best foreign film – at the Venice Film Festival in August 1972. Which, given this was Tinto Brass's home town was somewhat ironic. In a final twist, Kubrick's film was preceded in cinemas by an official trailer. With no dialogue or narrative, this mixed a quirky rendition of classical music, in full blown Pop-Art style, with rapidly intercut comic and violent scenes, elegantly composed shots of contemporary design, speeded-up sequences, black-and-white newsreel footage (including some of war atrocities) and explicit sexual imagery.[13] Kubrick had never done anything like this before. But Brass had in both *Nerosubianco* and *Ca Ira, Il Fiume Della Rivolta*. Given Kubrick's capacity for intensive research (for *Napoleon*, he watched every film ever made about the character to check how other directors had done the story), one wonders if he took a look at either of Brass's films, just to see how a rival might have treated the same material.[14]

Notes

(1)   On this see *The Guardian*, 16 October 2015.

(2)   Southern's recollections are contained in Lee Hill's 2001 biography *A Grand Guy: The Art and Life of Terry Southern*,

where somewhat expanded, it is stated that Southern was given a copy of the book by Cooper.

(3) For an account of this see *Sight and Sound*, September 1999, *Real Horrorshow: A Short Lexicon of Nadsat*, by Kevin Jackson. In an odd example of synchronicity with Brass, Jackson, who died in 2021, was working on a piece about Wilhelm Reich at the time of his death.

(4) See *The Independent*, 22 October 2011.

(5) From an interview available on line at https://www.lukeford. net/profiles/profiles/si_litvinoff1.htmandquotedathttps:// rjbuffalo.com/1968b-cl.html

(6) By early 1967, The Dave Clark Five had recorded 16 Top 30 hits in the *Billboard* Hot 100, against 15 for The Rolling Stones. US cinema audiences might have noticed the Stones, as one of many, in *The T.A.M.I. Show*, compared to which the Dave Clark Five had been seen in *Get Yourself a College Girl*, the TV special *It's What's Happening Baby* and numerous episodes of Jack Good's *Shindig!* as well as the Boorman film.

(7) *The Queen*, which includes appearances by Warhol, Southern and Edie Sedgwick, was, like *Nerosubianco*, a casualty of the aborted May 1968 Cannes Film Festival.

(8) See *The Daily Telegraph*, 3 May 2008.

(9) See *Rolling Stone*, 15 October 2015.

(10) On *Tantra: Indian Rites of Ecstasy* see *Groovy Bob: The Life and Times of Robert Fraser* by Harriet Vyner, 1999, p223-229. For more background on this peculiar episode see: https://pleasuresofpasttimes.com/kenneth-anger-lucifer-rising-1966-1981/ Vyner's book includes comments from Stash Klossowski circa 1967-1968, when he was dating Tina Aumont.

(11) See Stefano Iori, *Tinto Brass* (2000) also quoted at https://rjbuffalo.com/1968b-cl.html

(12) Paramount also backed *The Italian Job* which was popular in the UK but also, significantly, elsewhere. Paramount's most successful release in 1969 turned out to be *Paint Your Wagon* followed in 1970 by *Love Story*. Commercially, this indicated that London-based, counter-culture films were no longer cleaning up at the box-office in the way they had been a few years earlier.

(13) This can be seen at https://www.youtube.com/watch?v=9JIc_1v7i88

(14) Was Kubrick a plagiarist? On *Dr Strangelove* see https://www.wired.com/2018/03/geeks-guide-doctor-strangelove/ which states '...*the idea for the Doomsday Machine in Dr. Strangelove was inspired by the real-life thinking of Herman Kahn, one of Ellsberg's colleagues at RAND. 'Kahn's words are actually quoted in the movie, and Kahn himself wanted a cut, he thought he should get some royalties from this,' Ellsberg says. 'And Kubrick had to assure him that wasn't the way it worked...'*

9

'...TWO MONTHS OF PURE JOY AND LOVE OF LIFE...'

On the face of it the decision by Brass to pass up the chance to direct *A Clockwork Orange* (one of the great films of the twentieth century) in favour of *L'Urlo/The Howl*, a film almost no one saw, is so misjudged as to be up there with Decca's rejection of The Beatles in 1962, or, if a cinematic comparison were sought, Burt Reynolds turning down *Star Wars* in 1976. Suffice to say, as with most episodes of this type, it would not have seemed that way in June 1968.

When Brass and Sekers went to Rome to meet De Laurentiis it was to discuss the outline of the second of the films De Laurentiis had agreed to fund. According to Brass, who was clearly much influenced at that point by the rapidity of dramatic political events across the world, '...*I said to my producer, Dino De Laurentiis, that we should make the movie as freely as the time, in mood and spirit. The movie should feel like change as change occurs, much like the changes taking place at that time. There was no script. Scripts were written years later, but at the time of the shooting there was no script. De Laurentiis questioned me at the time, but I told him, if history runs, cinema can't keep walking...*[1] The film, therefore, had to be *of* 1968 and its attitudes, rather than something coincidentally shot at the same time. Repeating the approach taken with *Nerosubianco* he opted again for a female central character, confirming some years later '*...I try to express the thoughts of the woman because I find the female point of view more interesting... Women are naturally able to express feelings...*' Whilst editing *Nerosubianco* Brass approached Tina Aumont, who at that point was completing *Partner* for Bernardo Bertolucci. Based on Dostoyevsky's novella *The Double: A Petersburg Poem*, and updated to the present day amidst pro-Viet Cong students, it would premiere at the September 1968 Venice Film Festival with most critics noting its similarities to Godard's *La Chinoise*. Leaving this production to one side, though, Aumont was an attractive choice for a number of reasons. Firstly, and a valuable factor in selling any film she appeared in, she had immediate Hollywood name recognition. Her mother Maria Montez starred in a string of musicals during the 1940s and her father, Jean-Pierre Aumont, had been a significant figure in French cinema since the early 1930s. He had pitched up in the US after distinguished war service, and once he had returned to Europe in 1948 became one of the mainstays of French and European filmmaking. In the late 1960s he remained a name, co-starring in *Castle Keep* with Burt Lancaster and was still landing leading roles as late as 1992, 60 years after his career started.

As well as this, Tina Aumont was also regarded as a great beauty, quite possibly the next Bardot or Loren. As a teenager she was doing fashion shoots for *Paris Match*, was constantly featured in films and magazines and modelled for Christian Dior. By 1966 she was being shot by Chiara Samugheo, the leading Italian fashion and film set photographer, roughly the equivalent in her own country of David Bailey in the UK. The expectation that Aumont would ascend to mega-stardom led to many filmmakers then, and for some years afterwards, seeking her out for high profile roles. And indeed, her 1963 marriage – at 17, he was 36 – to Christian Marquand pulled her in precisely that direction. Marquand starred in many French and Italian films, and in between did occasional directing jobs, notably *Candy* in 1968. His sister, Nadine, was married to Jean-Louis Trintignant and he was a close friend of Marlon Brando and Roger Vadim. Not unsurprisingly, Aumont's own screen career took shape pretty quickly thereafter with co-starring parts in *The Game is Over* (directed by Roger Vadim 1966, alongside Jane Fonda) and the spaghetti western *Man, Pride and Vengeance* (1967, with Franco Nero). After finishing the latter, she hung out in Chelsea with Stash, aka Prince Stanislaus Klossowski De Rola, one of the great swinging 60s playboys and part of the Stones (and Beatles) entourage.[2] *Man, Pride and Vengeance* was particularly admired by Jean-Luc Godard who approached her that autumn to do *One Plus One/Sympathy for the Devil*. She declined in favour of *Partner* where her co-star was the radical leftist actor Pierre Clémenti. (It was actually reported in the Spanish magazine *Cine en 7 Dias*, in December 1967, that Aumont turned down Godard because '...*she wants to do something worthy and important...*'). By then she had divorced Marquand and moved in with the artist Frédéric Pardo, whom she had met whilst making the experimental trippy short *Visa de Censure No X*. Clémenti directed this and she also turned up in his next project *The Revolution is Only a Beginning, Let's Continue Fighting*, about the events of May 1968.[3]

This involvement with young agitprop French filmmakers was an additional attraction. Via Pardo and Clémenti, Aumont was associated (as were Nico and Jean Seberg) with 'the Zanzibar group' who between 1968 and 1970 shot 13 films, financed by Sylvina Boissonnas, a fabulously wealthy heiress. The group was led by Philippe Garrel, whose feature *Marie Pour Mémoire* won the top prize at Hyères Festival in April 1968. A generous patron, Boissonnas allowed her protégés to film on 35 mm, with no questions asked and without any contractual obligations. Her only requirement was that the cast – friends, actors, models, artists, musicians – were unpaid. At the same time as this she was providing financial support to the Exploding Galaxy Dance Troupe as well as a £500 donation to the Drury Lane Arts Lab to try and keep it open. In return, the Arts Lab served as a screening base for some of the Zanzibar group's avant-garde films that her largesse made possible, several of which were also shown at the Knokke Film Festival in Belgium, 1967-1968.[4]

After his success with *Marie Pour Mémoire*, Garrel quickly turned out *Le Révélateur* and *Le Lit de la Vierge*. The latter was filmed in Morocco without a script with post-production in Rome and featured Aumont immediately after *Partner* wrapped and prior to her starting work on *L'Urlo/The Howl*. Both of Garrel's films played mainly film festivals and were part of a now vanished canon of work: political/counter-culture material done in a denunciatory/avant-garde fashion with music, sex and challenging, hallucinatory visuals.[5] This type of renegade filmmaking chimed with the work of Brass at that time, and, indeed, with that of Peter Brook with *Tell Me Lies* (1966) and, of course, Jean-Luc Godard's output stretching from *Pierrot le Fou* (1965) via *One Plus One/Sympathy for the Devil* (1968) to *Wind from the East* (1971). *L'Urlo/The Howl* should be regarded as part of this ultimately short-lived genre, and when it was offered to Aumont, with the attraction that it included scenes shot in London, she accepted.

As her foil, the character who leads her through the action and points up the absurdities that she encounters in bourgeois society, Brass recruited the musician and actor Gigi Proietti. Head of the theatre company *Il Gruppo Sperimentale 101*, who did interpretations of everything from Shakespeare to Brecht, and even staged a play written by Picasso at one point, he had moved into film after a big hit with the 1963 stage revue *Can Can degli Italiani*.[6] On screen he was noted for *La Matriarca/The Libertine* (1968), with Jean-Louis Trintignant and had just finished *The Appointment* (1969). The latter was a really big film in its day... directed by Sidney Lumet, with Omar Sharif and Anouk Aimée from a script by fashionable US author James Salter and music by John Barry.

Proietti would later describe his time on *L'Urlo* as '*two months of pure joy and love of life*' and his ability to combine theatre, political comedy and satire whilst tackling themes such as corruption, crime, capitalism, racism and religion underpinned the approach Brass took in the film.[7] But, outside Italy he was less known than Aumont and the essentially farcical character he plays would be more common in the 1970s and 1980s in the theatre productions of Dario Fo. In fact, Fo's career – a screenplay writer who lived next door to Roberto Rossellini in Rome, who worked on various De Laurentiis projects (usually uncredited) and who, like Proietti, had his own radical theatre troupe – makes for an interesting comparison. In

1967, Fo staged *La Signora è da Buttare/Throw the Lady Out* about the US, the Vietnam war and the assassination of President Kennedy, and a year later was touring working-men's clubs with an overtly political routine. Fo's big breakthrough production would be the manic political comedy *Accidental Death of an Anarchist* (1970) which eventually arrived in the UK, to great acclaim, in 1979. Many of his plays and revues had music by Fiorenzo Carpi who mixed traditional folk tunes with contemporary (and often political) folk songs. Brass hired Carpi to do something similar on *L'Urlo*, and his material was conducted by Bruno Nicolai who at this point had just done the main title themes for *Django* (1966) and *Teorema/Theorem* (1968). Nicolai would do his work for Brass on *L'Urlo* at the same time as conducting Morricone's score for *Metti, Una Sera A Cena/Love Circle* (1969) a study of middle-class sexuality that starred, as so many films seemed to at that point, Jean-Louis Trintignant.

By casting Proietti in his film, therefore, Brass was approximately a decade ahead of the curve as far as getting a large audience in the UK and US were concerned. When discussing funding with De Laurentiis in Rome in June 1968 the choice of Proietti (who didn't speak English) was momentarily a problem, De Laurentiis insisting *'To be an actor, you should at least know English!'* He relented when Brass reassured him that English was relatively easy to learn by demonstrating how verbs are conjugated in the language. In the film itself the phrase *'break, broke, broken'* can be heard being repeated, partly as an in-joke in reference to this dispute and partly as a mantra on the deconstruction of the existing social structure.

Co-star Nino Segurini remained from *Nerosubianco*, playing the same type of part: the conventional husband, or in this case, as he appears in several roles, as a general representative of the forces of conformism, repression and statism. As ever, Brass used his usual crew with Alan Sekers in place for the sequences shot in London. The absence of a conventional script was seen as a positive, with Brass saying, 'In L'Urlo I wanted to create a new language, a changed language just as society and everything around us was changing... I just discussed the film with my cast and crew. I told them it was about a girl about to be married, who runs off with a stranger. Is this all a dream in the mind of this girl that lasts 1.5 hours or reality? In terms of the lines, either I wrote them down for the actors, fed them the lines or, occasionally, listened to their suggestions. Without a script, the set ran smoothly and without flaws. It was made just as I imagined.' In fact, the dialogue and situations we see on screen were a joint effort by him with Gian Carlo Fusco, Franco Longo and co-star Gigi Proietti. The end result, in which criticism of society is emotional rather than intellectual, and played with complete abandon by the cast, makes for an interesting comparison with Nerosubianco. If that film is Brass's Ulysses, then L'Urlo, with its dreamlike intensity, is his Finnegans Wake.

Shooting began in September 1968, about 4-6 weeks after Brass returned from Hollywood. By all accounts it proceeded quickly, at much the same speed that he had filmed Nerosubianco and Col Cuore in Gola. Editing and dubbing started in December 1968, but complications ensued. Firstly, De Laurentiis kept well away from the Italian tax inspectors and, with his financial affairs in their hands, it appears the finance for L'Urlo was much slower to access. Secondly, after starting the shoot at Cinecittà in Rome, the content of the scenes shot there (they were explicit, with a lot of full-frontal nudity) caused so much of a stir that the cast and crew eventually decamped to London,

Brass confirming this with the oblique comment '...*I wanted to feel free of all conditions in society and in the cinema industry. London in 1968 reflected that spirit. Actually, we started shooting in Rome, but we had many problems. We then moved to London where I didn't have these constraints and could invent new cinematic ideas...*' Later scenes were shot in France and Germany. Thus, the sequence of events shown in the film today does not follow the order in which the filming took place. Once again, because of these delays, trying to get a premiere at the May 1969 Cannes Film Festival became impossible, as did going back to Paramount to confirm his availability for *A Clockwork Orange*.

On screen we start with shots of the police baton charging demonstrators, see part of the celebrated Grosvenor Square demonstration and hear voices chanting '*Ho, Ho, Ho Chi Minh!*'. The camera focuses on the cover of Franz Kafka's 1919 novella *In the Penal Colony*, a topical inclusion as Frank Zappa recommended it be read before listening to his March 1968 LP *We're Only in It for the Money*, and UK actor Steven Berkoff presented it as a play at the Arts Lab, Drury Lane a month later.[8] Berto (Nino Segurini) is seen at a police station trying to get bail for his wife-to be Anita (Tina Aumont). It seems that she got arrested at the demonstration and has been detained. We cut to her having a shower, and learn that she was sexually assaulted whilst under arrest. Despite this, she and Berto decide to proceed with getting married. But, at the ceremony, Anita sees Coso (Gigi Proietti) beckoning to her, inviting her to abandon Berto. (Coso means 'thing' in Italian, and his character appears as a type of Greek chorus... part joker, part wandering musician.) Realising marriage is a bourgeois conformist trap, Anita runs away (complete in dress and veil) following Coso whom we see careering across Hungerford

Bridge – between Charing Cross and Waterloo – until they are united on the upper deck of a traditional red London bus. At which point the titles roll, nearly six minutes into the film, whilst the bus motors across open country.

Alas, the police are in pursuit. The bus ends up completely destroyed, and most of the passengers are killed. Alan Sekers remembers, '...I had to hire a bus. That scene, with all the extras dressed as policemen chasing the hippies and so on, was incredibly destructive and we incinerated the bus. You're supposed to have a permit if you're filming in the New Forest, but of course we didn't have one. (Typical with Tinto.) The fire and smoke from the bus was so dramatic that the real police turned up thinking there had been an air crash and I was pushed forward by Tinto to 'explain' what was going on. I had a bit of a stammer in those days and after a while the police gave up and just cleared off. Thankfully!'

Night falls and assorted hippies dance around the remains of the vehicle. Rather than remain with them, Aumont and Proietti wave down a car and are given a lift. They arrive, to the accompaniment of a ludicrous burst of spaghetti western music, at what appears to be a hotel. The receptionist/owner – a hugely obese man in leather sitting in front of a Paramount Pictures logo – books them in and they walk through a series of rooms. There is a blink-and-you'll-miss-it shot of *Tree Army Poem*, a miniature piece of verse (it is only 9 words in length) by Spike Hawkins, one of several British poets who rose to prominence in the 1960s.[9] It appears that Aumont and Proietti are actually in some type of elaborate sex dungeon. They walk from room to room through a variety of highly stylised erotic scenes, including some with quite elderly participants. None of the behaviour we see is spontaneous: it is theatrical, curiously joyless and there are two dominatrixes. The editing is exceptional and there is a great deal of high quality 1960s set design, suggesting that this was done at Cinecittà... and that this was the content that led to Brass, cast and crew quitting Italy. (*Playboy* magazine would later confirm '...*the movie's kinkiest scenes were shot in Rome, in Cinecittà studios...*')

They leave and end up in a wood where Proietti momentarily clowns around in the manner of Groucho Marx. A half-naked man, played by circus and street theatre performer Osiride Pevarello, appears, talking about nature. His family is living in a tree. They are preparing a meal and offer it to Aumont and Proietti who initially enjoy it until they are told that it is the remains of a missionary that the family have killed and cooked. They escape and a scene on a train follows, in which Proietti wears, like Sanders in *Nerosubianco*, Marcel Marceau-style make-up. Then, in an echo of *Col Cuore in Gola*, they end up on the immense pedestrian footbridge at Clapham Junction Station. From here Brass cuts to an Italian hilltop village, where they meet a man wearing a dilapidated barrel as his only clothing. This is clearly supposed to be the ancient philosopher Diogenes, who lived in a barrel, proclaiming that happiness could only be attained by being independent of society, even if this meant being outside normal family connections, giving up all property and not bothering about your personal reputation: views that chimed, to a certain extent, with some of the hippy philosophising of the late 1960s.

Once again, the forces of the state appear. There is newsreel footage of atrocities and a squad of soldiers, one of whom turns out to be Segurini, arrive. They attack the hippies and Brass edits in footage shot in and around the South Bank arts complex, opposite the Hungerford Bridge shown earlier, where amongst a lot of raucous political cabaret Tina Aumont is dragged away and raped by the soldiers and Carla Cassola, an avant-garde musician of some distinction, plays pianoforte. According to her, '...*Everything was improvised. Jokingly, I did some strange animal noises and played Tinto a tape of these sounds that I could do, and this interested him. He was shooting in an ancient town – Sermoneta, near Rome – and they had a pianoforte in the town square, so we did a scene with myself there. The title of the film L'Urlo ...it comes from those strange noises. In Italian it translates as "my voice", and in Basque the "Urlo" is a kind of ululating noise... The atmosphere on the set was crazy. There was a scene with some naked people in trees. Because it was so cold the day that we filmed that, they were all on drugs, which at the time quite shocked me*' [10]

Somehow both Aumont and Proietti escape and they meet a midget Napoleon in a sequence with a lot of weird bass voices and discordant electronic noise. Brass edits into the soundtrack speeches by Hitler and Mussolini whilst including in the footage scenes of Auschwitz, the Vietnam War and the Sharpeville massacre. Tina Aumont rouses the masses with a speech and things climax, in one of the most effective parts of the film, with images of the 1956 Budapest uprising and various scenes of street fighting edited to *Le Chant des Partisans*, the anthem of the French Resistance, composed in London in 1943 by Anna Marly, Joseph Kessel and Maurice Druon.

From here we cut to a long, tiled passage underground (actually the foot tunnel beneath the Thames at Greenwich) where Proietti and Aumont encounter an assortment of very peculiar-looking extras. With them, we move gradually into a scene where a crowd is dancing to a band. The sequence lasts about four-and-a-half minutes and is brilliantly shot, edited and dubbed by Brass. It all looks effortless but is clearly choreographed and actually quite hard to do. And administratively difficult too... the foot tunnel was administered by the Greater London Council which insisted that it remain open for pedestrians throughout the shoot. As a result, a member of the public can be briefly seen at one point encountering a semi-nude female dancer, and the scene also includes a completely naked young woman making what appear to be repeated attempts to sacrifice a chicken. Brass wanted Sam Gopal's Dream to be the live band, possibly because he remembered them from 'The 14 Hour Technicolour Dream' eighteen months earlier, where it would seem they made quite an impact with their mixture of guitar band rock and eastern instruments. (11) By chance, Brass ended up getting another group: Pete Brown and his Battered Ornaments. As Brown recollects, '... *The Sam Gopal Dream were originally intended to do The Howl. Tinto Brass had seen them and rated them – I knew them too from doing gigs alongside them at the Middle Earth and thought they were great. But on the day in question, they couldn't do it. So, Pete Sears, their guitarist, called me and asked if The Battered Ornaments could get down to the Greenwich Foot Tunnel with our gear, set up and play. It was the middle of the night. But it was paid, and quite well too, so we headed down there. I remember it vividly, particularly the girl with the chicken, but on the sound track it isn't us playing. The sound quality down there was probably abysmal and they used us to provide the atmosphere, but dubbed some library music on afterwards. Tina Aumont was absolutely gorgeous. There were lots of girls there, I think I took one home!'* (12)

This was all useful publicity for Brown and his band. A poet, lyricist, and regarded by some as the UK's equivalent of Ginsberg, he co-wrote the lyrics for Cream's international hits *Sunshine of Your Love* and *White Room* as well as seven other tracks on the albums *Disraeli Gears* and *Wheels of Fire*. Through 1967 and 1968 all of these sold heavily in the UK and US, making him an exceedingly well-known figure in the counter-culture. Striking out on his own musically, he and his group were signed by Peter Jenner and Andrew King – former managers of Pink Floyd – to their agency Blackhill Enterprises in October 1968, and immediately got a deal with EMI. Brown's timely inclusion in the film, the earlier split-second appearance of a Spike Hawkins verse (Hawkins and Brown were close friends, having first met in Liverpool in the early 1960s), and the use of a title that reminds one of Ginsberg's legendary poem, almost makes one think that one aspect of L'Urlo/The Howl might have been a deliberate attempt by Brass to show how important some of the key poets of the time were in a feature film.

Aumont and Proietti exit and emerge by a riverside where they escape on a speedboat. Alas, the boat explodes and they find themselves marooned on an island where they meet more hippies. Once more the police intervene, attacking the young people. The action here takes place on the remote Mediterranean island of Santo Stefano, where a maximum-security prison had been built by King Ferdinand IV of Naples in 1797. Brass's film was shot there three years after the facility closed, and its use as a location would have been understood by Italian audiences, as in real life San Stefano had been used, particularly during the fascist period, to incarcerate political prisoners, mainly socialists, communists and anarchists. Germano Longo plays the prison governor and Segurini turns up once more, this time as a sadistic guard. But, Aumont quickly inspires the inmates to revolt against the regime and they triumphantly escape.

We cut to Kensal Green Cemetery where Segurini appears again, this time as a gravedigger. Wandering amidst the

overgrown tombstones, Aumont and Proietti encounter a
black rights activist quoting Malcolm X and, bizarrely, a lion.
According to Alan Sekers, '...*It was a very old and quite toothless
lion. But Tina Aumont was terrified and completely stoned during
that scene...*' Next, we arrive in the UK countryside where yet
more hippies are milling around an open fire, many of them
naked. Aumont escapes again, now in a bridal veil and drives
off in a sports car, only to die in a car crash making a final
'howl' of her own and thinking of Segurini as she does so. A
priest then marries Aumont and Segurini (she semi-naked, he
in an ultra-straight business suit), with both of them making
meaningless, garbled vows before the police charge once more.
Finally, Proietti walks away, like a troubadour, muttering that
she was beautiful but crazy, and the film ends.

Notes

(1)   For this and many of the subsequent comments see http://
      filmint.nu/if-history-runs-cinema-can%E2%80%99t-
      keep-walking-an-interview-with-tinto-bras/
(2)   For background information on his life and times see
      http://dandyinaspic.blogspot.com/2012/03/prince-stash-
      klossowski-de-rola-1960s.html In terms of films Rola
      had supporting roles in *Les Démons de Minuit* (1961, with
      Charles Boyer) and *Le Dolci Signore* (1967, with Ursula
      Andress). In 1966 he released a single in Denmark, *Peace*,
      backed by Johnnie Dee and his Dee-Troit Sounds. Dee
      was a US songwriter who provided The Pretty Things,
      colleagues and rivals of The Rolling Stones, with a 1964
      hit, *Don't Bring Me Down*, thus completing a circle of sorts
      here. Like Rola, a figure of the 1960s, he married Janie

Jones in 1968, developed an interest in hard drugs and satanism and five years later was tried with her (and, unlike her, acquitted) of running a West End prostitution racket. The milieu described at the 1973 trial: violent crime, blackmail, sex, drugs, celebrities, politicians and rock musicians fits perfectly, as does that of Harvey Bramham earlier, with the setting of *Performance* and serves as a reminder of that side of the 1960s.

(3) *Visa de Censure No X* can be seen at https://vimeo.com/473622770

(4) See *London's Arts Labs and the 60s Avant-Garde* by David Curtis, 2020, p70.

(5) Garrel was subsequently taken up by Nico and Viva from Andy Warhol's circle and his next project, *La Cicatrice Interieure/The Inner Scar*, with Nico, would not appear until 1972, although it was completed a couple of years earlier. Images from it were used on the sleeve of her 1970 LP Desertshore.

(6) Directed on the stage by Giancarlo Cobelli, who appears in an acting role, as 'the revolutionary' in *Barbarella*.

(7) This quote is attributed to Proietti at https://www.dvddrive-in.com/reviews/n-s/poboxtintobrassblu.htm

(8) A Beatles satire which peaked at No 30 in the US charts. The Zappa quote is mentioned at Zappa wiki: https://wiki.killuglyradio.com/wiki/Franz_Kafka and in more detail at: http://www.tkinter.smig.net/Stuff/Kafka/index.htm One of the handbills advertising the Berkoff play can be seen very briefly on screen in Brass's film.

(9) A friend then of both Johnny Byrne, author with Jenny Fabian of the exposé *Groupie*, and Syd Barrett, Pink Floyd's original guitarist and lyricist, Hawkins had a slot

declaiming in 'The 14 Hour Technicolour Dream'. In *Syd Barrett: A Very Irregular Head*, Rob Chapman records that in the late summer of 1968 Hawkins was '...*working on an impossible film script that nobody could ever finish...*' In the autumn of 1967 Hawkins was supposed to film a promo-film for the Pink Floyd song *Scream Thy Last Scream*, which didn't, it would seem, appear either. Byrne was luckier. His TV play *Season of the Witch* was filmed in the summer of 1969. About a woman travelling around the UK and eventually finding herself, it starred Julie Driscoll and Paul Nicholas.

(10) Interview with Carla Cassola, 19 August 2020.

(11) Sam Gopal's Dream recorded an album, *Escalator*, October–November 1968, so their inclusion might have been intended to publicise that. Their manager at the time was Robert Stigwood; one wonders if he sent De Laurentiis another cassette tape of his latest band seeking exposure for them.

(12) Interview with Pete Brown, 24 February 2018. On Pete Sears, it appears he missed the sessions for *Escalator*, having moved on to Vamp by that point. He was replaced in Sam Gopal's Dream by Ian 'Lemmy' Kilmister, later of Hawkwind and Motorhead. For more on Brown and his career see *Shindig!* magazine No 78, April 2018.

10

'...A LUST-FILLED LABYRINTH OF PSYCHIC AND SEXUAL ABERRATIONS...'

There was an abundance of press coverage before and during the filming of *L'Urlo* beginning with a United Press release (13 September 1968) saying that *'Tina Aumont will shortly go to Rome to star in Tinto Brass's* The Howl' after which *Variety* (25 September 1968) noted *'...Tinto Brass will soon direct* L'Urlo (The Shriek) *with Tina Aumont for Dino De Laurentiis...'* Next, there was a spread by the set photographer in the 13 October 1968 edition of *L'Espresso* followed by another piece in *Tempo* on 9 November 1968.[1] All of these show sequences shot in Rome, though we know that Brass and his crew must have been in London by early November. He was, of course, also embroiled at this point in ongoing disputes with the Italian censors about *Nerosubianco*. At one point he returned to Rome from shooting *L'Urlo* in London to meet the censor board on Friday, 8 November 1968, only for it to be a fruitless journey: they banned the film anyway a few days later. Confirmation that *L'Urlo* was being shot in London came in *L'Espresso*, who ran an article on 24 November 1968 showing Proietti and Aumont on the upper deck of a London bus. That appeared a day after coverage in the Spanish magazine *Garbo* which stated that filming had been completed, with Aumont wearing make-up in one scene that made her look like a witch.

After further pieces in *Men* (25 November 1968), *King Cinemonde* and *Domenica del Corriere* (both December 1968, with the latter stating that some scenes were shot at Woburn Abbey) attention switched to Brass's struggle to get *Nerosubianco* a release certificate, this being covered in *ABC* (20 December 1968) and *Athos*, an Italian *Playboy-Mayfair* type publication (4 January 1969). By the time the latter appeared the censors had relented and Brass was in jocular form, ascribing his film censorship problems to the rapid turnover of governments in Italian politics. In other words, whichever version of the ruling Christian Democrats banned a film, the next version, always in office within six months, would allow it as part of clearing up what was left over from their predecessors. This had undoubtedly been the case with *Chi Lavoro e Perduto/Who Works is Lost* and would be so with *Nerosubianco*, but what Brass was offering in *L'Urlo/The Howl* would prove a bridge too far, even for Italy's expedient censor.

There was more coverage in *Riviera* (January 1969) and *Jolly Film* (February 1969) the latter publishing several shots of a black actress Linda Diatta, none of which appears in the version of the film available today. This repeated coverage in *Cinema X* (possibly late 1968) and seemed to imply that Diatta was virtually a co-star. There are also references to the appearance in the film of Leo Pistilli, although no footage of this person appears on screen. Was this actually Luigi Pistilli, a respected Italian actor of the period? However, as he regularly co-starred in quite significant productions, it seems inconceivable that he would have had all his scenes cut, and there are no references anywhere else to his involvement in *L'Urlo*. Nor, puzzlingly, is there a filmography for Leo Pistilli.

Royal (February 1969) focussed on the film as the latest to star Tina Aumont, and it appears that sometime around April Brass completed his cut. Pre-release coverage kept it in the public eye, notably *Oggi* (30 April 1969) and *New Kent* (June 1969) who had commissioned Chiara Samugheo to do a photo shoot of Aumont in Kensal Green Cemetery. As well as this, the July 1969 edition of *Playboy* carried a lengthy piece on Rod Steiger as a promo for *Three into Two Won't Go* (pointing out that his next role would be as Napoleon in De Laurentiis's *Waterloo*) and an artistic/erotic portfolio of Aumont about whom it stated, *'...Italy's great screen goddesses – Sophia Loren, Gina Lollobrigida and Claudia Cardinale – have all been home-grown heroines, but Tina Aumont promises to change that. Born in the US, 23-year-old Tina (daughter of French actor Jean-Pierre Aumont and Hispaniole-born actress Maria Montez) is riding the new wave to sex stardom in avant-garde Italian films... In L'Urlo, Tina portrays a freewheeling flower child named Anita, who searches for the ultimate liberation lifestyle. Toward that Elysian end, she and her lover, Carlo, drop out of society – and into a lust-filled labyrinth of psychic and sexual aberrations. Anita and Carlo force themselves to pass through repugnant scenes that can, in their view, completely free them as individuals. Says Tinto Brass, who wrote and directed the film, "...L'Urlo is about today's romanticism – the struggle between the consumer society and the new paradise..."* Most of L'Urlo *was filmed on location in London, Paris, Berlin and on the island of San Stefano; but the movie's kinkiest scenes were shot in Rome, in Cinecittà studios...'*

With the film complete, and lodged with the censors, the cast and crew dispersed. Aumont (together with Carpi and Nicolai) started work on *Giacomo Casanova: Childhood and Innocence/Infanzia, Vocazione e Prime Esperienze de Giacomo Casanova, Veneziano* with Leonard Whiting, formerly Olivia Hussey's co-star in Zeffirelli's *Romeo and Juliet*. Zeffirelli's film – which De Laurentiis produced – was one of the box-office sensations of the late 1960s, earning over 40 times what it cost, and winning several Academy Awards and BAFTAs. Much was expected of the Casanova picture, but a release outside Italy didn't happen for several years and it was barely seen in the US or UK. For his part, Proietti went off to do *La Fantastica Storia di Don Chisciotte della Mancia*, a children's TV series about the adventures of Don Quixote.

Months passed and *L'Urlo* failed to appear at either the Cannes Film Festival or later that summer. Despite Brass presenting three different versions of the film, each one 'tamer' than the last, all were rejected by the Italian censor on the grounds of gross obscenity. *L'Urlo/The Howl* was formally banned on 15 September 1969, quickly becoming something of a cause célèbre: a radical, liberated, taboo-breaking film that was being blocked by the establishment. A campaign to ensure its release started with the magazine *King* reporting (November 1969) that Brass, his crew and cast were all protesting at the failure to grant a certificate. Support came too – in the name of artistic freedom – from luminaries like fellow directors Michelangelo Antonioni and Mario Monicelli as well as Sergio Amidei, Rossellini's screenplay writer, and Carlo Lizzani, another Rossellini collaborator, at that point directing a couple of features for De Laurentiis.

That same month, Brass took his own cut of the film to London where he arranged a private, invitation-only screening for a select group that included Jane Fonda, Roger Vadim, Vanessa Redgrave and Franco Nero. They were impressed – Redgrave and Nero particularly so, as will be shown in the next chapter – but no release ensued. Eventually efforts were made for a premiere at the May 1970 Cannes Film Festival, but Brass withdrew it in favour of a formal entry in competition, alongside 26 other films including *Borsalino* and *The Conformist*, at the June 1970 Berlin Film Festival. Alas, bad luck struck again. US director George Stevens, as President of the Jury, objected to Michael Verhoeven's anti-Vietnam/anti-war film *O.K.* and persuaded his colleagues that it should be withdrawn from the event. A fierce dispute duly commenced about censorship, resulting in most of the other directors, including Brass, withdrawing their films (in the case of *L'Urlo/The Howl* after it had been screened) resulting in the abandonment of the event.[2] It appears that it was also shown a month later at the Taormina Film Festival (some magazine coverage of this, with shots of Aumont have emerged), but without winning a prize: these were awarded to Goldie Hawn, for *The Cactus Flower*, and John Schlesinger, for *Midnight Cowboy*.

A rare press review of the film appeared in *Variety*, whose correspondent had seen it at Berlin, on 1 July 1970: '*...One is bound to have mixed feelings about such a mixed grab-bag of a film as this latest by the unevenly talented Tinto Brass, a young Italian who's successfully rummaged through film libraries but lately come up with a style of his own. This irreverent nose-thumbing blast at modern manners and mores still has a familiar ring about it at times*

(Godard, Fellini, Pasolini and, inevitably, Buñuel) but a lot of it is fun once the spirit is assimilated and the intent becomes clearer. It could catch on here and there as a cult and college circuit item... But the outlook is limited at best, despite such fillips as nudity, cannibalism, gang rape, anti-clericalism, masturbation, necrophilia – you name it: it's all derisorily there to be mocked by the writer-director. Story-wise, it's a jumble and hard to follow at first as Brass takes off on a sort of odyssey through a present-day Dante's Inferno by following a young girl (Tina Aumont) who runs off with a stranger (Luigi Proietti) on the eve of her wedding to a middle-class square (Nino Segurini). The anti-establishment messages are all there, graphically or symbolically, on their joint journey. Some are amusing, others over-stated. Pic is ultimately pretentious, but more winningly so than some of Godard's increasingly boring recent pamphlets... Cast uniformly carries out director's intentions and Tina Aumont's disturbingly sultry beauty is an asset. Fiorenzo Carpi's music and songs fit well, and Silvano Ippoliti's camerawork (much of it on locations in England) is outstanding...'

This was a very generous estimation of a film that looks, on the basis of the version we have access to today, as if it were filmed in a haphazard way on a small budget. Almost all of it is shot outdoors in locations that wouldn't have cost anything, with a slender supporting cast that would have been modestly paid and a crowd of UK extras usually recruited, from his immediate circle of friends, by Alan Sekers. Even when a coup of some sort was pulled off – such as getting Cream lyricist Pete Brown and his band to perform in one scene – it wasn't exploited in any meaningful way. Given how famous Brown was in 1968-1969, why didn't this get publicised? Why did a film that had a musical input from four separate sources (Brown, Carpi, Nicolai and Carla Cassola) not produce a soundtrack album, or have even a single piece of its music released in any format? Cassola, for instance, was one of many associated with Italian experimental group MEV (Musica Elletronica Viva) whose debut album, *Friday*, appeared on the Polydor label in 1969. There are some peculiar electronic noises in *L'Urlo*, but Cassola has confirmed that none of them is by MEV.

The selection of Tina Aumont as the lead, the advance publicity in *Variety* and the pre-release publicity in *Playboy* all suggest a pitch to the US market. As does the commissioning of graphic artist Piero Ermanno Iaia, whose work ranged from Hitchcock's *Psycho* via Orson Welles's *The Trial* to Joseph Losey's *Secret Ceremony*, to prepare posters for a projected US/UK release. For reasons that are far from clear, though, once the Italian censors pulled the plug, attempts to distribute the film elsewhere were seemingly abandoned. Did De Laurentiis just write off *L'Urlo* as a bad job? Or was he so taken up with *Waterloo* that it got forgotten? If that was the case, and given that Brass clearly had access to his own copy of the film, why didn't the director just pay to have a couple of extra prints made and then release it himself via an art-house chain or the university cinema club circuit?

It isn't clear either which version of the film was screened by Brass in London in late 1969 or shown at Berlin and Taormina in 1970. Lobby cards from that period show a number of scenes not found in the 2009 DVD reissue. As mentioned, Linda Diatta appears to have been completely excised from the final cut. It may well be that Brass's original edit of the film was longer and more sensational: certainly, a great deal of explicit material ended up on the cutting room floor as he tried, and failed, to get a release certificate from the Italian censors. Standing back from this confusion and trying to reimagine the attitudes and expectations that existed in 1969 draws one to an interesting conclusion.

It is worth recollecting that in 1967-1968 Brass seemed to be exploring cinematically the same areas visually as bands like Pink Floyd and The Soft Machine did with their mixture of light shows, kinetic art and modern dance. He was overlapping with some of the same people who admired both groups and visiting the same locations where this 'scene' was likely to be found. Now, in 1969, he was orbiting Andy Warhol's circle and exploring the same territory as the 'Zanzibar group' of young, radical French cinéastes and activists.

After completing *Le Lit de la Vierge* in Morocco with Tina Aumont, for instance, Philippe Garrel spent a great deal of time in the US with Nico and Viva, whilst his colleague, Swiss artist Olivier Mosset, was working at Warhol's 'factory'. By the summer of 1968, Mosset had returned to France to make the four-minute short *Un Film Porno*, with Pierre Clémenti. A few months later Viva (and Louis Waldon) filmed Warhol's *Blue Movie*, which on its June 1969 release was hailed as the first explicit feature film. Scriptless and mainly a mixture of unsimulated sex and long discussions about the Vietnam War it earned $16,000 (five times what it cost to make) over a ten-day run at a solitary cinema before being confiscated, although Viva was assured that her performance was *'better than Vanessa Redgrave'*. By the time this level of notoriety had been reached Viva had appeared in Agnès Varda's *Lions Love and Lies*, alongside James Rado and Gerome Ragni, the writers of *Hair*. Varda's film had a fair bit of full-frontal nudity too, and was produced by Max Raab who would later produce *A Clockwork Orange*. Varda's film also used archival footage (much in the style of Brass) and had originally been intended as a starring vehicle for Jim Morrison, singer in The Doors. Finally, Aumont, Clémenti, Waldon and Viva were all in *Necropolis* (1970) which like *L'Urlo* mixes outlandish dialogue, nudity, violence, interesting set design and political comment. It was directed by Franco Brocani, who turns up as an actor in Mario Schifano's Rolling Stones project *Umano, Non Umano*.[3]

Looked at in this context, and based on the level of magazine and press coverage that it achieved through 1968 and 1969, the original cut of *L'Urlo* may well have been a much-talked-about, word-of-mouth sensation: a properly budgeted feature, with real actors that had extensive pornographic episodes and equated the sexual revolution with the political revolution of the day. Although *Blue Movie* is regarded now as '*the first adult erotic film depicting explicit sex to receive wide theatrical release in the United States*', Brass's film was shot and completed prior to Warhol's and is as deserving, if not more so, of critical reappraisal as an early example of the 'porno chic' phenomenon.

The only trouble was, in 1969 audiences couldn't see it. And the version that we have now, neither underestimated like *Col Cuore in Gola* nor neglected like *Nerosubianco*, is simply what it appears to be, an anarchic piece of street theatre, that makes overtly political points. It works as well, or as badly, as any other film of this type, and in the late 1960s there were quite a few examples to choose from. It contains three scenes that are exceptionally well shot and edited: the sex dungeon sequence (done at Cinecittà in Rome), the triumphant uprising of the people set to *Le Chant des Partisans*, and the sequence with Pete Brown and his Battered Ornaments in the Greenwich foot tunnel. It also has a fantastic part for a leading actress. Tina Aumont would later comment that whilst filming *Partner* for Bertolucci she and co-star Pierre Clémenti were carefully supervised to ensure that they didn't leave the set and take up positions on the barricades in Paris, whereas '...*Tinto left me full freedom to improvise and dress as I wanted...*' In fact, the notoriety that *L'Urlo* brought Aumont gave her career a huge boost. Between 1969 and 1977 she starred or co-starred, mainly in Italy, in a further 18 films. Her fee for *Casanova* with Leonard Whiting in 1969 was reported in the Spanish press as being 4 million pesetas, at the time roughly £32,000 and equal to about £1.2m now. It seems, then, that performing in Brass's banned film set Aumont on the path to being seriously rich.

L'Urlo finally got a release certificate from the Italian censors, or as it was put, was 'cleared for screening', on 12 April 1972. Given that, in July that year, *Tempo* magazine – in another piece on Aumont – referred to it as 'unfinished', one might conclude that the version the censors signed off was significantly different from Brass's director's cut. Cinema audiences had to wait until July 1974 to see it. A late flurry of accompanying publicity included *Panorama* magazine jocularly pointing out that in a world where Jodorowsky was a success, films that had been deemed un-releasable in 1968 were now being disinterred, and *Intrepido* described Proietti's character as a '*nonconformist Garibaldi*', whatever that meant.[4] The comparison with Jodorowsky, presumably a reference to his visually terrific, psychedelic/surrealist cult art-house epic *The Holy Mountain*, which premiered at Cannes in 1973, was actually quite flattering and yet another indication of the kind of filmmakers with whom Brass then tended to be bracketed.

Sadly, *L'Urlo* failed to emulate even the limited box-office takings of *The Holy Mountain*. Figures from 1976 indicate that its release was probably restricted to a run of a week or so in no more than 3-4 cinemas. The prints allowed into public circulation portrayed, and to a certain extent idealised, a hippy scene that was by then long gone. There was never an English language version and it quickly vanished from sight.

In the summer of 1969, though, Brass remained confident that he would move on to greater things.

Notes

(1) For many of the press comments that follow see https://tina-aumont.tumblr.com/

(2) See *The New York Times*, 4 July 1970. For more comment on this episode see https://www.berlinale.de/en/archive/jahresarchive/1970/01_jahresblatt_1970/01_jahresblatt_1970.html

(3) A copy of *Necropolis*, which runs for 2 hours, can be watched at https://www.youtube.com/watch?v=uQA11jUCQPE. The film came with a score by Gavin Bryars, a noted avant-garde composer.

(4) Jodorowsky's *The Holy Mountain* premiered in New York in November 1973. With his previous work, *El Topo* (1970), it found a niche audience at independent cinemas, usually screened during an all-night event.

11

'...I'D LIKE TO MAKE A MOVIE WITH YOU AND VANESSA...'

During his enforced absence from Italy, Dino De Laurentiis enjoyed a big hit with *Barbarella* which took $15.7m at the US box-office. It easily did better business than the likes of *Yellow Submarine*, *If*, *Petulia*, *Wild in the Streets*, *Head* and *Joanna* and in the pop-film stakes it was exceeded only by *Candy*, which grossed $21.1m. Unsurprisingly he quickly sought to capitalise on this with a sequel. By November 1968, only a month after the original's release, Paramount producer Robert Evans was stating that the working title of the follow-up would be *Barbarella Goes Down*, with the central character, unlike the inference in the title, continuing her adventures under water. But, with De Laurentiis incapacitated for many months by his tax difficulties, and then up to his neck in preparing and financing *Waterloo*, little of note happened until 7 May 1969 when *Variety* magazine announced, '*TINTO BRASS – Author* likes to blast social inhibitions and idols. Columbia released his Black on White *early this year with fair returns for a way-out pic. Brass recently terminated* The Shriek. *Both pix filmed in London for Dino De Laurentiis who now allows Brass to direct* Barbarella Goes Down.' [1]

Given that nothing transpired from this, it is hard to establish how much *Barbarella Goes Down* would have replicated the original, with its Terry Southern script, and all-star cast led by Jane Fonda, David Hemmings and Marcel Marceau. Information on the availability, or enthusiasm, of any of these for a second tilt at the 1962 comic book series is scarce. Without doubt, though, like *Barbarella* itself, it would have explored the same territory as Brass had in his previous three films. There would have been plenty of Pop Art, sexual imagery (including a Wilhelm Reich-style orgone box), music and outré set design. It would also have been big-budget. We should also note that the combination of Paramount, Southern and Hemmings echoes Brass's involvement the previous year with *A Clockwork Orange*, the importance of which today is usually minimised. As well as this, it is significant that the prospect of a third De Laurentiis film was being entertained despite the difficulties experienced with both *Nerosubianco* and *L'Urlo*. Brass clearly wasn't in bad odour with his main patron, and in the first half of 1969 he remained busy and well-regarded. *Col Cuore in Gola* finally reached the US in March, where Paramount distributed it, implying it was some sort of sequel to *Candy*, and it was also released in France a month later. *A Clockwork Orange* still hadn't been lined up for Kubrick, and a reasonable cut of *Nerosubianco* was sold at Cannes to Audubon, who, as noted by Variety, found that it yielded '*fair returns for a way-out pic*'.

Alas, any preparatory work that Brass did for *Barbarella Goes Down* came to naught as the tide quickly turned against him and that particular project. There were two major issues – firstly, Jane Fonda flatly refused to repeat her starring role and secondly, De Laurentiis became more and more preoccupied with *Waterloo*, which started filming in July 1969 and was at that point the most expensive film in the world. With *L'Urlo* being banned, after it had been recut several times, momentum was being lost, and to try and retrieve the position with Fonda, Brass brought a print of it to London for a special, invitation-only screening. Among those present at this event, which seems to have taken place in November 1969, were Jane Fonda, her husband Roger Vadim, whom Brass would have known from the Cinémathèque Française, Vanessa Redgrave, Franco Nero and Stephen Frears.[2] The point of the screening was to try to get Fonda interested in *Barbarella Goes Down*. She wasn't, however impressed she may have been by *L'Urlo*. Her latest film *They Shoot Horses Don't They?*, a serious drama, had wrapped in August 1969. It would be a box-office success and was later nominated for nine Academy Awards, including Fonda as Best Actress. She didn't want to go back to playing a sex kitten in a bikini involved in various ridiculous situations. Her politics were also coming to the fore. By late 1969 she was supporting the occupation of Alcatraz Island by Native Americans and, from April 1970, she would tour US Army bases performing an anti-war agitprop vaudeville revue with Donald Sutherland and Fred Gardner. So, instead of working with Brass, she opted to make *Klute* with Donald Sutherland, which began filming in the autumn of 1970.

However, all was not lost. After some discussion it turned out that Redgrave and Nero were agreeable to making a film like *L'Urlo*. Franco Nero says, '...*I knew who Tinto was before he approached me. In Italy he was considered a genius, a promising auteur. Everyone was talking about him after his film* Chi Lavora e Peduto... *One day he called me up and asked me to come to a screening of one of his films. It starred Tina Aumont and Gigi Proietti. After we had seen it, he said "I'd like to make a movie with you and Vanessa"...*' [3] So impressed were they by the version of *L'Urlo* screened that evening, that Redgrave and Nero accepted at once. Like Serge Gainsbourg and Jane Birkin, Yoko Ono and John Lennon, Mick Jagger and Marianne Faithfull, they were very much a 1960s power couple and, as well as pursuing their own careers, had already starred together in *A Quiet Place in the Country*, directed by Elio Petri and released in November 1968. Redgrave was known for films like *Blow-Up* and *The Charge of the Light Brigade* and was active politically, seen throughout 1968-1969 at many anti-war and anti-apartheid demonstrations. (Her activism eventually led her to the Workers Revolutionary Party in the early 1970s.) Nero's credits included *Django* (and a couple of sequels), *Man, Pride and Vengeance*, with Tina Aumont, Buñuel's *Tristana* and *The Battle of Neretva*. The latter starred Sergei Bondarchuk – the director of De Laurentiis's *Waterloo* – and was a massively expensive war film, personally approved by President Tito. Nero had been filming *Tristana* in Spain in September 1969, with Vanessa Redgrave present on the set after recently divorcing Tony Richardson. It must have just finished at the point they watched *L'Urlo*, and indeed Nero's reputation was sky-high around this point as he had also recently completed a starring role in the DH Lawrence adaptation *The Virgin and the Gypsy*. This would be voted the best film of 1970 by both the British Critics Circle and the New York Press, running for 18 months in London's West End and breaking box-office records in New York. With a couple of major stars signed up to a fresh project, Brass must have thought that attracting funding would be straightforward. But De Laurentiis couldn't oblige due to *Waterloo*, and hopes rested initially on Carlo Ponti, who at that point was expecting great things from his forthcoming production of Antonioni's *Zabriskie Point*.

Much awaited, work on this had begun as soon as *Blow-Up* scooped the Grand Prize at Cannes. After some deliberation, Antonioni hired Sam Shepard to do a script with Fred Gardner.[4] The plot had a couple of unknown actors, Mark Frechette and Daria Halprin, travelling across the US, filmed as an intensely alien environment, with various political points being made as they did so. By the time Brass was talking to Ponti, filming, which took a year, had been completed, and the soundtrack was being prepared. This involved an album worth of music from Pink Floyd (much of which wasn't used), contributions from The Kaleidoscope, The Grateful Dead and John Fahey. Even The Doors laboured over material only for Antonioni to reject the only song they produced.[5] Ponti and MGM, who produced, would have reasonably expected *Zabriskie Point* to emulate the success of *Easy Rider*, since both were films with a clear pitch towards young audiences in which characters traverse the US.

Alas, not foreseen was the impact the Manson killings had on public attitudes, and the effect this would have, in turn, on what type of films were financed by studio executives. *Easy Rider* (which Terry Southern scripted) turned out to be lucky: it was completed and screened prior to the carnage in Hollywood in July and August 1969 that saw seven people murdered. With Manson's trial not starting until July 1970, and the case attended by immense amounts of gruesome publicity, the fact that Antonioni's stars, Frechette and Halprin, lived in a commune with a dictatorial leader didn't play at all well, and people in general were no longer inclined to be indulgent towards the foibles of the counter-culture.[6]

Accordingly, when *Zabriskie Point* premiered in February 1970, it did so to poor reviews and lowish box-office takings. Ponti may not have taken an immediate decision to do so, but he dropped Brass's film pretty quickly after this, and rather than put money into another sprawling counter-culture film, opted instead to make *The Priest's Wife* with Sophia Loren and Marcello Mastroianni, a much more conventional venture. With *L'Urlo* still blocked, Kubrick now signed up for *A Clockwork Orange* and *Barbarella Goes Down* clearly never going to be made, this was a severe blow. But Brass was determined and with nothing else on the horizon, decided to plough on.

Quite when he made this decision is hard to pin down. Variety announced on 6 May 1970, '*He has a commitment from Vanessa Redgrave and Franco Nero to star in* Dropout *and plans to film it in London but can't find financing. It's the story of an Italian immigrant in London who breaks out of an insane asylum and runs off with a married woman*'. From this clipping it seems logical to assume that Ponti had changed his mind in March/April 1970, and the decision to self-fund the film was taken shortly afterwards. In the words of Franco Nero, '*Ponti tried to get a US company involved, but it turned out the US company wanted too much money and he couldn't close the deal... So Ponti withdrew and we – Vanessa, myself and Tinto – became the producers. There was no script. It was always just an idea with Tinto! It was never a big budget movie, in fact it had almost no budget at all and the entire crew couldn't have been more than 9-10 people, one of whom was*

Tinto's wife – Tinta – who ran the money side of things. She was part of the Cipriani family, so had access to funds that could be used to subsidise his films...'

Doing it as a DIY project involved shooting on 16 mm, improvising an awful lot (hence, the lack of any script whilst it was filming, though one was, apparently, written after the event) and using, even more so than was usually the case with Brass, cost-free, outdoors settings. What emerged was a smaller version, almost a violent charcoal sketch, of what might have been made had Ponti's money still been available. The plot was a variation on that of *Nerosubianco* and *L'Urlo*: a suppressed bourgeois woman (Redgrave) encounters a man (Nero) who shows her an alternative approach to life, via which she is fulfilled and learns to express herself in a more creative fashion. In a very late 1960s twist, it was decided that Nero would kidnap Redgrave from her idyllic suburban home whilst on the run from a lunatic asylum, having been certified insane by conventional society. Thus, the film skirts RD Laing territory: the man who liberates her is regarded as mad by 'normal' people.

Frank Windsor, then known to UK audiences for his work in the popular TV series *Z Cars* and *Softly, Softly*, co-stars as Redgrave's oppressive husband. *Dropout* was one of a trio of film roles he took around this time, the others being *Spring and Port Wine* and *Sunday Bloody Sunday*. (Redgrave, interestingly, had turned down the latter.) Actress Patsy Smart, also familiar then from TV work, appears in a small part. Like Windsor, she was taking roles in feature films, in her case John Boorman's *Leo the Last*, which like Brass's film is shot in various down-at-heel surroundings. On such a low budget, though, it was necessary to find a way to bulk out the cast without spending very much.

In this respect, Gigi Proietti came to the rescue, returning to London and bringing with him many of his colleagues from the Italian TV series *Le Fantastica Storia di Don Chisciotte della Mancia*. As well as Proietti himself, Carlo Quartucci (who actually directed the TV series), Mariella Zanetti and Zoe Incrocci all have acting roles in *Dropout*, whilst Roberto Lerici, who wrote the Italian series, eventually co-authored the script for Brass's film with Franco Longo. It isn't hard to see what the attraction might have been: an expenses-paid trip to London where they would spend a few weeks, making a film with Vanessa Redgrave and Franco Nero.

On the production side, Alan Sekers left to study art, and was replaced as assistant director by Stephen Frears. After an apprenticeship at the Royal Court Theatre, Frears had worked on films like *Morgan – A Suitable Case for Treatment*, *Charlie Bubbles* and *If...*, before directing the documentary *St Ann's Nottingham* and five episodes of the series *Tom Grattan's War* on TV. He was brought on board by Vanessa Redgrave, whom he knew from *Morgan – A Suitable Case for Treatment*, and when interviewed recently confirmed that he had been at the London screening of *L'Urlo*, with Fonda, Vadim, Redgrave and Nero.

The soundtrack was assigned to Don Fraser, a graduate from the Royal College of Music, where he studied alongside Andrew Lloyd-Webber and Rick Wakeman. Fraser had moved into scoring documentaries for Geoffrey Jones at the Shell Film Unit and got hired for *Dropout* after Vanessa Redgrave saw a performance of Christopher Logue's reworking from *The Iliad*, *Why Tears Achilles?* for which he had written some music. He remembers, '...*It caused quite a sensation and ran for 3 nights at the Royal College of Art. Vanessa came to the performance and it was*

she that introduced me to Tinto. They were about to start shooting
Dropout *and I kind of hung out with the crew... I remember at some*
point watching the World Cup around at my flat when we lost 2-3
to West Germany after being 2-0 up, very embarrassing when sitting
with an Italian film crew. Tinto just said to me one day, "You're doing
the music", that was it really...' [7]

Redgrave's interest in musical adaptations of Greek classics
actually went back to 1963, when she and Alan Dobie (who
performed regularly at the Royal Court Theatre in the 1950s
and 1960s) narrated a spoken-word album, *The Death of*
Patroclus, Book XVI of Homer's Iliad. Another Logue project,
this was released as a spoken-word album on 77 Records, a
label run out of Dobell's Jazz Record Shop at 77 Charing Cross
Road, London WC2. Logue was in fact quite a figure in the UK
scene, working with jazz drummer Tony Kinsey, mixing music
and poetry (in much the same way that Pete Brown would do
several years later), reciting at *Wholly Communion* and 'The 14
Hour Technicolour Dream' and being a friend of Mark Boyle.
By 1969 he was collaborating with John Lennon, Yoko Ono
and John Tavener on *Aspen 7 – British Box.* This appeared on
the obscure Roaring Fork label, which between 1965 and 1971
released various electronic music, spoken word and multi-media
performance art projects. Each of these, including something
from The Velvet Underground in 1966, came in a customised
box accompanied by booklets, phonograph recordings, posters,
postcards and even, in one case, a spool of Super-8 movie film.
Once again, as he had done in *Nerosubianco* and *Col Cuore in*
Gola, Brass was exploring, and recruiting from, the vibrant
London counter-culture of the time.

At the time he was appointed to do the score, Fraser was
working on the album *Half Baked*, by Liverpudlian singer-

songwriter Jimmy Campbell. Coincidentally, the cover of this almost echoes the atmosphere of the film: a man and a woman, in deliberately fantastic clown costumes, appear lost, or abandoned, in a wood. The same similarities are also apparent musically. On both the Campbell album and Brass's film, Fraser's music is understated folk-rock with simple arrangements. It was only a couple of years since The Freedom and *Nerosubianco*, but the draining away of optimism and generally downbeat atmosphere were palpable in a whole range of ways. The cover for *Half Baked*, for instance, was shot by Marcus Keef (aka Keith McMillan) who created a lot of album sleeves for the Vertigo, Neon and Nepentha labels in the early 1970s. Most of his images are of empty landscapes, abandoned debris and miscellaneous hippy artefacts implying the clear message that the party's over: something very much reflected in *Dropout*. Like Nick Saxton, Keef later moved into directing rock videos, and was responsible for many of the most popular of these from 1977.[8]

The England vs West Germany football match that so embarrassed Fraser took place on 14 June 1970. By then *Dropout* was already in production, *Variety* later reporting (on 15 July) that it had started shooting on 1 June. It had been a struggle, and money was so tight Brass himself would jocularly tell reporters, '*If you know what we spend, you won't write the film up!*' But despite many setbacks, he was now filming his fourth feature film in London. As to the plot... well, it features a lot of roaming around London, but unlike *Col Cuore in Gola* and *Nerosubianco*, what we see here are not the upmarket bits of a swinging city. Instead, we follow the central figures as they traverse a battered and ruined landscape and encounter a marginalised population of immigrants, striking workers, elderly meths drinkers, the homeless and the poor. As in *Nerosubianco* and *L'Urlo* the film is a study of a woman and her liberation. In *Dropout* the trigger for this is her chance encounter with a man who has escaped from a lunatic asylum, a course of action he takes to 'prove' to the authorities that he isn't mad.

The film starts with Redgrave, a bored housewife trapped in a conventional marriage, encountering a man (Nero) in her back garden, somewhere in suburbia. Nero, kitted out like one of the tramps in *Waiting for Godot*, initially asks her for food, but then breaks into her house and holds her at knife point. Her husband (Frank Windsor) is captured, stripped and tied up. Nero then absconds in the family car, taking Redgrave with him. It turns out Redgrave's character is called Mary Hopkins. The name would have been selected to underscore how clean-cut and conventional she is: Mary Hopkin being an angelic-looking, and angelic-voiced, teenage Welsh girl who signed to Apple records in June 1968 and had six hit singles and a hit album between then and 1970. Despite her Beatle connections, she was increasingly likely to be found on mainstream TV, and recorded quite a lot of very MOR material. The intended audience for *Dropout* would have immediately 'got' this reference, probably seeing it as an ironic comment on how the counter-culture, by 1970, was increasingly commodified and packaged.

Redgrave and Nero end up in a derelict/squatted house and the following day witness an industrial relations dispute at a factory. A lorry brings in strike-breaking workers and we see the police attack the picket line to the accompaniment of a busking/ukulele-style political song with a chorus that goes 'work, brothers, work'. From here we cut to Ladbroke Grove amidst various black community scenes whilst the folk-pop band Middle of the Road sing *The Sun is Shining in Jamaica* on the soundtrack. Redgrave and Nero visit a Black Power meeting, where the attendees seem suspicious of their presence, only for the police to arrive and break that up too. After a scene at a Salvation Army soup kitchen where Nero protests and starts a riot, they head back to derelict wasteland near a power station, possibly the one formerly at Barking Reach. Throughout this sweep across insalubrious parts of London the film's tone is that of improvised political slapstick, with deliberate vulgarity about bodily functions occurring against a soundtrack peppered with opera extracts. They end up in a doss house for the homeless where Redgrave's clothes are stolen and she takes to wearing a great coat over her underwear.

Fleeing again, she and Nero arrive at a complex of cavernous, nineteenth-century industrial buildings, where in another nod to Apple, the London Radha Krishna Temple jog through performing the *Hare Krishna Mantra*. Recorded with George Harrison as producer in July 1969, this was intended as an authentic corrective to the commercial version of the same tune featured in the stage musical *Hair*. Released a month later, it reached No 12 in the UK chart, as well as being a considerable hit in several European countries. Following some shots taken in what appears to be Smithfield Meat Market, they arrive back at the semi-derelict house where they encounter their landlord. There is an argument and Nero kills him, whether by accident or by design isn't clear. Redgrave and Nero flee again, this time back to Ladbroke Grove. Here they encounter Proietti and his entourage. Proietti is seemingly a pimp living in a grand house in a tumbledown area. This sequence, with its combination of shabby gentility and surreal dialogue, is not unlike much of the action in John Boorman's *Leo the Last*, a much-rated film in its day that was shot in north Kensington in late 1969, prior to the demolition of much of the area to facilitate the construction of the Westway urban motorway.

Whilst various types of music play – silent film piano riffs, trumpet solos and more opera extracts – Redgrave, Nero, Proietti and a couple of others visit the SPACE Studios at St Katharine Docks. Here we see in the background several sculptures and pictures by the Makkink brothers. Stanley Kubrick would later use these, with great effect, as props in *A Clockwork Orange*. Finally, a sequence is shot in an empty, derelict industrial building directly adjoining functioning railway lines (the most likely location for this appears to have been Bishopsgate Goods Yard) where a collection of meths drinkers and rough sleepers are sheltering beside a fire. Here Proietti sings *Do Not Cry*, in Italian.[9]

In the meantime, Redgrave goes back to her husband. She does various subservient, wifely things and also sings, with great irony, the national anthem. Her husband interrogates her and beats her. She leaves him again, returns to Nero and we see them, clearly very much in love with each other, on a train. They arrive at a port where they wait for a ship to take them away to another country, sleeping overnight in an abandoned WW2 gun emplacement as they do so. But her husband has followed them. The police arrive. On the beach the following morning, in a sequence shot at Camber Sands, Nero is arrested, and agrees of his own free will to return to the asylum. The point being made here, that it is his decision to do so, rather than that of society being imposed on him. He exits with the police. Redgrave is distraught, sobs and tries to follow. A shot rings out and she falls dead. We see Windsor, her husband, smiling sardonically and walking away. The film ends.

Shooting *Dropout* took, whichever account is relied on, no more than eight weeks, and possibly much less. As can be seen, a number of intriguing locations were used, not least SPACE studios. An acronym that stood for Space Provision Artistic Cultural and Educational, these were opened in early 1968 in the St Katharine Docks, after it had been closed by the Port of London Authority and transferred to the Greater London Council. There were plans to completely redevelop the site as soon as it shut, but it was clear that these would take time to come to fruition and the council agreed to lease the area for two years to a group headed by the artists Bridget Riley and Peter Sedgley.[10] The St Katharine Docks complex quickly became a creative hub for anyone looking for a studio and among those in residence were Graham Stevens (who did the inflatable sculptures seen in *Col Cuore in Gola* and *Nerosubianco*), Herman Makkink and Cornelis Makkink, the latter described as *'a mysterious and almost mythical figure of the 60s and 70s art scene'.*

The derelict warehouses and adjoining open spaces, where bombed buildings had been demolished, were also used for training purposes by the London Fire Brigade, some members of whom can indeed be seen in Brass's film, testing respirators. SPACE also attracted rock bands. The Rolling Stones were there for a photo-shoot, their last with Brian Jones, on 21 May 1969, and the images were used on the cover of their compilation album *Through the Past Darkly*.[11] Both Pink Floyd and The Soft Machine used the studios as a rehearsal facility, the latter in September 1969 prior to recording the music that accompanied performances of *Spaced*, a typical 1960s multi-media happening, at the Roundhouse. Hugh Hopper, bass guitarist in The Soft Machine, later recollected, 'We recorded chunks of music as a trio, in a converted warehouse in London's deserted ex-docklands that we used for rehearsals... It was grim: dead cats floating in the weed-choked docks and so on. My brother Brian came up at the weekend to add some sax blasts here and there, and we then spent a week or more playing around with tape loops and ancient mechanical aids to produce an hour and a half of finished tape' [12]

The footage of SPACE studios in Dropout is the only example of it in a feature film, and thus a fascinating time capsule. The appearance, in the background, of works by the Makkink brothers is also intriguing. We see the sculptures Christ Unlimited and Rocking Machine, by Herman, and a luxurious Pop-Art nude, by Cornelis, who apparently devised his work by projecting pornographic images against a wall, tracing their outline, and then copying the end result, with appropriate colouring, onto giant canvases. All three can also be seen in A Clockwork Orange. It seems that Stanley Kubrick saw, or heard, about the Makkink brothers and visited St Katharine Docks, buying a couple of pieces that were duly used as props in his film. Exactly when he did this is hard to pin down. The New York Times announced he had signed up to do A Clockwork Orange on 3 February 1970, so logically it would have been after this date, but prior to his beginning filming that September. However, we know that Brass, Redgrave, Nero and Proietti were at SPACE no later than July 1970, so it could be that they got there first. In any event Dropout was released a year prior to A Clockwork Orange, so it can claim to be the first film to show these works. Both directors were working against the clock, however: the SPACE studios lease ran out in December

1970 after which the artists dispersed to other premises. Brass caught them just in time.

Notes

(1) As noted at https://rjbuffalo.com/1969b-ba.html
(2) Fonda and Vadim had a daughter, Vanessa, named after Vanessa Redgrave: the four were friends.
(3) Interview with Franco Nero, 15 April 2019.
(4) Shepard, at this point in his career, had done a couple of experimental plays with Jacques Levy – later of *Oh! Calcutta!* – as well as a stint playing drums in The Holy Modal Rounders. Confusingly, the Fred Gardner listed here is different from the Fred Gardner who toured in in the anti-war show with Sutherland and Fonda: it was a pseudonym used by the Italian screenwriter Franco Rosetti.
(5) For an excellent account of Pink Floyd's abortive work on the score see: http://albumsthatneverwere.blogspot.com/2020/03/pink-floyd-zabriskie-point-soundtrack.html
(6) Frechette and Halprin were both members at one point of the Fort Hill commune, Boston, Massachusetts, run by Mel Lyman dubbed by *Rolling Stone* magazine 'the east-coast Charles Manson'. See: https://johnjburnslibrary.wordpress.com/2019/09/30/the-avatar-and-fort-hill-community/
(7) Interview with Don Fraser, 14 April 2019.
(8) For more on Keef/McMillan see: http://www.cvinyl.com/coverart/marcuskeef.php
(9) Substantially damaged by fire in 1964, Bishopsgate Goods Yard was abandoned by its owner, British Rail,

and declined into increasing dereliction over the next 40 years. The 1972 UK horror film *Death Line* was partly filmed in its wrecked interior.

(10) Like the Drury Lane Arts Lab, just prior to this SPACE were offered the former Marshalsea Prison in Southwark. Both declined, the Arts Lab moving instead to Robert Street, Camden. A short documentary film about how SPACE came to occupy St Katharine Docks can be seen at https://spacestudios.org.uk/our-story/

(11) These can be viewed at https://rollingstonesdata.com/2021/05/21/last-stones-photoshoot-with-brian-jones-may-21-1969/

(12) Quoted at http://www.calyx-canterbury.fr/hulloder/spaced.html

12

'...WITHOUT ANY DISCUSSIONS OR NONSENSE, WE DID IT. IT WAS JUST THAT SIMPLE...'

Trying, more than fifty years after its release, to describe *Dropout* is not a straightforward task. Unlike *Col Cuore in Gola*, *Nerosubianco* and *L'Urlo* it has had no DVD release, prior to that no formal video release and had disappeared from the cinema circuit, insofar as it was ever there, by 1976. The only viewable copy of the film that exists today appears to be a heavily edited version screened on Italian TV in the 1980s. This was copied onto videotape by a viewer (and not very competently either: there are two sequences where the screen is completely blank) and kept in their personal collection before finding its way into the possession of Ranjit Sandhu, the custodian of the Tinto Brass website.

But... enough of the film remains for us to be certain as to its beginning, ending and overall style. True, there are missing scenes, such as a shot where various skinheads confront a

room full of hippies, another where Franco Nero forces Frank
Windsor to undress, ties him to a chair, and absconds with
Vanessa Redgrave, and, towards the end, a much longer shot
at the dock where Nero and Redgrave are trying to find out
when their boat departs. The cut shown on Italian TV runs to
102 minutes, against 109 minutes when the film was released,
and nothing suggests that whatever was in the missing seven
minutes would change what the film looked like, even if it were
reinserted today.

As to the overall style, what we have is very much of its time,
and plays like a cross between the avant-garde surrealism of
Richard Lester's 1969 adaptation of Spike Milligan's *The Bed
Sitting Room* and one of Ken Campbell's bits of improvised street
theatre. To quote Stephen Frears, *'It all seemed to me so chaotic...
very anarchic, and part of me thought it ridiculous. And, of course,
it was done in this highly intellectualised atmosphere'.*[1] Like *L'Urlo*
it draws on the theories of RD Laing about madness, namely
in a world where nuclear extinction is possible, genocide has
already occurred, and the US is involved in a massive war in
Vietnam, who, exactly, are the mad? The people in asylums
or the politicians running the world? Such ideas were very
fashionable then, being aired in films like *Le Roi de Coeur/King
of Hearts* (1966), *Marat/Sade* (1967) and *The Committee* (1968).
Very much echoing this, *Dropout* invites us to regard Nero,
who has escaped from an asylum, as a sympathetic character,
without any information being provided as to his backstory or
how he came to be in the asylum in the first place.

Similarly, the scene where Redgrave and Nero visit what
appears to be a black consciousness-raising meeting, only for
the event to be broken up by the police, is both an echo of
John Boorman's *Leo the Last* (1970) as well as territory Vanessa

Redgrave would have been personally familiar with. In 1969 she had invited Black Panther Hakim Jamal to London, after meeting him in Hollywood, when filming *Camelot*. It was at a dinner party at Redgrave's house in 1970 that Jamal met Gale Benson, with whom he struck up a relationship. Gale, at that point, was the wife of Jonathan Benson, an assistant director on British films like *Bedazzled*, *Wonderwall* and *Women in Love* and Corin Redgrave had been best man at their marriage in 1964. Eventually, after about eighteen months together in London, Hakim Jamal and Gale Benson left to live in Trinidad with Michael X, former leader of the UK chapter of the Black Panthers, who had, of course, been present at the 1967 Roundhouse event *Dialectics of Liberation* with Stokely Carmichael, of the US Black Panther Party, and like Michael X, originally from Trinidad. It is hardly surprising, therefore, that *Dropout* features characters exploring and promoting black consciousness, in much the same way as Godard had done with Frankie Dymon Junior, another Michael X disciple, in *One Plus One* a couple of years earlier.[2]

The shoot ended in July 1970, after which, with a little money remaining from the budget, Brass, Redgrave, Nero and Proietti cobbled together, over a couple of weeks, the beginnings of another film, tentatively called *DNA*. Then, with their funds exhausted (and *DNA* incomplete), they dispersed. Vanessa Redgrave started work on Ken Russell's *The Devils* with Oliver Reed. Christopher Logue appeared in this too, and a year on would do the screenplay for Russell's next film, *Savage Messiah*. Stephen Frears began preparing his first feature, *Gumshoe*, with Albert Finney and Billie Whitelaw. Gigi Proietti returned to Italy, to a popular stage musical, *Alleluja, Brava Gente*.

Filming had been an enjoyable experience. Franco Nero recollects, '*Tinto was crazy about London and we went there and shot in 16mm which we blew up to 35mm for the cinema release. Off the set we went to Wheeler's restaurant in St James most nights and also watched a lot of live music at Ronnie Scott's. It was a wonderful experience. We improvised practically everything.*' As ever, Brass and his cohorts were enjoying the cutting edge of what London had to offer. Ronnie Scott's Jazz Club, at 47 Frith Street in Soho, was then, as now, the UK's premier jazz venue, though blues, funk and even occasional rock bands were also staged. It even had its own BBC2 weekly series, *Jazz Scene at the Ronnie Scott Club* which ran through 1969 and 1970, showcasing many acts. Whilst *Dropout* was being made The Soft Machine had a weekly residency there, and one wonders if their appearances coincided with the after-work relaxation of Brass and his team.

Whilst the editing and dubbing got underway, a piece about the film appeared in *The Los Angeles Times* on 2 September 1970. Written by Sally K Brass (no relation to Tinto... she had written about Jagger and *Performance* in the same paper in November 1968) it commented, '*...Italian director and producer Tinto Brass is making his fourth film in London and in true Italian style he has whipped around this sprawling metropolis dragging Vanessa Redgrave and Franco Nero through every city dump, slum, warehouse and garbage depot along the Thames. His latest film L'Urlo (The Howl) is the best example of his work to date...*'

The same article quotes Vanessa Redgrave as stating, '*...I saw his last film, he is a fantastic director. It's the first film that I've been around which is on every level that I am concerned about and that we are all concerned about...*' and goes on to confirm that the shooting schedule lasted six weeks and the suburban house, used as the Redgrave-Windsor residence, was in Putney and owned by a friend of one of the crew.

Further coverage came in *Variety* on 23 September, which reported that Oreste Coltellacci was co-producing. His company, Colt Produzioni Cinematografiche, had done the Franco Nero western *Le colt cantarono la morte e fu... tempo di massacro* which played the UK and US as *Massacre Time* and was marketed in some territories as a *Django* sequel, and in 1969 they shot the Klaus Kinski giallo thriller *A Doppa Faccia/ Double Face*, part of which was shot in London. Coltellacci's involvement may have come via Nero and would have brought some additional funds into play. More importantly, around the same time, Medusa paid for the European distribution rights. Founded in 1964 by Felice Colaiacomo and Franco Poccioni, they had handled distinguished films like *À Bout de Souffle/ Breathless*, *The Loneliness of the Long Distance Runner* and *La Voie Lactée/The Milky Way*, as well as a considerable volume of lesser material. Medusa were familiar with Colt Produzioni, having distributed their western *Due Volta Guida/Twice a Judas* (with Kinski) and it may be that *Dropout* was sold to them as a simple tie-in. It had three bankable stars so, one assumes, they were happy to pick it up and would have paid Brass, Redgrave and Nero for the distribution rights as well as the cost of manufacturing however many prints were required for the forthcoming release.

By the autumn of 1970, editing and dubbing was underway in Rome, though not without problems as the production continued to fly by the seat of its pants financially. According to Don Fraser, '...*I do remember after arriving in Rome to begin composing the score that there was no money in the music budget so Tinto simply called a music publisher who very happily paid for the score composition and recording... not an unusual situation back then...'* This suggests a fourth source of funding was now accessed, leading one to conclude that *Dropout* wasn't such a low-budget film after all. Fraser actually did the orchestrations for *Dropout* in a studio in London and the music tapes were then sent to the RCA studios in Rome where further work could be done on them. Fraser says today that he recorded around 40-45 minutes of music for the film and that Brass was *'Useful but not by any means over-pedantic and he allowed me to record options for certain scenes'.* The score included a couple of tracks Fraser had written and arranged for the Scottish folk-pop band, Middle of the Road, at that point resident in Italy and just signed to the Italian division of RCA. Originally from Glasgow, the group were known initially as Part Four, and later Los Caracas, in which guise they appeared on the Thames TV show *Opportunity Knocks* (as had the real Mary Hopkin), before following the same path to Europe as Mal Ryder, The Casuals and various others who found openings for themselves limited in the UK. *Dropout* wasn't their first film work. A couple of months earlier they had recorded material for the comedy *Il Prete Sposato* and by the time Fraser and Brass pitched up they had just finished work on *La Moglie del Prete/The Priest's Wife*. Both had soundtracks by Armando Trovajoli and the latter, ironically, was the film Carlo Ponti made rather than back *Dropout*, and resulted in Middle of the Road recording a couple of songs with Sophia Loren.

Ken Andrew, drummer with Middle of the Road recollects, *'...We were newly signed to RCA Italiana as featured artists, but they also used us as session singers on a number of films. The recording studio was, of course, well-known for soundtracks for feature films including many of the spaghetti westerns with Ennio Morricone.*

I believe we were one of the few English language singing groups attached to the RCA Studios in Rome and the RCA management volunteered us for the recordings. We were required to record only 2 songs: 'Do Not Cry' and 'Places'. I have no idea if we were the first option for the score but we did not hear of anyone else being offered the songs. We only recorded the 2 songs as above and the music bed was already recorded in London. We simply sang to these backing tracks... It was not really material that would have been appreciated by our live audiences. These songs were recorded before we had any of our pop hits and so they were somewhat too serious for our hit repertoire (sadly). We really liked the material, but at that time we were in the hands of our producers and their masters in the RCA Italiana boardroom. They set our musical direction for better or for worse. I am not complaining but we were not the master of our own musical career...' [3]

All of which sounds simple, and, in fact both *Places* and *Do Not Cry* appear on the LP *Middle of the Road*, released in Italy in March 1971. On this both are credited to Don Fraser and *Do Not Cry* is clearly listed as being from the film *Dropout*. *Places*, though, isn't and nor is it audible in the mangled, edited-for-TV version of the film that we have today. Perhaps it was included in a sequence that was subsequently edited out? It also credits W Blake, presumably the visionary, artist and poet William Blake, as co-author with Fraser. If so, then this was an adaptation of the type that Fraser had previously done with Christopher Logue. Blake was actually a popular source of inspiration at the time for many spoken-word performers: Argo produced an LP of his work being read by assorted actors, including Alan Bates and Richard Johnson, in 1964, and in 1970 Allen Ginsberg released *William Blake – Songs of Innocence and Experience* on MGM.

In fact, quite a lot of complications arise regarding *Do Not Cry*. For this Fraser used as lyrics the text of the last letter of Nicola Sacco, an Italian anarchist, prior to his execution in the US in 1927. Middle of the Road sing it in English, but it isn't in the film. The version that is, sung in Italian by Gigi Proietti, is entitled '*Non Piangere*', with the lyrics altered so that they become a tribute to Giuseppe Pinelli, an anarchist whose death in a police station in Italy occurred in December 1969. This was something of a political cause célèbre in Italy at the time, with Dario Fo staging a play, *Accidental Death of an Anarchist*, about it in December 1970. This became a global hit, reaching London, where it ran for a year and was adapted for TV in 1980, and Broadway, where it closed after 20 performances, in 1984. The tone throughout – agitprop politics and sociological comment played as farce – is similar to the approach Brass, Redgrave, Nero and Proietti took in *Dropout*. Nor was Fraser's choice of Sacco's letter unique to *Dropout*. A film of the famous Sacco and Vanzetti case was shot in Italy between August and November 1970 starring Gian Maria Volonte and Riccardo Cucciolla. Premiering in March 1971 it was a formal entry at that year's Cannes Film Festival (where Cucciolla won Best Actor award) and came with music from Joan Baez and Ennio Morricone. Baez used a modified version of the letter as the lyrics for her song *The Ballad of Sacco and Vanzetti*, released on RCA in October 1971.

In the version of *Dropout* that exists today, the score consists of eight or nine pieces of neo-classical music, composed by Fraser, a couple of Italian language folk-rock songs, sung in Italian, various opera extracts, two traditional London street songs and a track '*The Sun is Shining*', heard in the film and credited on the titles to Middle of the Road. But even something as apparently clear as this presents problems... no trace exists of Middle of the Road releasing a track of this name and one wonders if it wasn't part of a 'job-lot' of songs they recorded for use in Italian films that needed a UK band on the soundtrack.

Unlike *Nerosubianco* and *L'Urlo* there were no problems getting a certificate for *Dropout*, and a version running 109 minutes was released in France on 18 December 1970. On 13 January 1971 *Variety* announced that films distributed in the US by Titanus (who were handling *Dropout*) would be distributed instead by 20th Century-Fox, and, seemingly connected with this, Redgrave was interviewed by New York paper *The Journal-News* ten days later stating, '...*We knocked it off in three and a half weeks... Brass knew exactly what he wanted, he simply told us what to do, and without any discussions or nonsense, we did it. It was just that simple...*' No US release ensued, however, though the film did appear in Italy on 22 February 1971, and thereafter in Spain and Brazil.

By this point Redgrave, Brass and Nero had reunited in Italy to make *La Vacanza/Vacation* and the UK crew that had worked on *Dropout* disbanded. Fraser moved on to music production work with Carl Wayne, Sandy Denny and Peter Straker. For Denny he and Peter Elford wrote and composed the music in the short film *Pass of Arms*. He recollects, '...*I don't remember being asked to do the score for* Vacation *but in any event, I was getting pretty booked up with quite a few documentary commissions. Also, it was during this period that I was co-producing the film* Pass of Arms, *in fact we had made a recording of the song* Man of Iron *with Vanessa Redgrave, but then her agents got very snotty and were really controlling her career as only agents can... Sandy was great to work with... it was Chris Blackwell at Island Records who suggested Sandy record the songs we had written, he was one of the backers of the movie, Island got the publishing and recording rights in the score...'* [4]

The speed with which *Dropout* rapidly receded as a project was reflected in the lack of a soundtrack album for the film. Given the involvement of Fraser, the London Radha Krishna Temple, Middle of the Road and Proietti, this was extraordinary. Particularly so with regard to Middle of the Road. In November 1970 they released the Lally Stott song, *Chirpy Chirpy Cheep Cheep*, which promptly reached No 1 in the UK, Belgium, Denmark, Norway, Sweden and Switzerland, and stopped one place short of this in West Germany, the Netherlands, Austria and Spain. It was an absolutely massive hit and ended up selling ten million copies worldwide. That this wasn't capitalised on with a soundtrack album featuring their material for the film is surprising, to say the least: by way of comparison, their February 1971 sessions for the film *Il Sole Nella Pelle/Summer Affair* which featured them performing four Lally Stott-written tracks were released by RCA. So why not *Dropout?*

After a couple of years 20th Century-Fox decided not to exercise its distribution rights to *Dropout.* These passed to Scotia American, who handled the US release for material like *Giornata Nera per L'ariete/The Fifth Cord* (1971, with Franco Nero), *Milano Trema: La Polizia Vuole Giustizia/Italian Connection* (1973, starring Luc Merenda) and *Don Juan ou... Si Don Juan était Une Femme/If Don Juan Were a Woman* (1973, Brigitte Bardot). All these reached the US in 1975-1976 and around that time *Dropout* had a very limited screening there too. As for the UK, it appears to have been shown through the 1970s on the student and college cinema club network, an ideal forum for it, given its political stance.

But it remains the least visible of Brass's London quartet, never having been screened on TV in the UK and lacking a mention in either *Halliwell's Film Guide* or the *Time Out Film Guide*. Looked at today, what comes across is that for all Brass's expertise at ferreting out striking locations and props, and for all the energy and enthusiasm shown by the cast, the end result – though very much 'of its time' – is decidedly uncinematic. Which is not to say that it wasn't like an awful lot of experimental material that was made, performed or released then. The career of Günter Brus is a case in point. An Austrian artist, filmmaker, performer and writer, Brus specialised in shocking audiences with explicitly pornographic, obscene and highly sexual material. His *Kunst und Revolution* (1968) has, at one point, a man masturbating whilst singing the Austrian national anthem and his experimental films *Satisfaction* (1968), *Unverschamtheit im Grunewald* (1969) and *Manopsychotisches Ballett* (1970) explored similar themes and were inevitably banned everywhere. This is not, though, an exercise in obscurity. Brus does cross over into some of the terrain Brass explored during the 1960s, taking part in the Destruction in Art Symposium in London (9 -11 September 1966), an event that included John Latham; Jim Haynes and Barry Miles (both of *International Times*, and Haynes also involved with the Drury Lane Arts Lab); Yoko Ono; and Gustav Metzger.[5] So, yes, as a film *Dropout* is absurd (which may have been the point) and the material would have worked better had it been done as a stage revue with a strong political message. But, together with some of the scenes in *L'Urlo*, it was how some people did things then. Today we may simply conclude that, if it had been presented in the same way as *Accidental Death of an Anarchist*, it might have reached a larger and more appreciative audience.

Notes

(1)   Interview with Stephen Frears, 8 December 2020.

(2)   Dymon directed his own film at this time: *Death May Be Your Santa Claus*, shown at the Edinburgh Festival in August 1969. A *Nerosubianco* black man-white woman story, like Brass's film it had a score by a rock band, in this case Second Hand.

(3)   Interview with Ken Andrew, 28 May 2019.

(4)   Island released an EP from the film on 8 September 1972 containing two Fraser/Elford songs sung by Denny (*Here in Silence* and *Man of Iron*). The third track on the record was Christopher Logue reading Wilfred Owen's *Strange Meeting*.

(5)   The career of Brus can be studied at http://www.artnet. com/artists/g%C3%BCnter-brus/ Attempts to view his films on line are usually blocked. The Destruction in Art Symposium cost 10s (50p) to attend in 1966, equal to about £16.50p today. A poster for it is at: https:// walkerart.org/collections/artworks/destruction-in-art-symposium Gustav Metzger, with his theories of auto-destruction, was a key influence on the performances of The Who and Cream.

13

'...THE FILM WAS TO STAR JIM MORRISON AND HAD PROGRESSED QUITE A WAY...'

The autumn of 1970 saw Brass continuing to juggle various projects. There was hope that *L'Urlo* would get a release certificate after the Berlin Film Festival, he was editing *Dropout* and, remarkably, he was now approached and asked if he was available to make a film with Jim Morrison, singer of The Doors. The source of this fragment of information is Don Fraser, who recollects that whilst dubbing *Dropout* in Rome the prospect of this was raised, '...*there was serious talk of us doing a movie about Christ's Forty Days in the Wilderness, just up Tinto's street as to the fun he would have had showing, I assume, some very detailed temptation scenes. The film was to star Jim Morrison and had progressed quite a way... they (the producers and backers) would drop by the editing suite during post-production on* Dropout...'

Unpacking just how likely this was – with so many of those involved no longer being around to talk about it – is a challenging task. But there does seem to be something there. Morrison had moved into film in 1969 when he funded, shot and starred in *HWY: An American Pastoral* (aka *Highway*), a personal side project slotted in between recording the albums *The Soft Parade*, and *Morrison Hotel*.[1] Very much echoing *Easy Rider* and its successors like *Vanishing Point* and *Two-Lane Blacktop*, it was intended to pique interest in Hollywood and enable the raising of funds for a much larger project. But, as with Carlo Ponti's *Zabriskie Point* (for which The Doors composed a song, *Latin America*, only for director Antonioni to reject it) the murders carried out by the Manson Family in Los Angeles soured the attitude of both film producers and the wider public towards anything counter-cultural, meaning that something that a year earlier would have been a shoo-in suddenly became significantly harder to finance.

But Morrison was famous, charismatic and young, and The Doors were selling heavily across the US, the UK and Europe. The idea that Morrison should make a major feature film was an entirely reasonable one – after all, Jagger had done this with *Performance* and *Ned Kelly* – and screenwriter Larry Marcus was a keen advocate of Morrison doing likewise. With recent credits like *Petulia* and *Justine* to his name, Marcus visited Morrison in Los Angeles in June 1970, pitching to him an autobiographical story about a rock singer who had committed '*a public disgrace at the Albert Hall in London*'.[2] Alas, with Morrison facing an obscenity trial in Miami, the singer opted instead to travel to France, where he turned up on the set of Jacques Demy's film *Peau D'Âne/Donkey Skin*. He made the trip to show *Highway* to Demy and his wife Agnès Varda, hoping they, or someone they knew, might help finance its completion and expansion to a feature. Both Demy and Varda had shot films in the US in 1969, but neither saw much chance of doing anything with *Highway*, and Morrison returned empty-handed to the US.

On 20 September 1970, Morrison was duly convicted of indecent exposure and profanity at his trial in Miami. Sentenced to six months in prison and a small fine, he remained free on bail, pending the outcome of an appeal. With The Doors not due back in the studio for a further three months, Morrison and Marcus continued to discuss a major film project with Marcus recalling, *'We came up with a motherfucker of an idea, a marvellous film that we had to do, with a human being who wanted to vanish from the world and become zero... The hero was to have nothing to do with music... had kids and left it all behind... in his frantic search for zero (those were Jim's exact words) he went to Mexico for a few days and kept going. Ultimately the man was in the jungle in which no one else lived, alone... I got money for the film: like that! From Fred Weintraub. All Fred wanted was absolute living proof that Jim would do the film and he'd go with the money.'* This is more or less confirmed by Frank Lisciandro, Morrison's colleague on *Highway* and a noted US photographer. He recalls Marcus *'...had an idea – he had a treatment about a guy who retreats from society, and goes to a fishing village, like Morocco, and gets involved in a gypsy life...'* [3]

Whether it was Mexico, ending up in the jungle or Morocco, ending up with gypsies, this, with its premise of *'a human being who wanted to vanish from the world'* sounds roughly like the plot for Brass's *40 Days in the Wilderness*. The producer Marcus approached, Fred Weintraub, was at that point Executive Vice President of Warner Brothers overseeing the concert documentary *Woodstock*. Alas, the same month that *Dropout* was released, Morrison – who in his last couple of years was an intermittently functioning alcoholic – became abusive at a meeting to discuss progressing the Marcus film, which together with his preoccupation in the sessions for the LP *LA Woman*, meant taking the idea forward stalled abruptly. With Warner Brothers bruised by the reception given to *Performance* when it was released in the US in August 1970 (in the words of *The New York Times*, '*You do not have to be a drug addict, pederast, sadomasochist or nitwit to enjoy* Performance, *but being one or more of those things would help*'). The simple truth was nothing would be put into production by Weintraub unless Morrison sobered up and signed a contract. And, of course, like any other major studio, they had numerous other commitments at the time, including distributing Carlo Ponti's *The Priest's Wife*, shooting *Death in Venice*, and commencing Kubrick's *A Clockwork Orange* in the UK.

So, by December 1970, *40 Days in the Wilderness* fell back in the pecking order and at the end of the month *Variety* announced instead that Brass would direct *L'Evasione*, starring Gianni Morandi.[4] Details of this are scarce and the film was never made, by Brass or anyone else. Morandi was a very popular Italian singer, much like Cliff Richard in style, who had swerved into making simple pop musicals. At the point this announcement was made he was shooting *Il Provinciale*, a comedy, and his 11th starring role in 7 years. He was so mainstream that he represented Italy at the March 1970 Eurovision Song Contest, where Mary Hopkin competed for the UK. Quite what this was about, or whether it was even a jokey hoax press release, isn't clear. Either way Morandi was no obvious match for Brass.

Something that did happen, and was very much at the other end of the artistic spectrum from *L'Evasione*, was *I Miss Sonja Henie*. Brass travelled to Yugoslavia for the inaugural

Belgrade Film Festival, which opened on 9 January 1971 with a screening of *MASH*. Staged at the prestigious Dom Sindikata, a massive concrete and steel concert hall built for the Yugoslav Association of Trade Unions, the event was designed to showcase Marshal Tito's country as a relatively liberal communist state that was happy to serve as a cultural forum for both the western and eastern blocs as well as the 'non-aligned' nations, that Yugoslavia, with India and Egypt, sought to lead. Not that attendance at such a seemingly benign function was without its dangers. The visiting film industry luminaries were all accommodated at the same hotel, where the Czech secret police were waiting in a car outside to kidnap Milos Forman, one of the guests at the festival, and drive him back, suitably sedated, to Prague to face charges of abandoning his homeland without permission.[5]

On arrival Brass was approached in the hotel foyer by Yugoslav director and cameraman Karpo Godina and asked if he would direct a three-minute sequence in a compendium film, to be shot *that night* with six other directors: Forman, Buck Henry (actually best known for his screenplays, which included *The Graduate*, *Candy* and *Catch 22*), Mladomir Djordjevic, Dusan Makavejev, Paul Morrissey and US documentarist Frederick Wiseman. There were conditions. A camera would be set up in an attic flat and each of the directors would shoot a short sketch, based on scripts Godina had written, all of which had to include the sentence '*I Miss Sonja Henie*'. Godina patiently waited in the foyer for hours, speaking to each of the directors as and when they appeared. To his surprise they all agreed. Both Godina and Makavejev were part of the Yugoslav art movement Black Wave, which was similar to the famous Czech New Wave and Makavejev had just completed shooting

W.R.: Mysteries of the Organism, a film whose mixture of madcap satire, sex and documentary footage closely resembles Brass's *L'Urlo*.[6]

Despite the constraints – the flat was tiny and the lighting only worked in the entrance corridor and part of the main room – the film was complete by the following morning, helped on its way through the night by copious alcohol consumption by the various participants, who included the actresses Brooke Hayward and Catherine Rouvel.[7] Milos Forman's episode features himself, swathed from head to foot in bandages, and is clearly a tribute to American screenwriter and novelist Dalton Trumbo's film *Johnny Got His Gun* which at that point had been finished, but not yet released. (It premiered at Cannes in May 1971.) Brass's contribution, which contains a lot of shouting and banging on the flat door, is actually quite funny, and as a bizarre exercise in instant dissent, executed in a typically central European absurdist style, the completed film works brilliantly.

But why Sonja Henie? She was a glamorous Norwegian ice-skater who starred in a string of Hollywood musicals in the 1930s and 1940s, excerpts from one of which, *Sun Valley Serenade*, with the Glenn Miller Orchestra, are briefly intercut here. The plots in her films were so escapist and undemanding that they make for a bizarre juxtaposition with the goings-on in each of the directors' segments. Perhaps the intention was to say something about the packaged, opulent Hollywood approach that usually dominates cinema. Makavejev's film *W.R.: Mysteries of the Organism* also has a subplot involving a Josef Stalin look-a-like ice skater... so is *I Miss Sonja Henie* riffing on this in the expectation that *W.R.: Mysteries of the Organism* would be banned? If that was the intention it was entirely successful, as both films were frowned on by the Yugoslav authorities. Makavejev's film was only allowed a few carefully selected screenings in its home territory, even though it became one of the staples of late-night screenings on the independent cinema network in the UK and US through the 1970s and 1980s. *I Miss Sonja Henie* vanished completely, it would seem, and was not publicly screened until 2009. Brass's involvement with this, as with his being considered for *A Clockwork Orange*, confirms once again his standing in cinema circles at that time. Unlike how he would be regarded in later years, in 1971 he was seen as avant-garde and quite the equal of Milos Forman, Dusan Makavejev, Buck Henry and Paul Morrissey.

Following this unexpected diversion, Brass returned to Italy where he made another film with Nero and Redgrave, using $100,000 of their own money. This was guaranteed by Ital-Noleggio, the state-owned Italian film distributor, and *Variety* announced on 27 January 1971 that it would be shot entirely in Italy, the first such Brass film to do so for six years. Franco Nero confirms, '...*We did another film* (La Vacanza), *but filmed this in Italy in the region around Venice. The dialogue was entirely in Venetian dialect, which Vanessa learnt until she was word perfect. Usually, the films were always dubbed in whatever language was required for whatever country they were being shown in, that was common in those days...*' Further information was provided in *Variety* on 3 February 1971 '...*Over on the Adriatic, Giovanni Tinto Brass has gathered Vanessa Redgrave, Franco Nero and newcomer Fany Sakantany for a start on* The Vacation...' Who was Fany Sakantany? The *Variety* piece implies she was a co-star. In fact, she has only a small part and was originally a model, winning one of the 1968 heats for Miss Greece. The real co-stars in the film are Corin Redgrave, Margarita

Lozano and Leopoldo Trieste. *La Vacanza* is a more substantial and considered piece than *Dropout* and relies much less on impromptu improvisations and walk-on participation by members of the public. Even so, Brass's links to London and its counter-culture were not completely extinguished. In fifth place in the cast is Contessa Veronica, formerly a performer at the Roundhouse with Mark Boyle's New Sensual Laboratory (where she appeared on 29 September 1967 with The Jeff Beck Group and Ten Years After) and, like Ms Sakantany, essaying a career in acting.[8]

Whilst *La Vacanza* took shape, *40 Days in the Wilderness* remained a possibility. Larry Marcus persisted with Morrison, and by early 1971 was trying to get the film set up in Italy, which provides a confirmation of sorts that Brass, as Fraser recollects, was intended to be the director who could carry off such a project. Films with either a religious/biblical plot such as Pasolini's *The Gospel According to St Matthew* (1964) or a contemporary drama with religious parallels like Buñuel's *La Voie Lactée* (1969) were well-known (and successful) in Europe, so looking at the Marcus-Morrison film in that context does make some sense. By March 1971, Morrison had moved to France, and discussions continued, initially with him staying at the Hotel George V, which he said '...*looks like a red-plush whorehouse...*' and later at L'Hotel, Rue des Beaux-Arts, favoured by Mick Jagger, and formerly the final residence of Oscar Wilde.[9]

In the meantime, *La Vacanza* proceeded according to plan. A film in which, like *L'Urlo* and *Dropout*, the main character is presumed to be mad, like *L'Urlo* it has its share of absurd situations and surreal juxtapositions and was shot mostly with direct sound. Atmospherically it resembles a fairy tale.

Redgrave is a peasant girl who gets committed to an asylum before being released for a month to see if she can function in 'normal' society. She meets various characters (gypsies, an English travelling underwear salesman, and so on) whilst battling for her freedom against the police, local fascists and criminals. The music, by Fiorenzo Carpi, back working with Brass after *L'Urlo*, is quite affecting and includes a couple of numbers by Gigi Proietti as well as both the Redgraves doing an ironic *Oh What a Lovely War*-type song.

By the time *La Vacanza* had wrapped (May 1971), Morrison, after moving again to a three-bedroom apartment at 17 Rue Beautreillis, and visiting Jacques Demy and Agnès Varda once more, had left for London with his girlfriend Pamela Courson. Here they stayed at a hotel in Hyde Park, which they hated, after which Courson took up with the Count de Breteuil, a wealthy French drug-dealer, post-Jagger partner of Marianne Faithfull and holder of a spare set of keys to the house Keith Richards and Anita Pallenberg owned in Cheyne Walk.[10] (Richards and Pallenberg were in the south of France at that point, where the Rolling Stones were limbering up to record *Exile on Main Street*.) At a loose end, Morrison met up with Michael McClure, a poet and actor who'd just finished a supporting role in the Peter Fonda western *The Hired Hand*, and can be glimpsed uncredited in Varda's *Lions Love*. It seems that, not content with *Highway* and whatever interest Larry Marcus could rustle up in Italy for *40 Days in the Wilderness*, Morrison also had plans to film McClure's novel *The Adept*, about which he had said, eighteen months earlier, when he and McClure were working on it as a screenplay '...*If I do anything in films it will probably be this script called Saint Nicholas that Michael McClure and I wrote based on his novel* The Adept *which hasn't been published yet. It's a contemporary story about a couple of dope dealers that go to the desert to make a score and if I, if I do anything that'll probably be the first project...'* [11]

By June 1971, producer Elliott Kastner, whose credits included such big-budget literary fare as *A Severed Head* and *X, Y and Zee*, had passed on *The Adept/Saint Nicholas* and it was being mulled over instead, allegedly as part of a three-picture deal with MGM, by St Regis Films, a decidedly smaller outfit headed by William Belasco. But none of this was either worked on, or discussed very much, in London. Instead, McClure and Morrison went on drinking binges in Soho, drove on one occasion all the way to the Lake District in a taxi and eventually moved into the Cadogan Hotel at Sloane Square where French photographer Alain Ronay joined them. Finally, Morrison, Courson and Ronay returned to their apartment in Paris. Drinking and drug-taking on a prodigious level continued until, on 3 July 1971, Morrison died, with speculation on precisely how this happened continuing for decades afterwards.

Once again, everything had evaporated for Brass. Another tantalising project had failed to crystallise. A month later he admitted that the curtain had come down on his time as an independent auteur directing pop-culture films. He wound up Lion Films, announcing that he would next direct a studio commission, some sort of thriller. No details were given. Ironically it was just as *Ca Ira, Il Fiume Della Rivolta/Thermidor* finally opened, to good reviews, in the US. Complete with a commentary from Ben Gazzara and Irene Worth, its release became possible when Altura, who distributed some very distinguished material by the likes of Orson Welles and Luis Buñuel, picked it up after the Italian censors had denied it a licence.

In the meantime, there was still work to be done getting *La Vacanza* into the public domain. It premiered at the Venice Film Festival in September 1971 in competition with *The Devils*, *The Last Movie* and Liliana Cavani's *L'Ospite/The Guest*, the latter, about a woman released from a mental hospital who tries in vain to fit into society, not dissimilar to Brass's film. Among the other work being screened there was *The Arp Statue*, by Alan Sekers, now making films whilst studying at the Central School of Art, and happy to renew his acquaintanceship with Brass. His hour-long effort, a series of photographs filmed using a super-8 camera, over which a narration had been dubbed, would also be shown at the London Film Festival a few months later with *The Spectator* proclaiming, '*But technically the most stimulating film that I've seen is a work of Alan Sekers called* The Arp Statue. *Using entirely still photographs, the movie elaborates on several complex themes and stories; although the whole tends to be over-subtle, not to say confusing, its sheer inventiveness kept me watching and waiting for more. It has genuine wit, too.*' [12]

Brass was in luck. *La Vacanza* ended up beating *L'Ospite* to win the prize for best Italian film, though not without causing considerable controversy. *The New York Times* noted on 5 September 1971, '*The 1971 Venice Festival had its stormiest session yesterday evening when a section of the audience loudly voiced its objection to a delirious Italian entry,* La Vacanza, *which was itself deafeningly noisy.* La Vacanza *stars Vanessa Redgrave and Franco Nero and has to do with a peasant girl who suffers more outrages at the hands of the Establishment than were visited on de Sade's Justine. One must have a heart of stone not to laugh at her humiliations, all of them grotesquely pictured. Sold by her parents – as a mare – to a miller to whom they are indebted, she finds true love when she runs away and meets an understanding poacher in the woods. Her later* aspirations to win the affections of Count Claudio result in her being incarcerated in a lunatic asylum and later being sent to work in a factory full of vibrating sewing machines. Events here run to a high sexual pitch. At this point a cry of "Schifo" – "Disgusting" – was heard in the auditorium. That set off a chorus of "Basta" – "Enough" – and the rest of the film became inaudible, though it equalled its spectators in noisemaking. It concluded with most of the players being machine-gunned by the police. Not to be outdone, the movie's director, Tinto Brass, greeted the dissatisfied house with an obscene gesture when the house lights rose. La Vacanza is probably the squawkiest of all talkies. Its dialogue in Venetian and Milanese dialects is accompanied by snare drums, bugle calls, nightwatchmen's whistles, agonised shouting and gunfire...'

Venice was Brass's home town, of course, so perhaps winning an award there with his ninth feature film in eight years was not that surprising. But there were many who thought it had real merit. Franco Nero recalls: 'The critics liked La Vacanza and Vittorio De Sica saw it and told me "...it was a little masterpiece..."' In anticipation of decent box-office receipts a soundtrack album appeared in October 1971 with two tracks sung by Vanessa Redgrave as well as the couple that featured Gigi Proietti. Some care, and presumably some expense, was taken with the material, on which Fiorenzo Carpi was assisted by the vocal group 4 + 4 di Nora Orlandi. Proietti's songs were also released as a single.[13] Alas, distributor Ital-Noleggio delayed the film's release until April 1972, and when it finally did appear provided inadequate publicity. La Vacanza wasn't the hit some might have thought possible. It was eventually screened in France (April 1975) and Spain (July 1979) but didn't travel much beyond that. Franco Nero admitted many years later '...Both Drop Out and La Vacanza got cinema releases *but only played to low audiences. Basically, they were experimental films and they didn't make us any money...'*

The failure of Brass to get anywhere with Morrison and *40 Days in the Wilderness* produced a final, unlikely, connection to one of the groundbreaking films of the early 1970s. After Morrison's death Alain Ronay moved into a room at Agnès Varda's house, where, with Bernardo Bertolucci, he helped her write the script for *Last Tango in Paris*. Originally intended to star Jean-Louis Trintignant (who had been in Bertolucci's previous film, *The Conformist*, with Pierre Clémenti) this was about an American in exile in Paris, spiralling down via an intense affair with a (much) younger woman, to his eventual death. Clearly influenced by Morrison's demise, *Last Tango in Paris* eventually starred Marlon Brando and Maria Schneider. It began filming in March 1972, with Pauline Kael proclaiming on its release that *'...The movie breakthrough has finally come...'* [(14)] With box-office takings over 70 times what it had cost to make, commercially this was the polar opposite of *Nerosubianco* and *L'Urlo*. The constant troubles he experienced with censors, distributors and producers must have been a great disappointment to Brass. Had *40 Days in the Wilderness* been made, the combination of a decent budget, Warner Brothers distributing and Morrison starring could well have been the ingredients that would have finally positioned him within the UK-US mainstream. But, like *A Clockwork Orange* and *Barbarella Goes Down*, it turned out to be just another idea that failed to come to fruition.

And, whereas Redgrave, Nero and the rest of the cast could, and did, move on to other work, the limited income produced by *La Vacanza*, and its predecessors, was a financial problem for Brass. His wife Tinta continued to keep the family afloat with her earnings from the Cipriani restaurant business, but there were limits to how much could be used to subsidise Tinto's career. He needed a hit, a big commercial success.

Notes

(1) *HWY: An American Pastoral* can be viewed at https:// www.youtube.com/watch?v=H2vNXCm13d4 Apart from a public screening in Vancouver in March 1970, it remained largely unseen for almost forty years.

(2) See *The Lizard King: The Essential Jim Morrison* by Jerry Hopkins, 1992.

(3) See *Rolling Stone*, 5 August 1971 at https://www. rollingstone.com/music/music-news/james-douglas-morrison-poet-dead-at-27-40343/

(4) See https://www.rjbuffalo.com/1971a-ev.html

(5) Forman notes at https://milosforman.com/en/movies/i-miss-sonja-henie *'...I received an invitation to the film festival in Beograd. Yugoslavia was sort of a renegade, but still – it was a communist country. Therefore, I wasn't too enthusiastic about it. In those days from time to time the Czech secret police hijacked emigrants and took them back to their homeland where they were taken to court. I was afraid of that, but a friend of mine, Dusan Makavejev, convinced me that they were going to take care of me and everything would be fine. And everything really went fine, I could walk around and I watched the movies, until the day when at about 2 a.m. someone suddenly started knocking at my door – and there was Dusan saying: "Do not ask me anything, pack your luggage but leave it here. We are going to take care of it later. At five o'clock you must be ready at the back door of the hotel. I'll pick you up." I asked why and he told*

me to have a look out of the window. Two cars which the secret police had been using at that time were parked there. It was easy to understand that they hadn't come to admire the beautiful architecture. Therefore, I left the hotel at five in the morning using the back door, and Dusan gave me a lift to the railway station, as he didn't dare to take me to the airport. On the train I was accompanied by his friend till I crossed the Austrian border...' The film can be viewed at https://www.youtube.com/watch?v=_hKbQ0SNRkc

(6) *W.R.: Mysteries of the Organism*, in which the theories, therapies and beliefs of Wilhelm Reich are aired, reached the UK in October 1971 at the now vanished Academy Cinema, 165 Oxford Street. Similar to Kenneth Rive's Gala Berkeley Cinema, this exhibited many ground-breaking films.

(7) Hayward, formerly married to Dennis Hopper, was in Warhol's *Tarzan and Jane Regained... Sort of* (1964); Rouvel was in *Benjamin...The Diary of an Innocent Boy* (with Pierre Clémenti), *Borsalino*, *Les Assassins de L'Ordre* (with Jacques Brel) and much else.

(8) Email from Peter Prentice, 4 January 2021. Contessa Veronica (aka Veronica Gardiner) also appeared in *Casino Royale* (1967), *Popdown* (1968) and *Zeta One* (1969) before moving to Italy where she appeared in Brass's film and *The Statue* (1971). She had many other uncredited roles.

(9) For more on this see: https://www.loudersound.com/features/l-a-woman-and-the-last-days-of-jim-morrison

(10) Breteuil, who died in 1972, comes across as being rather similar to Harvey Bramham. See https://www.archyde.com/jean-de-breteuil-the-camel-of-rock-stars-who-was-after-the-death-of-jim-morrison/. According to Faithfull

'...Jean was a horrible guy, someone who had crawled out from under a stone. Somehow I ended up with him ... it was all about drugs and sex...'

(11) Quoted at https://recordmecca.com/item-archives/doors-st-nicholas/ McClure was playwright in residence at the Magic Theatre, San Francisco throughout this period.

(12) See *The Spectator*, 20 November 1971 available at http://archive.spectator.co.uk/article/20th-november-1971/17/cinema Sekers's film was further reviewed in *The New York Times*, 4 September 1971.

(13) Orlandi, one of very few women working in film music composition in Italy, is credited with 16 film soundtracks between 1966 and 1973, including *The Sweet Body of Deborah* (1968) and *Double Face* (1969), both now highly regarded and reissued on CD.

(14) Quoted at https://www.loudersound.com/features/l-a-woman-and-the-last-days-of-jim-morrison

14

WHAT CAME NEXT

When Brass collected his award for *La Vacanza* at the Venice Film Festival, he probably didn't envisage that his next film wouldn't be released until 1976, and it would be one of only four he would complete over twelve years, a stuttering career trajectory that would eventually see him abandoning mainstream cinema. For the time being he was busy, at least according to the trade press, on projects like *Order and Sex Discipline* and *History of Italy*. The former, announced in March 1972, was to star Macha Méril, a French-Ukrainian actress who had appeared in films by Godard and Buñuel as well as co-starring with Montgomery Clift in *The Defector*. Like the latter, supposedly a satirical overview, it was never made. Both came and went whilst Brass was a jury member at the June 1972 Berlin Film Festival, mulling over the merits of Pasolini's *Canterbury Tales* (which won the main prize), *The Bitter Tears* of *Petra von Kant*, *Hammersmith Is Out* and Jacques Brel's *The Bar at the Crossing* among others. That done, he was named to direct *The Borgias* from a Wolf Mankowitz script and starring Fernando Rey. This was budgeted at $8m-$9m and he worked on it for around 10 months before it finally collapsed in May 1973. After a gap in which he directed in theatre and did a TV commercial, his name next cropped up in April 1974 in connection with *Stormtroopers*, a farcical WW2 comedy.[1] This finally got made – two years later – by a different director, and amidst the ensuing confusion and lack of employment he tried to put together *Punch* (based on the puppet) with Gigi Proietti, only for that to fold too.

Finally, in January 1975 he was thrown a lifeline by Ermanno Donati, the producer who'd given him *Col Cuore in Gola/Deadly Sweet* nearly a decade earlier. Donati brought him in to direct *Salon Kitty*, replacing Sidney Lumet who had opted instead to do *Dog Day Afternoon*. Based on a book by German author Peter Norden about a brothel the SS had run in Berlin, this had a script by Ennio de Concini, a stalwart of Italian cinema and famed at that point for *Hitler: The Last 10 Days*. Donati provided a decent budget and the production values, with retro art-deco sets by Ken Adam, who had just come off Kubrick's *Barry Lyndon*, were excellent. The cast was strong too. The stars were Ingrid Thulin and Helmut Berger, both of whom had appeared in *The Damned*, with Teresa Ann Savoy and Bekim Fehmiu as the most notable of the co-stars. For the first time since *Nerosubianco*, Brass had everything in place – money, actors, script and setting – and the end result is quite entertaining. There are so many musical and dancing sequences that the film itself is heavily reminiscent of *Cabaret*, which it would often be shown alongside at late night screenings in art-houses in the years to come. It's a perfectly reasonable example of the Nazi-chic genre that existed in the 1970s and Brass, in the same way that he had in *Thermidor*, *Nerosubianco* and *L'Urlo*, intercuts newsreel footage and plays around, amidst an abundance of explicit nudity, with Reichian ideas, namely that perverse sex is a version of perverse politics (fascism) and vice versa.

It premiered in March 1976, and the critics were generally aloof, with the *Time Out Film Guide* noting '...*this predictably speculative slice of Nazi sex is aimed squarely at the box-office...*' But in a world that appreciated *The Damned*, *Cabaret* and *The Night Porter*, *Salon Kitty* had its admirers and ended up getting the widest release yet of a Brass film, appearing across Europe, the UK, US and Japan and drawing good audiences wherever it played. More importantly, its success and sexual frankness were noted by Bob Guccione who quickly brought in Brass to direct his immense and explicit epic *Caligula* starring Malcolm McDowell, Helen Mirren, Peter O'Toole, Sir John Gielgud and Maria Schneider. The owner of men's magazine *Penthouse*, Guccione had branched out on his own after putting money into films made by other studios, notably commercial hits like *Chinatown*, *The Longest Yard* and *The Day of the Locust*. Franco Rossellini, the nephew of Roberto, produced, a family connection that quite possibly helped Brass. After an early script by Lina Wertmüller was discarded, Gore Vidal came on board on the basis that he had worked (with many others) on *Ben-Hur* in the late 1950s and his 1964 novel, *Julian*, about Emperor Julian (360-363) contained a considerable amount of sexual material. And, of course, he was the author of the 1968 satirical masterpiece *Myra Breckinridge*, an energetic exploration of transsexuality, feminism, machismo and sexual deviation.

For *Caligula*, though, he would be disappointed as Guccione eventually judged that Vidal's screenplay had far too much homosexual content: hardly the market that was being aimed for.[2]

As he usually did, and helped by the enormous budget at his disposal, Brass worked quickly. Elaborate sets were built, and with Guccione's agreement, Vidal's script was rewritten, and the sexual content was expanded to include orgies and a great deal of female nudity. The latter caused problems with Maria Schneider, who was distancing herself from films with sexually explicit scenes after her experiences on the set of *Last Tango in Paris*. Brass replaced her with Teresa Ann Savoy, from *Salon Kitty*, adding John Steiner, Leopoldo Trieste, Osiride Pevarello and Adriana Asti to the cast at the same time. More significantly, the script alterations led to an immediate dispute with Vidal, who sued and had his name removed from the project, the credits eventually stating that the film was '*adapted from a screenplay by Gore Vidal*'.

Filming went well and was completed by December 1976. By all accounts Brass struck up a good relationship with Malcolm McDowell and, when viewed today, the sections of the film made by Brass are visually magnificent.[3] As with *Yankee* and his earlier London quartet, care is taken in how the shots are set up, and there is a great depth and richness to what is on the screen with the soundtrack – dialogue, music and background effects – being mixed in perfectly to match this. Back in 1966 Brass had commented to Alan Sekers '*...I know I can't direct actors... but if I shoot at a ratio of 100 foot for every foot used, I know I'll get something I can use...*' There was truth in this, and it usually worked, but if he thought this would pass muster on *Caligula*, he was mistaken. Instead, Guccione stated acidly that Brass had shot enough film to '...*make the original version of Ben-Hur about 50 times over...*'. After the first hour had been assembled in rough-cut, Guccione locked Brass out of the editing suite and began changing the structure of the entire film by deleting key scenes, using different takes and filming pornographic hard-core sex sequences with several Penthouse Pets. These were then edited into Brass's footage wherever Guccione considered them appropriate.

Brass sued, and an Italian court ruled that, as director, he had the right to edit the film. But he never did, and ultimately, he disowned *Caligula*, not that his hostility had any impact on how the film progressed. Realistically there could have been screenings for the media and critics by mid-1977. Instead, the next two years were full of continual publicity about the Brass and Vidal litigations, Guccione's opinions about these (and them), breathless newspaper and magazine articles about the explicit nature of what would finally be released, the difficulties this would pose with the censors and the burgeoning cost – which rose from $3.5m to an unprecedented $17.5m. With the exception of McDowell most of the cast disassociated themselves from it. Peter O'Toole was even difficult about recording his dialogue, eventually agreeing to do this in Canada where he was on location filming *Power Play* with David Hemmings.

There is some evidence that Brass knew from early on that working with Guccione would be problematic, but assumed he would be able to navigate his way through any issues and still end up being able to make his version of the film. Helen Mirren records that around April 1976, '...*Before we started filming, I went to New York for a dinner Guccione was throwing for us on the top floor of the Penthouse building – the penthouse of the Penthouse – and the whole cast was there, and Tinto Brass, the director, and* the designer and the producer. Bob Guccione had a certain innocence about him; an American naivety and decency about him. I rather liked him. He was completely up front about who he was. And he was very proud about all this talent he had pulled together. I was sitting at the table next to Tinto when Bob made a toast, raising his glass, saying, "We have the best actors in the world in this movie; we have the best designer; we have the best composer; we have the best writer in the history of literature ...", and, at that moment Tinto Brass leans over and says quietly to me, "To make the worst movie"...' [4] If Brass really felt he could bypass Guccione, he was quickly disabused of this. The immediate effect of his enforced removal from the film, and the allegations that were bandied around about his budgetary incontinence and general contrariness, was to make him unemployable.

A 3½-hour version of the film was eventually shown at the May 1979 Cannes Film Festival. Edited down to 2 hours 36 minutes it premiered, in six separate cinemas, in Rome on Sunday 11 November 1979. For the next four days it broke box-office records but was then confiscated by the police and banned, a pattern that would often be replicated in other countries. It premiered in the US in February 1980 and opened across Europe in the months that followed. The critics were ferocious in their condemnation, though *Time Out* did state '... *dotted throughout there are glimpses of what might have been: Caligula enquiring of an ebbing Gielgud what it's like to die, a death machine that operates like a combine harvester, some exotic sets in Italo-barbaric style...*' In fact, many people who went to see it at the time noted it appeared to be two separate films, edited together in a not particularly competent way. On the one hand a quite well made high-budget Roman epic with decent acting... on the other, hard-core porn scenes with no relationship to the rest of the plot.

But who cares about the critics or discriminating audiences? *Caligula* took $23m at the box-office, subsequently rising to $30m with video sales. It became the highest-grossing independently produced pornographic feature film ever made. As well as in the US, it was a financial success in France, Germany, Switzerland, Belgium, the Netherlands and Japan, and to ensure a release in censorious areas, a 1 hour 45-minute version, without the explicit sexual material, became available in 1981. For those who wanted a keepsake from a great night out Penthouse Records released a double album soundtrack, *Caligula: The Music*. Recorded at Motown Recording studios in Los Angeles, in between sessions by Michael Jackson and The Commodores, it included, incongruously for a film set in the first century AD, a soft-rock dance track with synthesisers. [5] There was even a tie-in paperback novelisation, *Gore Vidal's Caligula* by William Johnston (using the pseudonym William Howard). As an exercise in marketing 'product' and extracting money from the public, Guccione's *Caligula* scored highly... and ultimately didn't damage the reputations of its participants in quite the way they may have envisaged.

But until the money rolled in, Brass, ousted from the editing suite and damned publicly by Guccione, found work hard to come by. In August 1977 he tried with Vincenzo Siniscalchi, co-producer of *La Vacanza*, to do *Punch* again, this time as a starring vehicle for Malcolm McDowell. Plans were made to film in Italy and London but it didn't happen; McDowell opted instead to make *The Passage* in which he played a ludicrously sadistic SS officer, looking exactly like one of the cast in *Salon Kitty*. After this there was talk of a thriller, *The Pig Advantage*, and when this came to nothing, Brass fell back, as he had a decade earlier, on funding and directing his own work. What emerged was *Action* which he shot in London in May 1979. With Luc Merenda and Adriana Asti, this picks up where *Dropout* left off... a very downbeat, edge of the city portrayal, full of drab locations and peculiar characters. Anyone expecting a return to *Deadly Sweet* or *Attraction* (or even *The Howl*) will be disappointed, as, although this is London at the end of the 1970s, when new wave music was quite popular, there is no trace of it here, though the two main characters do meet a nasty gang of Kings Road punks who do unspeakable things to them on a piece of waste ground.

Dramatically, *Action* is done as a film within a film within a film, with many well-shot sequences. The final section, with a trio of characters set in a petrol station on the edge of a rundown area is very effective, and plays not unlike Serge Gainsbourg's 1976 film *Je t'aime mois non plus*.[6] Alan Sekers returned as production manager and confirmed that much of *Action* was shot at Beckton, an immense post-industrial landscape that, in another of Brass's intersections with Stanley Kubrick, served as the main set for *Full Metal Jacket*. (7) But is *Action* any good? Well, Brass fans think it an excellent example of his work, it has some striking scenes, and for anyone else it passes the time. Luc Merenda was a big star in France, Germany and Italy, appearing in 21 spaghetti westerns, action thrillers, mafia thrillers and giallos between 1970 and 1979 and Adriana Asti had been in both Bertolucci's *Before the Revolution* and Buñuel's *The Phantom of Liberty*. The cast do what they can with the material, much of which looks improvised. Neither Merenda nor Asti had filmed in London before, so one suspects that was the attraction for them in accepting such a hit-and-miss, modestly budgeted production. The truth was, ground down by the protracted litigation over

Caligula, Brass was not in a good place temperamentally whilst filming and somehow this seeped into the finished product. Released across Europe from January 1980, one assumes that it got its costs back.

A year later, with many now eyeing the takings enjoyed by *Caligula*, Brass was back in demand and was lined up to make *Boudoir*, an adaptation of de Sade. Jesús Franco had shot a version of this in 1969 as *Eugenie... The Story of her Journey into Perversion* with Maria Rohm. Harry Alan Towers, who wrote and produced that, now wanted a larger, more explicit film extracted from the same source. In fact, *Boudoir* had been doing the rounds since 1977 as something starring, at various times, Pierre Clémenti, Tomas Milian and Fernando Rey. It collapsed in 1982, at which point Towers began raising funds for Brass to make *Fanny Hill*, with Giovanni Bertolucci co-producing. But when Brent Walker got involved as co-producers, Brass was ousted in favour of Gerry O'Hara, and the film went ahead without him, starring Lisa Foster, Oliver Reed, Shelley Winters and Wilfrid Hyde-White.

When this happened, Bertolucci, who'd had a major success as producer of *The Conformist*, agreed to fund Brass directing *The Key*. Announced in February 1983, it was based on Junichiro Tanizaki's 1956 Japanese novel, *Kagi*. Tanizaki was known for exploring eroticism and elaborate sexual themes in his work and Kon Ichikawa had filmed it previously as *Odd Obsession*, in which guise it shared the Jury Prize with Antonioni's *L'Avventura* at Cannes in 1960. The material itself was ideal for Brass who it appears had been keen to make the film for many years. The action was shifted to Venice in 1940, and Frank Finlay and Stefania Sandrelli (who appeared alongside Jean-Louis Trintignant in *The Conformist*) starred.

Finlay was selected after Brass had seen him in the London stage production of *Amadeus*. Ennio Morricone was brought in to do the score.

Despite being withdrawn from the Venice Film Festival and having the usual trouble with the censors, *The Key* premiered at the San Sebastian Film Festival, in Spain, in September 1983 and was released across Europe through 1984. It was a very substantial commercial hit, and its success led to Brass making all his subsequent films in the same erotic, soft-core style. Between 1985 (*Miranda*) and 2006 (*Monamour*) he completed twelve such productions, of which Bertolucci produced eight. This period, lasting about 20 years and starting in the mid-1980s, was the time when censorship was relatively relaxed, video releases were easier to obtain and the internet had not yet appeared and collapsed the market for films of this type. Alongside *Salon Kitty* and *Caligula* these are the films that most people associate with Brass. They are certainly the ones that made him the most money, and they also comprehensively blotted out his earlier period as an innovative, experimental and intellectual auteur. He might have carried on, but in 2005-2006, at the age of 73, he suffered two misfortunes. Giovanni Bertolucci, his producer, died and a little later his wife passed away. Then, in 2010, he suffered an intracranial haemorrhage, which effectively ended any remaining chance of him making films.

Notes

(1) *Stormtroopers* first appeared as a strip cartoon in 1968. Drawn by Bonvi (aka Franco Bonvicini) it was satirical and anti-war, making Brass the ideal director to transfer

such 'pop' material to the big screen. Perhaps he should have stayed with the project: the film was successful enough to spawn a 1982 sequel *Stormtroopers 2 – All to the Front*.

(2) Vidal's *Julian* was in fact optioned for a film by producer Elliott Kastner in the mid-1960s. The project got as far as a first draft screenplay, by Vidal, in 1969 but went no further.

(3) Note the comments of McDowell at https://www.hobotrashcan.com/2008/10/02/one-on-one-with-malcolm-mcdowell/ *'...We did some good work in that film, believe it or not. There are still sequences of it that are incredible. It doesn't really hold together brilliantly I think as a terrific film, it's sort of very flawed. The cuts are a bit weird and I don't know what happened with the editing. It went through many processes and many editors and Guccione had his cut and I don't know what happened afterward. It was a bit of a mess. But there are still pieces in it that I think are very good. And, you know, it's sort of amazing to find these great actors – Helen Mirren, John Gielgud, Peter O'Toole – in this film of debauchery. But that's what it was about and historians of that particular era say it's a very accurate rendition of what was going on in Rome. It's history...'*

(4) Quoted at https://penthousemagazine.com/history-page4/

(5) The ubiquity of disco music at this point extended to other films. *Just a Gigolo*, set in WW1 and the 1920s and 1930s (and with a screenplay by Ennio de Concini who did *Salon Kitty*) featured Manhattan Transfer and The Village People and *Escape to Athena*, a WW2 prisoner of war drama, had Heatwave playing on the end credits.

(6)   The 1976 film *Je t'aime mois non plus* starring Jane Birkin and Joe Dallesandro largely takes place at a truck stop/petrol station/café on a peripheral piece of waste ground surrounded by wrecked vehicles.

(7)   The gas-producing works at Beckton, for many years the largest in the world, closed in 1971, after which the area (covering approximately a square mile and with many redundant buildings) became de facto a large-scale outside film set. Amongst the features partially shot there were *Brannigan* (1975), *For Your Eyes Only* (1981) and *1984* (1984).

15

THE NATURE OF FAME

Our view of the past, and our assessment of what was popular then, is quite simple to establish, at least initially, when dealing with cinema. We have access to viewing figures, and some data about the costs, profits and losses associated with particular films. We know which films won awards and were highly regarded, as well as which were spoken about and either disregarded or dismissed utterly. Much of this was summed up in the handy compendium guides that began appearing from the mid-1960s: in the UK *Halliwell's Filmgoer's Companion* (joined from 1977 by *Halliwell's Film Guide*), and a bit later *The Time Out Film Guide* (1989).[1]

We may remember what was screened on TV, and when. We may have either seen something in a cinema, or caught it on TV a few years later. Our views on either may still be clear. Film music too conjures up memories. A small network of record shops specialised in film soundtrack albums, often stocking copies of these for many years after the film itself had come and gone. The small number of such items that were big sellers in their day will be remembered, and listed as such in music guides and compendiums. Formerly, there were also the various analogue film libraries (some, like the BFI institutional, most commercial) that maintained catalogues of 16mm and 35mm films for distribution to the main cinema chains, and, importantly, the network of independent picture houses and film societies for connoisseurs of material beyond the mainstream.

This interlocking network of books, vinyl records and celluloid film underpinned everything, and was easily navigable by anyone interested in cinema. By the early 1980s opinions on the great directors, great films, great music and great stars of any given decade had, it seemed, all been pretty much arrived at. Overturning them retrospectively would never be an easy task.

The idea that someone of interest and quality might have been overlooked, by just about everyone, seemed unlikely, and if such cases existed, surely it was just down to bad luck? Around 1980 for instance, RJ Sandhu couldn't find a single print of any of Brass's films available for exhibition in the US, nor were any of them even available on video. For my part, the first I knew of him was in connection with *Caligula*, the scandal and publicity surrounding which was difficult to avoid in the early 1980s. I was a regular attendee at the Scala, King's Cross, the ultimate UK art-house independent cinema. Both *Caligula* and *Salon Kitty* were screened there during its heyday, *Caligula* in its botched form, twice, both in 1983 and *Salon Kitty* 17 times between 1983 and 1993. But of his earlier films? Nothing.[2]

By the early 1990s, with the renewed interest in UK psychedelia, the music of three decades earlier was being revisited. Some of the attention from this dribbled Brass's way via the 1994 reissue of The Freedom's debut album, *Nerosubianco*. But his films from that period remained unseen. He was never accorded a BFI retrospective and neither *Col Cuore in Gola* or *Nerosubianco* received TV screenings and the kind of kudos awarded retrospectively to the likes of *Wonderwall* or *The Touchables*. In fact, around about this time, roughly between 1990 and 2005, when first Channel 4 and then Channel 5, in a last gasp of activity before the internet swept everything aside, showed rarely screened late night films, Brass did actually become slightly better known in the UK by virtue of a couple of appearances on *Eurotrash*. These concentrated, though, on his post 1983 reputation as a director of soft-core films.[3] DVD reissues of his better work didn't appear until 2007 when *Yankee* got a German release, followed in 2009 by Cult Epics putting out *Col Cuore in Gola*, *Nerosubianco* and *L'Urlo*. Finally, in 2011, a young German director Alexander Tuschinski submitted a study of *Nerosubianco* for his PhD thesis, having correctly identified it as a groundbreaking work, and one that ought to have received far greater acclaim.

This led a year later to the Hollywood Reel Independent Film Festival staging a retrospective of Brass's early films, screening versions that had been restored in collaboration with Tuschinski. It brought a limited recognition, but many, particularly feminists, still decried his attitude to sex. Whilst it is true that his earlier quartet of London films are all built around strong central female characters, his later productions, particularly those made between 1983 and 2006, are clearly soft-core. Though well enough made as pieces of cinema, they have an abundance of nudity. By no means all of this nudity is female, however. So, is Brass really exploitative? Is it just the case that he likes showing lots of nudity? Certainly, his descriptions of visiting brothels in Italy pre-1958 (when state-regulated brothels were abolished) sound more like someone dipping into a heterosexual version of the type of sex-with-no-strings gay nightclubs that can be found in most city centres today, rather than anything grimly unpleasant and non-consensual. According to Brass these were sociable establishments, with a vast historical pedigree stretching back to antiquity and a friendly non-judgemental clientele. There was sex to be had, if you wanted it, and any that was had was undertaken discreetly off-set, so to speak, but a lot of the attraction in visiting was to hang out with like-minded liberal people and know that for a few hours you were escaping the straitjacket of conventional society. As to what his intention was, particularly post-1983, when making his films, Alan Sekers, a lifelong friend, was very clear in 2018 that Brass was *not* a pornographer, and described him instead as Rabelaisian, which seems a good summary.

If we accept that, and given his approach to sex and nudity, one wonders if Brass ought to be regarded as a kind of 'straight', heterosexual version of Fassbinder. Like Brass, Fassbinder directed quickly, turning out 24 features in 13 years, most on limited budgets. Other similarities between them are a casual approach to the credibility of their plots, a greater reliance on improvisation than was usually the case, striking sets, an interest in art-deco design and glamour, and a careful selection of the type of music needed to accompany the action. They were also related through their libertarian politics with both looking at the legacy fascism had bequeathed their respective countries. Other comparators might be Russ Meyer and John

Waters, both of whom used sex and nudity in a satirical fashion. Like Brass, Meyer and Waters had difficulties working within the mainstream and both are fondly remembered now for specifically 'pop' films that capture the essence of 1960s culture: *Beyond the Valley of the Dolls* (1969, Meyer) and *Hairspray* (1988, Waters) respectively. It is interesting to note that Meyer's output appeared through the 1960s and 1970s, Fassbinder's almost exclusively in the 1970s and Waters's sporadically between 1969 and 1988, after which he directed only 5 films in 16 years, to diminishing financial returns. Considering all of this, and Brass's own career trajectory, it does rather suggest that guerrilla filmmaking of the type all four directors were best known for faded away at the end of the 1980s.

Brass was clearly at his most distinctive in the 1960s and 1970s, with the films he shot in London between 1967 and 1970 being something of a high point artistically, if not commercially. With the UK, on the back of the *Bond* franchise and The Beatles output, briefly the epicentre of world filmmaking how does he compare with his many contemporaries? Out of the US directors who filmed in London we would remember Stanley Donen for *Bedazzled*, Richard Donner for *Salt and Pepper* and *Twinky*, Cy Endfield for *Universal Soldier* and Jack Smight for *Kaleidoscope*. Of the various European auteurs, Godard did *One Plus One* and *London Sounds* and Antonioni *Blow-Up*, whilst the other directors who dropped into the UK at that time, Truffaut, Gérard Oury, Alberto Lattuada, Mario Monicelli and Michele Lupo, used its studios and locations to shoot parts of *Fahrenheit 451*, *The Brain*, *Matchless*, *Girl with a Gun* and *Seven Times Seven* respectively. Brass, in contrast, made four London-based films. With the possible exception of Godard, a commitment to the city that nobody else attempted.

Nor is it just the number of films that Brass made in London that marks him out. Most of his contemporaries featured footage of various aspects of the contemporary fashion and music scene. However, with the exceptions of Antonioni and Godard, they did it mostly in an incidental way. Brass, in contrast, invariably had it up front and central in his work. As a result, his London quartet today contains important and, in many cases, unique footage of Granny Takes a Trip, Indica Gallery, 'The 14 Hour Technicolour Dream', the Exploding Galaxy Dance Troupe, Samantha's Discotheque, Yoko Ono's *Cut Piece*, the Mr Fish 'man skirts' worn by The Freedom, Tariq Ali speaking at Trafalgar Square, the Mark Boyle Light Show with Graziella Martinez at the Roundhouse doing a unique performance of *Son et Lumiere for Bodily Fluids*, Axiom Gallery, Quasar Khanh's inflatable furniture, SPACE Studios at St Katharine Docks, Graham Stevens's inflatable plastic sculptures and the London Radha Krishna Temple. It's hard to think of this range of cultural material being available anywhere else.

We should consider too whom Brass worked with during this period and those with whom he was connected by no more than a couple of degrees of separation. In the former category are Dino De Laurentiis, Carlo Ponti, Armando Trovajoli, Mal Ryder, Guido Crepax, Stephen Frears, Vanessa Redgrave, Jean-Louis Trintignant, Franco Nero, Ewa Aulin, Tina Aumont, Fiorenzo Carpi, Bruno Nicolai, Gigi Proietti, The Freedom, Pete Brown and the Battered Ornaments, Don Fraser and Middle of the Road. Among the latter would be Monica Vitti, Bob Monkhouse, Steppenwolf, Procol Harum, The Rolling Stones, Pink Floyd, The Soft Machine, The Bee Gees, Jane Fonda, Radley Metzger, Viva, Andy Warhol, Nico,

Pierre Clémenti, David Hemmings, Robert Stigwood, Roger Vadim, Jean-Luc Godard, Christopher Logue, David Bowie, Buck Henry, Paul Morrissey, Dusan Makavajev, Milos Forman, Dario Fo, Jim Morrison, Bernardo Bertolucci, Stanley Kubrick, Jacques Demy, Agnès Varda, Malcolm McDowell, Harvey Bramham, Sandy Denny, Fairport Convention, Glyn Johns and Eddie Kramer.

This is quite a haul, and indicates what an interesting figure he was at this point. But assessing his true value is more than just considering how many people's address books Brass may have been listed in at some point in the distant past. The intellectual depth and influences that he manages to incorporate into his best films – James Joyce, Wilhelm Reich, opera, Pop Art, experimental theatre and political cabaret – were rarely attempted elsewhere. Could it be the case that Brass's embracing of these areas actually precluded him from gaining serious artistic and critical acclaim, despite the virtues and accomplishments of much of his work? Is he too difficult a 'fit' for the critics and organisations that adjudicate and curate what is considered 'good' in culture? Politically too, he came with problems. He wasn't mainstream, even in Italy, and his point of view and opinions would be puzzling, especially to Anglo-Saxon audiences. Brass's amalgamation of radical politics and sexual freedom, seen most acutely in *Nerosubianco*, for instance, would later feature in the policies of the Radical Party, a group that Brass supported. An Italian green-left movement it was anti-nuclear, anti-NATO, pro-civil liberties and anti-clericalist. Enjoying modest electoral success, one of their elected deputies (between 1987 and 1991) would be the singer, model and sex film actress Ilona Staller aka *La Cicciolina*. Like Brass she appeared too on *Eurotrash* in the

1990s, and there are even parallels, if one wishes to consider them, in their respective careers: Brass's family were originally Austro-Hungarian, Staller was Hungarian; Brass began in mainstream cinema and moved latterly into sex films, Staller did likewise; Brass was interested in deploying a great deal of music in his films, Staller had a recording contract with RCA; Brass was interested in Pop Art throughout his career, Staller married the US Pop artist Jeff Koons, who exhibited explicit phots of them (*Made in Heaven*) at the 1990 Venice Biennale. Which is not to suggest that Staller has any artistic merit per se, but rather to highlight how odd this must seem to US or UK commentators.

With Brass no longer directing it is still hoped by some that his reputation may rise as his work is reconsidered retrospectively. There are hopes, or rather there were hopes in 2018-2019, that Alexander Tuschinski would be allowed to re-edit *Caligula*, his best film, to conform more properly with Brass's intentions. This now seems to have been dropped as a project by Penthouse in favour of a re-editing by Edmund Merhige that conforms to Gore Vidal's script. No release date for this has been given. In the meantime, a 'director's cut' has appeared on DVD, containing an interview with Malcolm McDowell. Online reviews for this suggest it is mainly a repackaging of the already released film, rather than a reinterpretation of it using material deleted by *Penthouse*. As ever, the reviews differ widely, some proclaiming it brilliant (and comparing it favourably with *Game of Thrones*) and others insisting it is junk that isn't worth watching. If dealing with Penthouse is too tiresome, perhaps reconstructing a director's cut of *L'Urlo* or producing pristine quality new prints of *Nerosubianco* might be attempted? The negatives and footage for both still exist in the vaults.

Tinto Brass is not the only film director to move from artistic credibility to blatantly commercial projects. Actors, too, often have career trajectories that take them from critically acclaimed portrayals to a multitude of rent-paying roles. Some of this is just down to how the wheel of fortune turns. As Orson Welles, who surely suffered more than most from the vicissitudes of the film industry, memorably stated, '...*Nobody gets justice. People only get good luck or bad luck...*' The last words here though belong to Franco Nero who acknowledged, when interviewed for this book, that Brass's failure to break through to the mainstream was due to the limited returns his mainstream films generated: '...*This was the main reason Tinto eventually did other types of film! I just did those two films with him. Some years ago, he asked me to do another film and sent me the script but I said "Tinto, this is too exaggerated!" There was far too much sex. And then he got ill. Tinto is unique. An original person!*'

Notes

(1)   Mention should also be made of David Shipman's *The Great Movie Stars – 2 The International Years* (1972). Among its many biographical synopses are accounts of the careers of Jean-Louis Trintignant and Vanessa Redgrave mentioning, very briefly, their performances in *Col Cuore in Gola*, *Dropout* and *La Vacanza*. In contrast the entry for Monica Vitti in the same volume discusses *Il Disco Volante* at greater length. Neither *Nerosubianco* nor *L'Urlo* feature in the book because there are no entries covering the careers of Anita Sanders, Terry Carter, Tina Aumont or Gigi Proietti.

(2)   See *Scala Cinema 1978-1993* by Jane Giles, 2018.

(3)   Brass was featured twice on *Eurotrash*: 8 October 1993 and 14 July 2000. The series was broadcast in the UK by Channel 4 TV between 1993 and 2004 offering a weekly summary of bizarre and comic events across Europe. He was in good company. Other directors who appeared during the show's run included Just Jaeckin, Menahem Golan, Paul Verhoeven, Pedro Almodovar, Russ Meyer, John Waters, Michael Winner, Jesus Franco, Alejandro Jodorowsky and Lars von Trier.

ADDENDUM

Much of this book discusses the narrow line between success and failure, something Tinto Brass would certainly have been aware of during his early career. The narrative also sets out the back story behind his projects, much of this information not being widely known. It also shows how, like all directors, he worked on many ideas that failed, for whatever reason, to come to fruition.

One film that did come to fruition was *Sympathy for the Devil*, directed by Jean-Luc Godard and almost produced by two of the crew from *Nerosubianco*, Alan Sekers and Nick Saxton. By way of illustrating the many wonderful things that happened in the 60s that are now fading from the collective memory as their participants gradually depart this mortal coil, Alan Sekers remembers events thus:

'It was the summer of 1967 and I had just left film school, and in between Tinto Brass's projects I was working for Eleni Collard, a Greek lady who had set herself up as a film producer, operating out of a basement in Gloucester Place. She had a job for me as an assistant location manager for The Inn Way Out, a film she was preparing about London pubs. A short drama, it was painfully slow and dull and wasted on a rather good cast.

When principal photography was over, she told me of her plans for her next film. She wanted to work with the Beatles and the French director Jean-Luc Godard. It seemed a big step up for her: had she even seen any of his films? With the impetuousness of youth, I told Nick Saxton, a colleague from film school who had just worked on the documentary Anatomy of Violence, and we decided that what she needed was to hire both of us because we knew his films backwards. She was comfortable with that and she somehow raised the money to fly Godard to London and to put him up at the Dorchester with his then partner, actress Anna Karina.

We went over to the hotel to have coffee with him. I remember thinking that this was a strange place for a revolutionary artist to be staying. To understand how green we were, at one point we asked Godard if he had a subject that he wanted to make a movie about. From behind his half-tinted glasses, and with a Gitane (maïs sans filtre) glued to his upper lip, he replied something like this "Today, so many people are offering me the possibility of making a movie that I have exhausted all my ideas" and then added, "So what I do now, is I think I take two subjects that I am a little interested in and I begin to make two movies, with the eventual certainty to cut them together to make one movie. Logically, then, if the subjects are far enough from each other, the only connections I will find will appear profound." He took another drag from his Gitane... and Eleni, Nick and I all nodded sagely.

I don't remember who called Apple, the Beatles' management company, but they were very interested to meet Godard and invited us to come to their office in the West End. At that time, the Beatles were probably the most famous people in the western world. Godard, Anna Karina, Eleni, Nick and I were shown into a rather corporate meeting room where we sat around a large white table and were introduced to Neil Aspinall, Derek Taylor and Peter Brown, the team of minders and advisers that the Beatles had assembled over time. They told us that John could not make it, but Paul would join the meeting presently. The chat was desultory until Paul arrived. He looked round and sat down right opposite Anna Karina and smiled at her winsomely. I watched her smile back. I also watched Godard watching her watching Paul. He looked pained, and the introductions and small talk continued. At some point, the Beatles' minders suggested we go to a nearby preview theatre, where they could show us their own film that they had nearly finished, Magical Mystery Tour. I remember thinking it really wasn't very good.

Next day, Nick was inveighing against Eleni. "She doesn't understand anything. She will never make anything happen. Why don't we take the project from her? We could go to Paris, persuade Godard he'd have better producers in us, and tell the Beatles the deal has changed, and we're away!" I knew that this was all wrong, morally and in every other way, but Nick persuaded me, saying this was how real film producers work. The vision of a smooth path forwards after we had committed the theft was seductive. So, Nick and I went off to Paris seeing ourselves as junior media executives, and called Godard's offices to fix a meeting. The most fun thing about going there was seeing the acolytes: all wearing half-tinted glasses, all with unlit Gitanes (maïs sans filtre) hanging from their upper lips and all very cool.

Godard himself seemed a little surprised to see us, but he told us, "If you can get the money in place, it can work". And then he dropped a bombshell. "But I am thinking of not working with the Beatles. I like more the Rolling Stones." Nick and I nodded enthusiastically but we began to feel things were running out of control. We returned to London and, it being the 60s, we somehow knew the Stones manager's lawyer well enough to meet him in his consulting rooms. He told us that if the Stones were going to be involved in the project in any way, we should get out while we could. It would be a toxic experience that would corrupt everything around it and we'd be lucky to get out alive.

We did as the lawyer suggested, and a few weeks later both of us were working on Nerosubianco. In truth we had no choice: we would never have been able to find the money. And eventually Iain Quarrier, an actor who worked on the Apple film Wonderwall, stole the project. He was a friend of Roman Polanski and he raised the money and arranged for the film, Sympathy for the Devil, to premiere at the London Film Festival in November 1968. Unknown to Godard, Quarrier had recut the ending. At the press conference, Godard shouted that the audience should demand their money back, and punched Quarrier in the face, causing pandemonium. Not long after that, Polanski's new wife Sharon Tate invited Quarrier to a party at her house in Hollywood. He was there working on Vanishing Point but was running late and went to another party instead... and so survived the murders.

When I decided to make my own movie in 1970, I was casting around for a subject. I was 21 and wanted to make a really profound film. But I couldn't think of anything profound. And then...I thought of Godard and his tactic. I decided to go one better: find three subjects that having nothing to do with each other, record all three and turn them into one film. This was The Arp Statue which was shown at the Venice Film Festival in 1971. Back then, I thought it was really, really profound.

Ah well...'

BIBLIOGRAPHY

BOOKS

Rob Chapman *Syd Barrett: A Very Irregular Head* (2010)

David Curtis *London's Arts Labs and the 60s Avant-Garde* (2020)

Jane Giles *Scala Cinema 1978-1993* (2018)

Lee Hill *A Grand Guy: The Art and Life of Terry Southern* (2001)

Jerry Hopkins *The Lizard King: The Essential Jim Morrison* (1992)

Claes Johansen *Procol Harum: Beyond the Pale* (2000)

Michael King and Robert Wyatt *Wrong Movements: A Robert Wyatt History* (1994)

Roger Manvell *New Cinema in Britain* (1968) (Entry on *Separation*)

Barry Miles *London Calling: A Countercultural History of London Since 1945* (2010)

Dileep Padgaonkar *Under Her Spell: Roberto Rossellini in India* (2008)

Julian Palacios *Lost in the Woods: Syd Barrett and the Pink Floyd* (1998)

David Parker *Random Precision: Recording the Music of Syd Barrett 1965-1974* (2001)

David Shipman *The Great Movie Stars 2: The International Years* (1972) (Entries on Jean-Louis Trintignant and Vanessa Redgrave)

Paul Stoller *The Cinematic Griot: The Ethnography of Jean Rouch* (1992)

Janet Street-Porter *Fall Out: A Memoir of Friends Made and Friends Unmade* (2006)

Christopher Turner *Adventures in the Orgasmatron: Wilhem Reich and the Invention of Sex* (2011)

Harriet Vyner *Groovy Bob: The Life and Times of Robert Fraser* (1999)

ARTICLES

Alexander Tuschinski *Nerosubianco: The film that almost could have changed Hollywood-cinema of the 1960s* (2011)

The Spectator, 20 November 1971 (review of Alan Sekers's film at 1971 Venice Film Festival)

The Photographers' Gallery *Loose Associations* Vol 3 Issue I (2017) (Article on Roger Mayne)

Shindig! 69 (July 2017) (Article on *Tonite Let's All Make Love in London*)

Shindig! 78 (April 2018) (Interview with Pete Brown)

Shindig! 88 (February 2019) (Article on The Freedom and *Nerosubianco*)

FILMS AND TV MATERIAL

Trailer for *Canal Grande* (1943): https://www.youtube.com/watch?v=L3kAqmqFIBw

Spatiodynamisme (1958): https://www.youtube.com/watch?v=dO0pffhB9SU

India, Matri Bhumi (1959): https://www.youtube.com/watch?v=FLrfyIBLOdA

L'Italia non è un paese povero (1960): https://www.youtube.com/watch?v=kaQ8Uy34rsE

Speak (1962): https://vimeo.com/159652068

A Whiter Shade of Pale (1967): https://www.youtube.com/

watch?v=z0vCwGUZe1I

BBC TV *Man Alive - What is a Happening?* (1967): https://www.
youtube.com/watch?v=kOC13xE9gwE

Anatomy of Violence (1967): https://www.youtube.com/
watch?v=88M60oBU-Ms

Ah Sunflower! (1967): https://allenginsberg.org/2011/07/iain-
sinclair-ah-sunflower-footage-asv-10/

Visa de Censure No X (1967): https://vimeo.com/473622770

Love You til Tuesday (1969): https://vimeo.com/211318045

Necropolis (1970): https://www.youtube.com/watch?v=uQA11j
UCQPE

Space Studios – Our Story (1970): https://spacestudios.org.uk/
our-story

HWY: An American Pastoral (1970): https://www.youtube.com/
watch?v=H2vNXCm13d4

A Clockwork Orange Trailer (1971): https://www.youtube.com/
watch?v=9JIc_1v7i88

I Miss Sonja Henie (1972): https://www.youtube.com/watch?v=_
hKbQ0SNRkc

Col Cuore in Gola (1967), *Nerosubianco* (1968) and *L'Urlo* (1969)
are all available on DVD from Cult Epics.

Drop-Out (1970) and *La Vacanza* (1971) have yet to become
commercially available.

INTERVIEWS AND CORRESPONDENCE

Mal Ryder 9 April 2016

Pete Brown 24 February 2018

Mike Lease 9 December 2018

Alan Sekers 15 January 2019

Don Fraser 14 April 2019

Franco Nero 15 April 2019

Bobby Harrison 1 May 2019

David Mairowitz 23 May 2019

Ken Andrew 28 May 2019

Barry Miles 31 May 2019

David Cobbold 17 September 2019

Carla Cassola 19 August 2020

Stephen Frears 8 December 2020

Peter Prentice 4 January 2021 (re: career of Contessa Veronica)

Tinto Brass, *Film International* interview 24 February 2011

Bob Monkhouse, *Guardian* interview 20 August 2020

WEB SITES

On the career of Tinto Brass: www.rjbuffalo.com

On The 14 Hour Technicolour Dream: www.ukrockfestivals.com

On the career of Tina Aumont: https://tina-aumont.tumblr.com

INDEX

●LDCASTLE BOOKS

POSSIBLY THE UK'S SMALLEST
INDEPENDENT PUBLISHING GROUP

**Oldcastle Books is an independent publishing company formed
in 1985 dedicated to providing an eclectic range of titles with
a nod to the popular culture of the day.**

Imprints vary from the award winning crime fiction list, NO EXIT
PRESS (now part of Bedford Square Publishers), to lists about
the film industry, KAMERA BOOKS & CREATIVE ESSENTIALS. We
have dabbled in the classics, with PULP! THE CLASSICS, taken
a punt on gambling books with HIGH STAKES, provided in-depth
overviews with POCKET ESSENTIALS and covered a wide range in
the eponymous OLDCASTLE BOOKS list. Most recently we have
welcomed two new sister imprints with THE CRIME & MYSTERY
CLUB and VERVE, home to great, original, page-turning fiction.

oldcastlebooks.com

| OLDCASTLE BOOKS | KAMERA BOOKS | HIGHSTAKES PUBLISHING
| POCKET ESSENTIALS | CREATIVE ESSENTIALS | THE CRIME & MYSTERY CLUB
| NO EXIT PRESS | PULP! THE CLASSICS | VERVE BOOKS